THE *ODYSSEY* IN ATHENS

A volume in the series

MYTH AND POETICS

edited by Gregory Nagy

A full list of titles in the series appears at the end of the book.

THE *ODYSSEY* IN ATHENS

Myths of Cultural Origins

Erwin F. Cook

CORNELL UNIVERSITY PRESS

ITHACA AND LONDON

First published 1995 by Cornell University Press.

Printed in the United States of America

♾ The paper in this book meets the minimum requirements of the American National Standard for Information Sciences—Permanence of Paper for Printed Library Materials, ANSI Z39.48-1984.

Library of Congress Cataloging-in-Publication Data

Cook, Erwin F., 1957–
The Odyssey in Athens : myths of cultural origins / Erwin F. Cook.
p. cm.—(Myth and poetics)
Includes bibliographical references (p.) and index.
1. Homer. Odyssey. 2. Athens (Greece)—Religious life and customs. 3. Epic poetry, Greek—History and criticism. 4. Odysseus (Greek mythology) in literature. 5. Epic poetry, Greek—Religious aspects. 6. Mythology, Greek, in literature. 7. Homer—Knowledge—Greece—Athens. 8. Erechtheum (Athens, Greece) I. Title. II. Series.
PA4167.C58 1995
883′.01—dc20 95-9557

For Tanya:
My *Apologoi*

Contents

Foreword

Gregory Nagy

The "Odyssey" in Athens: Myths of Cultural Origins, by Erwin Cook, brings a new dimension to the study of connections between mythology and poetics in the Homeric *Odyssey.* The author argues that the evolution of this epic was conditioned by rituals as well as myths, specifically by the civic rituals of the city-state of Athens, culminating in the festivals reorganized under the rule of the Peisistratidai, from around the middle until toward the end of the sixth century BCE. According to Cook, the Homeric *Odyssey,* which he sees as a performance tradition explicitly rivaling the *Iliad,* finally became crystallized into a text in Athens. He views the process of Athenian state formation, including the development of civic festivals, as coextensive with the crystallization of this Homeric text.

In the complex of myths and rituals encompassed by the civic festivals of the archaic Athenian calendar year, the author reconstructs a fundamental interplay between two concepts, *biē* 'force' and *mētis* 'intelligence', analogous respectively to the concepts of "nature" and "culture" in the discourse of anthropologists. As Cook shows, the same opposition of *biē* and *mētis,* or of nature and culture, is played out in the overall composition of the *Odyssey*—both in the fantastic tales retold by Odysseus himself in Books 9 to 12 (the so-called Apologoi) and in the story about his revenge against the suitors after his homecoming to Ithaca.

These concepts are not mutually exclusive, however. Although nature excludes culture, culture does not necessarily exclude nature. To put it another way: although nature is distinct from culture so long as it is excluded from it, nature can also be included in culture writ large. In Athenian myth and ritual, as in the *Odyssey,* the very origins of culture are explained as an ultimate fusion of *mētis* with *biē*. Such fusion is symbolized in the myth of a primordial accommodation between Athena and Poseidon after the *mētis* of Athena wins out over the *biē* of Poseidon. In the symbolic world of Athenian myth and ritual, the goddess and the god had struggled over the possession of Athens, over the very identity of that city. The victorious goddess, champion of culture, redefines that culture through her victory over the elemental forces of nature, championed by the defeated god. Through Athena's accommodation with Poseidon, culture now includes nature and is thus reinvented in Athens.

On the acropolis of Athens, there was a sacred precinct known as the Erechtheum, shared by Athena and the prototypical hero of the Athenians, Erechtheus. Like Odysseus, this civic hero had Athena as his champion and Poseidon as his prime antagonist. Within the Erechtheum were two key ritual objects, a lamp and an olive tree, both essential features of a "charter myth" that told of a primal struggle between Athena and Poseidon for the identity of Athens. In the Homeric *Odyssey* as well, we find the lamp and the olive tree of Athena, key features of the epic plot. As Cook argues, the innermost sanctum of Athena at Athens can be viewed as the ritual and mythological impetus for the poetics of the epic that is the *Odyssey*. Moreover, the sacred festival cycle of archaic Athens, rounded out at the end of every calendar year in the central idea that civic order, temporarily dissolved, must be reaffirmed in an act of violence, finds its ultimate epic expression in the struggle between a just Odysseus and the unjust suitors, culminating in the definitive reassertion of kingship for the hero and of sovereignty for the state. To that extent, the mythology of Athens becomes the poetics of the *Odyssey*.

Acknowledgments

This book has had a long gestation. I developed my reading of the *Odyssey* as a civic ritual text while attending a lecture course given by Walter Burkert at the University of Zurich in the spring of 1982. An early draft was written in Freiburg, Germany. There I was invited to present Chapters 1, 3, and 5, part 2, in the winter of 1986 at a colloquium on the transition from orality to literacy sponsored by Wolfgang Kullmann. My heartfelt thanks go to Professor Kullmann and to the other participants in the colloquium for their insights, and to Knut Usener and his family for their kind hospitality throughout my stay. I also benefited greatly from Professor Burkert's written comments on Chapter 5, part 2, in January 1987, and from those of Professor Kullmann on Chapter 1 in July 1988.

On my return to the United States I solicited and received comments from virtually the entire Classics Department at the University of California, Berkeley. Special thanks are due to J. K. Anderson, Anthony Bulloch, Philip Damon, Mark Edwards (of Stanford), Yvonne Feinleib, John Ferrari, Helene Foley and Alan Griffiths (both of whom were visiting the department at the time), Mark Griffith, Anthony Long, Donald Mastronarde, Andrew Riggsby, and Ronald Stroud. Richard Janko read the manuscript in the summer of 1990 and gave detailed suggestions for revision. Here at the University of Texas I cajoled Thomas Palaima and Barbara Goff into reading Chapter 5. To Thomas Hubbard, who provided expert guidance as I wrote the Introduction, I also owe many an insightful conversation on topics ranging from Foucault to poitrine de veau. Simon Goldhill read and commented generously on the first draft of the book (excluding Chapter 5), as did Marcel Detienne and an anonymous reader of the penultimate draft. To Hardy Fredricksmeyer fell the labor of proofreading the manuscript. Bruce Hartzler provided the index. Charles Segal graciously made available to me an advance copy of his own book in this series.

I am deeply grateful for the time and energy that these scholars invested in my work. Most of all I thank Gregory Nagy for his patience, insight, and support during the last stages of revision.

E. F. C.

THE *ODYSSEY* IN ATHENS

Introduction

When Horace wished to illustrate how to begin an epic poem, he chose the *Odyssey* (*Ars* 136–45). Modern critics have been less generous. D. M. Jones, for example, declares that "we need have no esteem for the composer of this prologue, whose inspiration, after a good first line, has so lamentably failed."[1] Indeed, the majority of scholars in this century who treat the *Odyssey*'s introductory verses share his opinion, if not quite his vehemence. The arguments most often deployed against these verses find their source in Analysis, a text-critical approach popularized by Friedrich August Wolf at the close of the eighteenth century.[2] The traditional aim of Analysis is to isolate textual strata belonging to different periods. In so doing it hopes to recover a pristine text of Homer, known as the Urtext, that had been altered and enlarged with the insertion of additional, or "interpolated," verses. This text was assumed to have an author, an individual poet named "Homer." The poet responsible for altering the Urtext is generally called the *Bearbeiter,* and his handiwork is detected by the criteria of linguistic, factual, logical, and thematic inconsistency. In the Introduction to the *Odyssey,* Analysts find the proem to be factually inconsistent, and the divine assembly thematically inconsistent, with the events of the *Apologoi,* the first-person narrative of Odysseus' adventures in Books 9–12.[3] The Homeric poems

[1]Jones, 21.

[2]Literature on the so-called Homeric Question is vast. See in particular Dodds (1954); Davison (1962); Lesky (1967); Heubeck (1974).

[3]I label verses 1–10 as the proem, verses 1–21 as the prologue, and the prologue together with the first divine assembly, verses 1–95, as the introduction. Rüter includes

soon found advocates among scholars known as Unitarians. By defending the integrity of the text, Unitarians seek to prove that it is the creation of a single poet. I survey Analytic attacks and Unitarian defenses of the *Odyssey*'s Introduction in Chapter 1. For convenience I will adopt the shared conventions of previous scholarship and refer to the written text that has come down to us as the *Odyssey* and to the authorial personality as Homer.

Relatively few classicists resort these days to the pure Analysis of Wolf and his followers, yet it is seldom acknowledged that the suppositions, aims, and methods of the Analysts lie at the heart of more than one modern critical approach to Homer. Students of intellectual history find evidence of widely divergent cosmologies in the *Odyssey* and assign them to different periods in the development of Greek thought. As we shall see, the divine assembly of Book 1 is at the center of this controversy. Similar arguments have been advanced to explain alleged internal discrepancies in the nature of Homeric society and the material culture. Most important for my purposes are the Neoanalysts, who concede that we have the work of Homer largely intact.[4] The Neoanalysts seek to demonstrate that various Iliadic episodes derive from the so-called cyclic epics, thus effectively replacing the *Bearbeiter* with extra-Homeric tradition. Such accounts can even be assumed to be oral rather than written, so that Alfred Heubeck has seen Neoanalysis as a way of reconciling traditional Analysis with the Parry-Lord school of oral poetic criticism.[5] The diachronic model of Wolf, with its Urtext and *Bearbeiter*, gives way to a synchronic model in which Homer is seen to be drawing on one contemporary epic tradition as he composed in another.

It is now possible for Analysts to consider themselves Unitarians and Oralists, and for Unitarians and Oralists to practice Analysis. Corresponding to this blurring of critical categories is a resurgence in the popularity of Analytic method, as can be readily observed in the two most recent full-scale commentaries on the *Odyssey*. For example, Stephanie West argues that the Odyssean proem is modeled on the *Iliad*, and that it was designed for an earlier version of the poem devoted to Odysseus' wanderings. Heubeck argues that a number of formulaic expressions in the *Odyssey* are modeled on their Iliadic counterparts, and

---

the divine assembly in the prologue, whereas I see the assembly as formally distinct from the first 21 verses and emphasize its role as a commentary on the opening Ithacan narrative.

[4] Kullmann (1965, 1981, 1984); Clark; M. Edwards (1990); *IC* 5.15–19; Seaford (1994) 154–59.

[5] Heubeck (1978); see Clark, 379; A. Lord.

that individual episodes of the *Apologoi* are derived from the Argonautic Saga. Even traditional Analysis has its champions in Manuel Fernández-Galiano, who assigns much of Books 21 and 22 to the *Bearbeiter,* and in Roger Dawe, whose comprehensive study of the poem singles out the prologue and Books 11, 20, 21, and 24 as substantially or entirely interpolated. Yet whatever its form, Analytic argument still tends to be based on the assumption that influence proceeds in one direction: often the modern Analyst merely replaces interpolation with appropriation. Moreover, the direction of influence still tends to be established by negative criteria such as factual inconsistency. This is the frequent though by no means inevitable price of criticism based on establishing priority.

American scholars have recently proposed a somewhat different model, which I shall call intertextual.[6] The intertextual approach is necessarily synchronic, but is less interested in proving dependency than in investigating the interaction between contemporary poetic traditions as revealed in our written texts. The pioneering work in this regard is Gregory Nagy's *Best of the Achaeans,* which has shown that the Homeric traditions are aware of and allude to one another.[7] More recently Pietro Pucci has gone a step further in arguing that such allusions can be specific to the written text of the poems.[8] Nagy's own theory, that the texts of Homer crystallized over the space of two centuries, provides a theoretical basis for Pucci's interpretation that is compatible with the Parry-Lord model.[9] Coextensive with the process of textual fixation was a shift in the transmission of the Iliadic and Odyssean traditions from poets who composed as they sang to rhapsodes who recited. It is during this penultimate stage in the process—the final stage being commitment of the text to writing—that text-specific allusion first becomes possible. In Chapter 5 I suggest that this penultimate stage was reached at Athens by the second quarter of the seventh century B.C.E. and that the *Odyssey* achieved its written form by the middle of the sixth century. Competitive performances at the Panathenaia would have greatly contributed to the stabilization of the Athenian text of Homer. Peisistratos' own involvement in the Panathenaic festival doubtless gave rise to the

[6] For the term see Pucci (1987).

[7] See also Redfield (1973).

[8] Pucci (1987).

[9] Nagy (1982) 43–49 (revised as [1990] chap. 3, 36–47); Nagy (1989) 31–38; Nagy (1992) 33–52. My larger argument leads me to conclude that the mid-seventh century would be the earliest plausible date for a dictated text that became the primary source of our manuscript tradition.

tradition that he authorized a recension of the Homeric poems. I consider it likely, though unprovable, that our own manuscript tradition is ultimately based on a reference text used during the Panathenaia and treated as authoritative by the Alexandrian editors of Homer.[10]

My own approach to Odyssean intertextuality most closely resembles Pucci's. I depart from Pucci, however, in assuming the priority of the Iliadic text to that of the *Odyssey*. In other words, I believe that only the *Odyssey* makes allusions that are text-specific, although both traditions can and often do allude to each other. I have reached this conclusion with some reluctance, and it is not a consequence of my theoretical orientation but based solely on my inability to find convincing examples of Iliadic allusions to the actual text of the *Odyssey*. Thus I argue in Chapter 1 that the proem to the *Odyssey* echoes its Iliadic counterpart in order to emphasize the difference between the heroes and gods of the two epics.

I am chiefly interested, however, in expanding the range of intertextual research to include the relationship of Homeric epic to ritual. The model I am proposing can be seen as an application of Albert Lord's model of interaction between poetic performance and context.[11] Specifically, I treat the *Odyssey* as a performance medium within a specific ritual cycle at Athens. It is my contention that the *Odyssey* and Athenian ritual grew up together and continued to write each other—often in ways that we can no longer recover—until the text of our poem achieved canonical status. Thus, the crystallization of the Odyssean tradition into a written text, the growth of Athenian civic ritual, and the process of state formation in Attica were simultaneous and mutually reinforcing developments. By placing the *Odyssey* in the context of Athenian ritual I am able to offer a motive for preserving not simply a performance of the *Odyssey* but a specific kind of *Odyssey*. The poem emerges not as a flat text but as a ritual program with a social function.

Since I locate the *Odyssey* in place and time, I find Nagy's theory that Homeric epic crystallized gradually over time the most plausible way of accounting for the origin of the written texts and for the *Odyssey*'s allusions to the text of our *Iliad*. A more traditional explanation for the allusions would be that the author of the *Iliad* or possibly an apprentice of his composed the *Odyssey*. Perhaps the *Iliad* had become fairly stan-

[10] For recent discussions see Jensen; Ballabriga; Nagy (1992); Stanley 279–93; Seaford (1994) 144–54.

[11] See especially A. Lord.

dardized after a lifetime of performance? Be that as it may, the fact that the *Odyssey* never directly refers to events recorded in the *Iliad* suggests that the Iliadic text had reached a sufficient degree of fixity to render such avoidance both possible and desirable.[12] Both Homeric poems by contrast regularly appropriate material from other epic traditions such as those of the *Aithiopis, Cypria,* and *Nostoi,* whose texts had yet to achieve canonical status. Under either of the above scenarios, it would have been no more difficult for the Odyssean proem to allude to the *Iliad* than to episodes within the *Odyssey* itself. And if it were possible to drive home the themes of the *Odyssey* by contrasting them with those of the *Iliad,* then we have supplied both opportunity and motive for alluding to it.

I began the project that developed into this book by investigating the structure of Odyssean narrative. This led me to study the effects achieved by parallelism between verses, scenes, episodes, and still larger sequences of narrative. From my work I concluded that the *Odyssey* is informed at all levels of composition by a series of contrasts that can be placed under the rubric of *mētis* and *biē,* or 'cunning intelligence' and 'violent might.' In the human sphere this polarity is seen in the struggles of Odysseus with Polyphemos, the suitors, and even his own crew. Among the gods, Zeus and Athene are aligned with *mētis* and Poseidon with *biē,* chiefly in the context of their opposed attitudes toward Odysseus. Thus, in the divine assembly of Book 1 Poseidon's hatred of Odysseus conforms to a patriarchal system of retributive violence that contrasts with Zeus's own view of human suffering and the role of the gods in it. When Poseidon first appears in the poem, he raises a storm that destroys Odysseus' raft and nearly drowns Odysseus himself (5.282–381). As Odysseus swims to Scherie, Athene twice inspires in him the stratagems by which he saves his life (5.426–40; see also 5.381–87 and 491–93 with 465–77).

In the so-called enchanted realm of Books 9–12, commonly referred to as the *Apologoi,* Poseidon's more primitive outlook in the divine assembly manifests itself in his support of a savage, the Cyclops Polyphemos. In fact, throughout this realm the polarity between *mētis* and *biē* attracts to it an opposition between Greek culture and all that is not Greek culture or, for convenience, "nature." This is not to find a uniformity of conception where none exists. In the adventures before

[12] This is often referred to as Monro's law, for which see Nagy (1979) 20–21; Ford, 158–60. With Ford's argument compare that of Hubbard (1992).

Circe, Odysseus encounters a broad spectrum of alternative cultures; yet the position of these cultures along the spectrum is registered by their relative inferiority to the Greek. And the more closely the inhabitants of the enchanted realm are identified with nature, the closer they come to being simple embodiments of *biē*. This process culminates in the scarcely personified Charybdis, an even greater threat than Scylla, the daughter of Krataiis, or 'Ineluctable Force'.

As I reviewed the history of Homeric scholarship, I realized that my reading of the *Odyssey* was based on passages that had long been the focus of Analytic debate. Thus, although I endeavor to resolve a number of these *cruces* in terms of the polarity between *mētis* and *biē,* I believe that the Analysts were intuitively right to insist on their interpretive significance. Nor did I set out to write a polemic against Analysis, and I have myself not hesitated to employ Neoanalytic method to relate the *Odyssey* to the various traditions on which it draws. Indeed, an aim of my work has been to show that some of the most influential modern critical approaches taken by the Anglo-American and Continental schools of Homeric scholarship converge without coercion in a synoptic reading of the *Odyssey.* My results have important implications for the origin of the texts that have come down to us: surely our *Odyssey* is in the fullest sense "traditional" if complementary results are obtained by intertextual readings of its Introduction, structural analysis of the Introduction and *Apologoi,* Structuralist analysis of the *Cyclopeia* (9.106–566) and of the Thrinakian episode (12.260–425), and a ritual interpretation of the Ithacan sections of the poem, in particular the Revenge (Books 13–24).

Since Zeus and Athene are aligned with *mētis* and Poseidon with *biē* in the *Odyssey,* I investigated Greek myth and cult for parallels. My aim was to anchor the polarity in a specific Greek context. This led to some surprising results, for I found that Zeus and Poseidon seldom occur together in myth or cult, Athene and Poseidon regularly. In fact, as I discovered, Poseidon is united with Athene in cult more often than with any other god. Still more important, the relationship between these gods is invariably antithetical: Poseidon represents the *biē* of nature, Athene the technological *mētis* that makes natural *biē* available for human use or protects humans from it. The evidence from cult thus supports my interpretation of the gods' opposed roles in Homer. The cults of the Erechtheum, however, offer a number of significant parallels to the Revenge, and the fate of Erechtheus closely resembles that of Odysseus. Most striking of all perhaps, the Erechtheum boasts two artifacts, an olive tree and a sacred lamp belonging to Athene, that are highly restricted in cult, but appear in the home of Odysseus. From this I concluded that the *Odyssey* acquired the form in which it has come down to us in the context of Athenian civic cult.

Since I have attempted to chart the development of the opposition between *mētis* and *biē* throughout the poem, I reserve the actual correlation between the *Odyssey* and the cults of the Erechtheum for the concluding chapter of the book. The opposed attitudes of Poseidon and Athene in the *Odyssey* take on an entirely new perspective, however, when viewed in an Athenian context, as does the larger opposition between *mētis* and *biē*. It will be useful, then, to preface my discussion of the Introduction and the *Apologoi* with a brief summary of my argument in Chapter 5.

At Athens, Poseidon and Athene are opposed in two different ways. First is the story of their contest for the patronage of the city. Both gods offered tokens in support of their claim, Athene the first cultured olive tree and Poseidon a wave of the sea. In historical times, Athene's tree was located in the Pandroseion, a sacred precinct attached to the Erechtheum, and the wave within the Erechtheum itself. Poseidon's gift is a natural element which he uses to punish the citizens of Attica for his loss in the contest by inundating the countryside. The gift of Athene, by contrast, is an obvious and frequently exploited symbol of culture. The domestic olive is also a technological product, and as such is ideally suited to be a gift from Athene, a goddess of technology. As the 'Tree of Fate', or *Morios* of Athens, the olive tree also embodies the well-being of the city. Athene's lamp, which was housed in the Erechtheum and fed by olive oil, served a similar function, as did the olive wood statue, or *xoanon,* of the goddess. On one level, the Athenians' preference for the olive in the contest amounts to a decision to organize politically.

The association of Athene with olive trees in cult is essentially restricted to Athens and its satellites. Yet the olive tree is repeatedly associated with Athene's support of Odysseus in the *Odyssey.* Thus, Odysseus finds an olive wood staff upon praying to Athene for vengeance on Polyphemos, the savage offspring of Poseidon. The staff is explicitly related to a series of technological innovations—a ship's mast, fire-hardened spear, drill, and a steel axe and adze—as Odysseus uses it to overpower the Cyclops. When Odysseus finally reaches Ithaca, he and Athene plot their revenge on the suitors while seated beneath an olive tree. The scene of recognition between Odysseus and Penelope is formulated in such a way that an olive-tree bedpost represents the *Morios* of Odysseus' household, just as Athene's tree in the Erechtheum is the *Morios* of the city. Finally, Athene guides Odysseus and Telemachos by the light of a golden lamp as they hide the weapons in the palace on the night before the *Mnesterophonia,* or 'slaughter of the suitors'. The light emanating from the lamp serves as a guarantee by Athene that with her active support the house of Odysseus will survive the threat posed by the suitors. The golden lamp in Book 19 and the olive tree in Odysseus' bedroom are indices of Athene's cult in the Erechtheum and have analogous ritual and poetic functions.

The opposition between Athene and Poseidon that began as a contest for Athens also manifests itself in her patronage, and in his antagonism toward King Erechtheus. Although the constellation of the hero with his divine patron and antagonist is broadly attested, the *Odyssey* and Athenian cult are the only two occasions on which Athene and Poseidon are so related. In myth, Erechtheus is known for defending Athens against an invasion led by Eumolpos, the son of Poseidon. Eumolpos leads the invasion in order to avenge the defeat of his father in the contest with Athene for Attica. Erechtheus successfully defends the city and kills Eumolpos, whereupon Poseidon kills him in revenge. Athene compensates Erechtheus for his sacrifice by awarding him cult honors on the Acropolis as Poseidon-Erechtheus.

As I have already suggested, my approach assumes that the *Odyssey* and Athenian cult developed together and influenced each other over the space of many years; the *Odyssey* did not simply "write" Athenian cult nor did Athenian cult simply "write" the *Odyssey.* In many places the direction of influence cannot be determined with any certainty. For example, it seems impossible to prove that the cult of Poseidon-Erechtheus is prior to the text of our *Odyssey* or vice versa. What is clear, however, is that the *Odyssey* must have resonated deeply with Athenian audiences as soon as Erechtheus was united in worship with Poseidon as his ritual antagonist. On the other hand, there are good reasons to suppose that the cult of Athene in the Erechtheum is a survival from the Mycenaean period. Although Athene's presence in the home of Odysseus and the partial restriction of her support to the local context of Ithaca can also be viewed as a Mycenaean survival, I find it likely that Athenian cult has indeed directly influenced the *Odyssey* at several points. Again, however, by an organic model which views the *Odyssey* and Athenian cult as developing together, priority is less important than the symbiotic relationship which they achieved. For Athenian audiences of Homeric performance the *Odyssey* was a ritual mimesis of their most important civic cults.

It remains to position the correlation between the *Odyssey* and Athenian cult in the context of my larger argument. In the first chapter, I analyze the structure of the opening scenes of the *Odyssey.* I show that these scenes are organized by a series of oppositions between groups of typologically related characters. These include Odysseus and the crew, whose fates are contrasted in the proem, and Zeus and Poseidon, whose outlooks on the role of the gods in human suffering are contrasted in the divine assembly. The sea god's persecution of Odysseus thus need not be reconciled with Zeus's own claim that mortals bring suffering on themselves, or with his portrayal of the gods as seeking to avert suffering rather than cause it.

The themes of the divine assembly exert a normative influence on the narrative which does not, however, flatten the characters into simple representatives of good and evil. We need look no further than *polumētis,* or 'greatly cunning', Odysseus himself, who retains some of the features of the trickster figure from which he is typologically and genealogically descended.[13] *Mētis,* or 'cunning intelligence', is an ambiguous quality in that it is at once responsible for civilization and a tool of deceit. While "lying and deception are acceptable tactics" against one's adversaries, they can also be viewed as criminal acts when directed against the members of one's own social unit.[14] It is precisely the negative potential of *mētis* that marks Odysseus' character outside of Homeric tradition. The *Odyssey,* however, largely suppresses the moral ambiguity of Odysseus' character while emphasizing his identification with Olympian values.[15] To claim that the suppression is somehow imperfect because traces of the original trickster remain implies that the *Odyssey* would be a greater work of art if it were a morality play.

At first, the polarity between *mētis* and *biē* that unifies the contrasts informing the Introduction remains latent. The proem merely declares that Odysseus was a clever man of wide-ranging experience. Whereas

[13] Odysseus is the grandson of Autolykos in the *Odyssey*. The tradition of Sisyphos' paternity is recorded in the *Cypria* and receives frequent mention in the tragedians, for which see Jebb at S. *Ph.* 417; Pearson at S. *Fr.* 567; Seaford at E. *Cyc.* 104. See also Plutarch, *quest. graec.* 43; Hyginus, *Fab.* 201. Theognis, 702–12, relates that Sisyphos returned from Hades due to his cleverness. Kullmann (1965) 41, note 1, argues that the tradition of Sisyphos' paternity was known to Homer.

[14] Beidelman, 233; see also Pitt-Rivers, esp. 11.

[15] For the characterization of Odysseus, see Stanford (1954) 8–24; Rutherford; Kullmann (1985) 10; Segal (1994) 109, 197, 200, 219–20. For the ambivalent nature of *mētis,* see the classic study by Detienne and Vernant (1974). For the moral neutrality of deceit in ancient Greek culture, see Stanford (1954); Beidelman, 233. On Odysseus' pedigree as a trickster, note that competing genealogical traditions made Odysseus son to Sisyphos and grandson to Hermes or, as in the *Odyssey* itself, grandson to Autolykos. The ambiguity of Odysseus' character can also be explained in terms of his status as a stranger throughout the poem (on the ambiguity of strangers, see Pitt-Rivers, chap. 5).

he suffered greatly at war and on the sea, his crew perished on account of their own *atasthaliai,* their 'reckless acts'. The significance of this condemnation of the crew is revealed in the divine assembly when Zeus insists that humans are responsible for their actions. The assembly also links the fate of the crew to that of the suitors by the paradigm of men who perish by their own "reckless acts." In the human assembly that follows in Book 2, Telemachos demands that the suitors leave the palace, with the result that the suitors openly align themselves with *biē.* At this point, we are able to see Odysseus' struggles with the suitors in terms of a *mētis-biē* polarity and to retroject that same polarity onto the proem. On the other hand, the opposition between Poseidon and the other Olympian gods, which began as an ethical contrast in the divine assembly, returns in Book 5 when Athene's *mētis* saves Odysseus from the *biē* of Poseidon.

Intertextual readings of the *Odyssey* and the *Iliad* lend support to my interpretation. It has long been recognized that the proems of the two Homeric epics are similarly structured. These similarities have been variously accounted for as accidents of formulaic composition or as the result of the Odyssean poet's emulation of his predecessor. The latter explanation belongs to an analytically inspired model that views Odyssean echoes of the *Iliad* as derivative. I replace this model with one in which polemic is the key to Homer's allusive art: the *Odyssey* consistently asserts its views and its claim to greatness at the expense of the *Iliad.* Thus, the structural parallels between the proems correspond to a striking contrast in the character and destiny of Odysseus and Achilleus. This contrast in the protagonists of the epics ultimately reinforces the opposition between *mētis* and *biē* that informs the Odyssean proem. Similar results are obtained when we compare the divine assembly following the Odyssean proem to the assembly that begins *Iliad* 24. In this case, it is the behavior and outlook of the gods that are contrasted in the context of parallel narrative structures. In the *Odyssey,* the alignment of *mētis* with Greek cultural norms results in a theodicy, while the *Iliad,* the poem of *biē,* is populated by gods who cause undeserved suffering.

In Chapter 2 I argue that the *Apologoi* illustrates and further defines the opposition between *mētis* and *biē* announced in the prologue. I begin by observing that the enchanted world represents an anti- or antecultural Paradise intimately associated with the sea and its figurehead Poseidon. Cultural representatives are distinguished by their capacity to subordinate physical force to intelligence, both internally and in their external environment, while intelligence is subordinate to force in representatives of nature. As a consequence, the identity of the poem's characters as civilized can be determined by their capacity to restrain their own behavior. Whereas Odysseus ultimately survives and returns to civilization through self-restraint, the crew, as they have done throughout the adventures, succumb to their physical urges on Thrinakie and are for this destroyed. Thus, to the larger theme of "nature" and "culture" belongs an opposition between physical urges and restraint, in the form of reason, social law, and piety. These oppositions ultimately return us to the ethical themes of the divine assembly.

The episodes of the *Apologoi* collectively reinforce the centrality of improper eating as a marker of unrestrained and uncivilized behavior. Yet the *Apologoi* is not simply an example of early Greek ethnography. It serves the important function of providing a commentary on the Ithacan narrative. In particular, the *Cyclopeia, Nekyia,* and Thrinakian episode add a perspective to Odysseus' struggles with the suitors on Ithaca that would otherwise be unavailable to us. The *Cyclopeia* uses cannibalism to illustrate the unrestrained behavior of Polyphemos and links the theme of improper eating to that of improper hosting. In the *Nekyia,* Odysseus learns from Teiresias the spiritual condition on which his return will be based: he must restrain himself and his men from eating the cattle of Helios on Thrinakie. After they arrive at Thrinakie, the crew sacrifice the cattle in Odysseus' absence and in doing so pervert the sacrificial ritual.

Odysseus fought at Troy for ten years to recover Helen, an improperly courted wife; for the next ten years repeated violations of the laws that govern civilized eating threaten his return to Ithaca. The last such violation, by his own crew on Thrinakie, is analogous to that of the suitors, who create a false Paradise by ravaging Odysseus' herds in his absence. Odysseus returns home to punish both crimes against the laws of hospitality—crimes which he has fought his entire adult life. The *Apologoi* can be read as an apology by Odysseus to his Phaiakian hosts as to why he must go home rather than remain on Scherie. His return from the enchanted realm results in the Ithaca's return from conditions endemic to that realm. By subordinating the *Apologoi* to the Ithacan narrative as a commentary on it, I conform to Aristotle's classification of the *Odyssey* as a tale of revenge by a returning hero (*Po.* 1455b10–11) while showing that the adventures nevertheless play a vital role in the poem as we have it.

Structural analysis of the *Apologoi* reveals that its narrative architecture reinforces the thematic centrality of Odysseus' journey to the Underworld, the *Nekyia.* From this analysis it emerges that the tales are arranged by two different patterns of organization relating Thrinakie to the *Cyclopeia* and to the Aiolian episode respectively. Detailed prosopography of the *Apologoi* confirms the centrality of the *Nekyia,* and hence the validity of the structural analysis, by showing that it divides the adventures into two distinct groups. While the adventures following the *Nekyia* involve divine females, those preceding it depict alternative societies. Together, the *Cyclopeia* and the Aiolian and Laistrygonian episodes create a hierarchy of civilization in which the Aiolians are the cultural equivalents of the Phaiakes and the Cyclopes their exact opposites, while the Laistrygones occupy an intermediate position. It is important to observe in this context that only the border realms of Scherie and Aiolie approach the standards of Greek culture as defined by the poem itself.

Comparative analysis of the *Cyclopeia* and the Thrinakian episode confirms their structural correlation by showing that they belong to a family of myth in which cattle represent the source of life. As such, the cattle oscillate in the tradition between complementary poles, being now in control of a chaos-demon, now in the possession of the sun god. In the Greek sphere, cattle are regularly appropriated for human use as a source of nourishment. At the same time, the Thrinakian episode is also linked to the Aiolian by a common structuring pattern that relates Cylopes-Aiolians-Laistrygones to Scylla-Thrinakie-Charybdis. As we have just seen, the members of this first triad are also related to the Phaiakes, the internal audience of the *Apologoi,* by their relative affinity to the norms of Greek culture. While the *Cyclopeia* comments on the social conditions that develop on Ithaca, Odysseus' experiences among the Phaiakes, a people who occupy the opposite end of this cultural spectrum, look forward to the restoration of order and prosperity after his return.

Polarity becomes actual conflict in the *Cyclopeia,* in which Odysseus, the protégé of Athene, attempts to establish *xenia,* a 'guest-host relationship', with Polyphemos, the son of Poseidon (Chapter 3). When Odysseus blinds Polyphemos he earns the wrath of Poseidon, which is in fact a defining aspect of Odysseus' own character. Whatever its true etymology, it is clear that the Greeks heard in Odysseus' name the verb *odussesthai,* meaning 'to hate'. Thus Homer first mentions Odysseus by name with the statement that Poseidon "raged incessantly against godlike Odysseus, before he reached his land" (1.20–21). Odysseus is not simply the "man of hatred" in a generic sense but is introduced as the object of a specific kind of hatred. Odysseus acquires that identity in the *Cyclopeia,* in the context of a struggle in which *mētis* is aligned with Greek culture and *biē* with the savage race of Cyclopes. When Odysseus escapes from the cave of Polyphemos, however, he yields to his own anger and in typically heroic fashion identifies himself to his victim. In so doing he assimilates himself to the very forces that he opposes. Moreover, this scene of revenge and assimilation acts as a paradigm for his later punishment of the suitors. Odysseus is at once the hater and the hated for punishing characters who violate the laws of hospitality.

The *Cyclopeia* also provides us with a unique opportunity to test the theories concerning the relationship of the *Odyssey* to its tradition. Wilhelm Grimm's demonstration that the *Cyclopeia* conflates two separate folk-tale traditions permits us to speak of a uniquely Odyssean account that exerts a limited influence on the tradition. Confirmation of Grimm's theory is provided by Lutz Röhrich, who observes: "The medieval versions [of the folk tale] depart widely from the Homeric text in Book Nine of the *Odyssey*. Previously, however, scholars had failed to notice their striking and significant correspondences with other ancient Mediterranean traditions independent of Homer. Such traditions are attested in part by recently discovered archaeological evidence, in particular the early vase paintings."[16] Justin Glenn gives the theory further support by cataloging some twenty story elements unique to the *Cyclopeia*.[17] If these elements were taken from a strand of the folk-tale tradition that had been celebrated to any significant extent in either time or place then we should fairly expect at least some of them to be attested by the extant variants. I am able to build on Glenn's findings by demonstrating that each of the features that distinguish the *Cyclopeia* from the folk-tale variants are motivated by the single aim of privileging the technological and ethical advantages of Greek civilization over the savage existence of the Cyclopes. The comparative material reveals that Odyssean tradition could thoroughly reshape a folk tale to its specific purposes while keeping the basic structure of the story intact.

In Chapter 4, I use my findings in the preceding chapters to refute the theory that traditional narrative carries with it the necessary consequence of thematic inconsistency. In particular, this theory cannot be used to support the argument that the behavior of the gods in the enchanted realm contradicts the theodicy of the divine assembly. I then turn to a formal analysis of the Thrinakian episode, where I show that Thrinakie echoes the themes of the Introduction so as to underscore the guilt of the crew. The crew's guilt is further emphasized by the fact that they pervert the sacrificial ritual when they slaughter the cattle of

[16] Röhrich (1962) 60.
[17] Glenn (1971).

Helios. Parallels with the Egyptian adventure of Menelaos, narrated in Book 4, support the view that the crew have already earned the anger of the gods before they sacrifice the cattle. On the other hand, structural parallels between the *Cyclopeia* and the Thrinakian episode relate the vengeance of Poseidon on Odysseus to the punishment of the crew by Zeus. This correspondence reproduces in detail the opposition between Poseidon and the other Olympian gods found in the Introduction. The opposition returns in the divine council-scene of Book 13, in which Poseidon deliberates punishing the Phaiakes for transporting Odysseus to Ithaca.

I conclude with a survey of the cults and myths in which Athene and Poseidon are paired (Chapter 5). Detailed analysis of evidence from Athens, Corinth, Sparta, Olympia, and Trozen demonstrates that the polar opposition which I have found between these gods in Homer has many precedents in Greek religious thought. Since I am chiefly interested in exploring the relationship between the *Odyssey* and the cults of the Erechtheum, I relegate the correlative material to Appendix 2. Pindar's Olympian 13 is of particular interest because its treatment of the Bellerophon myth offers some striking thematic parallels to the *Cyclopeia*.

In the contest of Athene and Poseidon for the patronage of Athens, the *mētis* of Athene is associated with civilization and the *biē* of Poseidon with an elemental and potentially hostile nature. The war between Erechtheus and Eumolpos provides a sequel to the contest in which the social order is threatened and reaffirmed with an act of war. The ritual analogue to the war, the Skira, belongs to a cycle of year-end festivals in which the order of society is dissolved and reconstituted. The Odyssean Revenge narrative conforms to the synchronic ritual pattern in its depiction of Ithacan society, and to the mythic pattern in its use of violence to restore order. The concept of culturally generative violence is a paradox embodied by Odysseus himself.

CHAPTER I

Dialectics of Enlightenment

Nowhere has Analysis yielded more anomalies, real or supposed, than in the *Odyssey*'s opening verses, and nowhere are the issues at stake of greater importance for a synoptic interpretation of the poem:

ἄνδρα μοι ἔννεπε, Μοῦσα, πολύτροπον, ὃς μάλα πολλὰ
πλάγχθη, ἐπεὶ Τροίης ἱερὸν προλίεθρον ἔπερσε·
πολλῶν δ᾽ ἀνθρώπων ἴδεν ἄστεα καὶ νόον ἔγνω,
πολλὰ δ᾽ ὅ γ᾽ ἐν πόντῳ πάθεν ἄλγεα ὃν κατὰ θυμόν,
ἀρνύμενος ἥν τε ψυχὴν καὶ νόστον ἑταίρων.
ἀλλ᾽ οὐδ᾽ ὣς ἑτάρους ἐρρύσατο, ἱέμενός περ·
αὐτῶν γὰρ σφετέρῃσιν ἀτασθαλίῃσιν ὄλοντο,
νήπιοι, οἳ κατὰ βοῦς Ὑπερίονος Ἠελίοιο
ἤσθιον· αὐτὰρ ὁ τοῖσιν ἀφείλετο νόστιμον ἦμαρ.
τῶν ἁμόθεν γε, θεὰ θύγατερ Διός, εἰπὲ καὶ ἡμῖν.
ἔνθ᾽ ἄλλοι μὲν πάντες, ὅσοι φύγον αἰπὺν ὄλεθρον,
οἴκοι ἔσαν, πόλεμόν τε πεφευγότες ἠδὲ θάλασσαν·
τὸν δ᾽ οἶον, νόστου κεχρημένον ἠδὲ γυναικός,
νύμφη πότνι᾽ ἔρυκε Καλυψώ, δῖα θεάων,
ἐν σπέσσι γλαφυροῖσι, λιλαιομένη πόσιν εἶναι.
ἀλλ᾽ ὅτε δὴ ἔτος ἦλθε περιπλομένων ἐνιαυτῶν,
τῷ οἱ ἐπεκλώσαντο θεοὶ οἶκόνδε νέεσθαι
εἰς Ἰθάκην - οὐδ᾽ ἔνθα πεφυγμένος ἦεν ἀέθλων
καὶ μετὰ οἷσι φίλοισι - θεοὶ δ᾽ ἐλέαιρον ἅπαντες
νόσφι Ποσειδάωνος· ὁ δ᾽ ἀσπερχὲς μενέαινεν
ἀντιθέῳ Ὀδυσῆϊ πάρος ἣν γαῖαν ἱκέσθαι.

(1.1–21)

Tell me, Muse, about the man, he of many turns, who many times
was driven from his course after he sacked the holy city of Troy.
He saw the cities of many men, and came to know their way of thought,
and many were the pains at sea that he suffered in his heart
striving to win his spirit, and the return of his companions.
But not even so did he save his companions eager though he was,
for they were destroyed by their very own reckless acts,
fools, who devoured the cattle of Hyperion Helios,
and he in turn took from them the day of their return.
Of these things, from whatever point, divine daughter of Zeus, tell us
also.
Then, all the others, as many as escaped sheer destruction
were home, having escaped both war and the sea;
but him alone, yearning for his return and his wife
a sovereign nymph detained, Calypso, the radiant goddess,
in her hollow caves, desiring him to be her husband.
But now when the year arrived in the revolving seasons,
the gods spun for him to return home
to Ithaca—not even there did he escape from his trials,
even among his friends—but the gods all pitied him,
apart from Poseidon, who raged incessantly against
godlike Odysseus, before he reached his land.[1]

The following comment by Stephanie West belongs to a long tradition of criticism: "Despite the care which has obviously been bestowed on its composition, this is, as has often been pointed out, an odd opening for our *Odyssey*."[2] It is the view of Analytic scholars that the proem, or at least parts of it, once introduced an epic devoted to Odysseus' wanderings. The earlier epic, however, corresponds only loosely to the adventures narrated in Books 9–12 of our poem. These conclusions rest on the following assertions: the proem only describes the events from Book 5 to the beginning of Book 13, is inaccurate in what it does describe, and awards undue emphasis to the Thrinakian episode, in which Helios punishes the crew for eating his cattle.[3]

Reference to the Thrinakian episode in verses 6–9 of the proem is open to censure on all three counts. Dawe, for example, faults the poet for choosing a relatively insignificant episode and for claiming that the

[1] Translations are my own unless otherwise noted.

[2] *CHO* 1:68.

[3] *CHO* 1:68; see Peradotto, 76. A rehearsal of Analytic attacks on verses 6–9 can be found in Rüter, 49–52, to which should be added those of Schadewaldt (1960) 874, note 21.

crew were responsible for their destruction: "It [the proem] evinces a solicitude for his comrades which is strangely out of keeping with their background role in the poem as a whole. It pays particular attention to one episode (the cattle of the Sun) which is by no means the one which has most impressed posterity, and it passes a judgement on the comrades' behaviour which is of a severity hardly merited by anything in the story as it is actually told to us."[4] Such criticism is not based on a specific feature of the proem, but on an interpretation of the *Apologoi.* I will address the accuracy of the proem as a description of the adventures and the significance of the Thrinakian episode in Chapters 2 and 4. For the moment suffice it to observe that there is nothing in the actual verses to betray a poet whose inspiration has failed him.

Stephanie West finds two reasons to question the appropriateness of these verses as an introduction to our poem. First, the Thrinakian episode is ill-suited to represent the other adventures: "None of the *speciosa miracula* which we associate with Odysseus—Polyphemus, Aeolus, Circe, the Sirens, Scylla and Charybdis—is mentioned. We do not expect a comprehensive summary of what is to come; but if the poet's purpose was, as it would be natural to suppose, simply to indicate enough of his theme to catch his audience's attention, his choice of detail is strange."[5] In her judgment, the proem also misrepresents the Thrinakian episode, the other adventures, and the guilt of the crew, by suggesting that Odysseus loses his entire crew on the island. In so doing, it exaggerates the importance of Thrinakie: "The emphasis given to this episode . . . is striking. In fact this severe condemnation of Odysseus' companions is not borne out by the narrative. Eleven of his twelve ships are destroyed by the Laestrygonians, through no fault of the victims, and even on board Odysseus' own ship there are several casualties before Thrinacia is reached."[6] It is true that only seven percent of the crew die off Thrinakie, so that a factual discrepancy does exist: *the* crew do not perish as a result of eating the cattle of the sun, only the majority of those who sailed in Odysseus' own ship. But to claim that the episode is therefore overly emphasized implies that significance amounts to a simple body-count.

Even if we chose to downplay the inaccuracy of verses 6–9, we are still left with a number of important questions: why does the poet single

[4] Dawe at *Od.* 1.1–10.

[5] *CHO* 1:68–69.

[6] *CHO* at 1.7–9. The issue of whether the crew is in some sense responsible for their destruction in the Laistrygonian harbor is somewhat more complex than West supposes (see below, Chapter 2).

out this one episode for mention and why does he devote almost half of his ten-verse proem to it? In other words, does the Thrinakian episode have a significance commensurate with the expectations raised by the proem, and how—if at all—does the proem serve to introduce the *Odyssey* as we have it? A related and no less important issue concerns the prominence given the theme of Poseidon's wrath in the opening narrative. Once again, it is argued that the god's prominence is out of all proportion to his influence in the actual events of the poem and his behavior is, moreover, at variance with the portrayal of the gods in the divine assembly. Poseidon is thus assigned to the Urtext and the assembly to the *Bearbeiter*.[7]

Analytic scholarship has demonstrated beyond any doubt that if a poet were to single out an episode from the adventures for mention in the proem, then Thrinakie is a less than obvious choice. Any attempt to address the larger issues of the poem must explain its selection and the emphasis placed on it—and on the wrath of Poseidon. As a way out of this impasse I suggest that we first reorient the discussion and ask whether these references to Thrinakie and Poseidon can be justified by their local function in the opening narrative. To this end I will analyze the Introduction in terms of its narrative structure and thematic development. I will then build on the results of my inquiry to address issues of accuracy and significance in subsequent chapters.

The Antiphonal Structure of the Prologue

Homer conducts the initial exposition of the *Odyssey* with a series of balanced contrasts, as shown in the outline on the facing page. The proem, verses 1–10, is enclosed by a ring observing chiastic word-order: "the man to me please tell o Muse / Goddess . . . please tell us also" (*andra moi ennepe Mousa / thea . . . eipe kai hēmin*).[8] As the proem concludes, we are prepared for a tale devoted to the wanderings of Odysseus after the Trojan war. At the poet's invitation, however, the Muse selects the last month of the adventures as the starting point of the story and

[7] For the significance and outlook of Poseidon and his role in the poem, see, for example, Woodhouse, 39–40; Jacoby (1933) 189–90; Focke, 156–61; Heubeck (1954) 84–85; Jones, 11–12; Reinhardt (1960) 69–73; Rüter, 44–45, 89–90; Fenik (1974) 208–30; Clay (1983) 229–30; *CHO* at 9.526–35; Peradotto, 62–63; Dawe at *Od.* 1.20; Segal (1994) chap. 10.

[8] Bassett (1923) 340.

A) Prologue
1) A proem announcing the theme of the *epos* (1–10):
a) a clever man who wandered and suffered at sea after sacking Troy;
b) his companions perished by their own reckless acts.

2) The situation on earth as the story begins (11–19a):
b) all the Greeks who had escaped destruction were home
a) except him alone, whom Calypso was detaining against his will; not even when he returned home did he escape from suffering.

3) The attitude of the gods towards the suffering of 'the man' (19b-21):
a) all the gods pitied him,
b) except Poseidon, whose hatred was unrelenting toward godlike Odysseus.

B) The Divine Assembly
4) The situation on Olympos as the story begins (22–27):
b) Poseidon was away, feasting with the Aithiopes,
a) and all the other gods were together in the house of Zeus.

indicates that events on Ithaca belong to it (verses 11–19).[9] The poet will narrate the story outlined in verses 11–21 in his own voice. To Odysseus falls the adventure story that the poet set out to tell.

Verses 11–19, describing the initial situation on earth, are enclosed by a second ring: "they were at home, having escaped / but not even there [at home] did he escape" (*oikoi esan . . . pepheugotes / oud' entha pephugmenos*). This second ring heightens the contrast between Odysseus and all the other Greeks at verse 11: "on the one hand, all the others / but him alone" (*alloi men pantes / ton d' hoion*). The prologue concludes with a reference to Poseidon's hatred of Odysseus (19–21) that balances the vengeance of Helios on the crew in the final verses of the proem (8–9).

The collective reference to the Greeks "on the one hand, all the other men" (*alloi men pantes*) that begins the second ring, is echoed by a collective reference to the gods "but the gods all pitied him" (*theoi d' eleairon hapantes*) at verse 19. The latter clause introduces a third ring that closes with "but at the time all the other [gods]" (*hoi de dē alloi*) at verse 26. Whereas the second ring explains the location of the Greeks who fought at Troy, the third ring begins with the attitude of the gods towards the sufferings of Odysseus and continues with their whereabouts. The comprehensive statements beginning the second and third ring are each

[9] On the Muse's reorientation of the opening narrative, see Pedrick.

followed by an immediate qualification: "all the other men . . . but him alone," and "all the gods . . . apart from Poseidon."

Finally, the entire prologue, verses 1–21, is enclosed by a fourth ring, "man / godlike Odysseus" (*andra / antitheō Odusēi*), that introduces one of the poem's ruling leitmotifs: as in the cave of Polyphemos, on Scherie, and on Ithaca, the hero is introduced anonymously as one who has lost everything, and acquires his name only after his character has been defined by his actions.[10] As important, "godlike Odysseus" receives his name with mention of a god's wrath. Syntactically, the word Odysseus is introduced to the poem as the object of a verb meaning to hate, *meneainen*. More is at work here than a pun on the word Odysseus, or 'the hated': the anger of his ritual antagonist, Poseidon, defines Odysseus' thematic identity.[11]

The prologue concludes with "the gods all pitied him / apart from (*nosphi*) Poseidon" (19–20). This is answered by the verses introducing the divine assembly: "but he [Poseidon] had gone off to the Aithiopes who live far away. . . . but the others were assembled together in the home of Olympian Zeus" (22–27). A contrast between Poseidon and the other gods that begins with their attitudes toward Odysseus is thus emphasized by its repetition in the verses that follow. The inherent symmetry in this pair of contrasts is heightened by the syntax and language, which link them thematically. Especially noteworthy is the use of *nosphi,* or 'apart', at verse 20. The adverb regularly implies physical separation and is only here in the *Odyssey* employed in a transferred sense. As Klaus Rüter observes, "Poseidon is absent due to the isolation in which he finds himself through his hatred of Odysseus, while the compassion of all the other gods results in their assembly at the house of Zeus."[12] In fact, the wrath of Poseidon results in the isolation of both himself and Odysseus from their respective social units. The poet emphasizes Odysseus' own situation by separating "the hero, first from his Comrades, then from the other heroes of the *Iliad,* and finally from the civilized world."[13] Nor is Poseidon merely absent from Olympos, but is located at the ends of the earth, among the Aithiopes, a people who

[10] For the ring structure, see Rüter, 42. For the motif of concealment and delayed identification see Rüter, 47; Thornton, 124–28; Fenik (1974) 5–60; Pucci (1982) 49–57; Bergren, 43; Peradotto, 101; Goldhill (1991) 1–36.

[11] For ritual antagonism see Nagy (1979) 142–53; Nagy (1990) 12. For the poet's derivation of Odysseus' name, see *Od.* 1.62, 5.340, 19.405–12. See discussion with further references in Clay (1983) 27–29; Peradotto, 120–70; Goldhill (1991) 24–36; Segal (1994) 33, 90–91.

[12] Rüter, 53.

[13] Bassett (1934) 108.

do not belong to the Greek cultural sphere. Here, as throughout the poem, physical location is a correlate of one's spiritual condition.

The organization of the prologue serves an obvious narrative function: its chiastic and antithetical arrangement of individuals and groups permits a seamless transition from one topic to the next. An initial pair of contrasts relates the fate of a single man, Odysseus, to that of two groups of men in their return from Troy. A second pair opposes the attitude and whereabouts of a single god, Poseidon, to those of the other Olympians. Also worth noting is the elliptical manner in which Homer alludes to the demise of the crew and to the anger of Poseidon. In the former case, the cause is described but not the circumstance, and indeed we hear nothing further of Thrinakie or the cattle of Helios for another five books. In the latter case, the fact of Poseidon's anger is mentioned but not the cause: pity and hatred, Poseidon and all other gods, are simply juxtaposed with Odysseus at the center of their attention. It is as if the poet's immediate expository aim were simply to establish a series of contrasting relationships.

The pity of the gods is the force that sets events in motion; and although I have been able to expose a principle of antithetical organization in which the crew and Poseidon participate, the foregoing analysis offers nothing more than a formal explanation of their function. Moreover, the Muse's own reorientation of the story so that it includes the struggles of Odysseus on Ithaca could lead us to conclude that Thrinakie is only significant for a version of the *Apologoi* that we never actually receive.

In the discussion that follows, I argue that the prominence awarded Thrinakie and Poseidon is not an accident of Homer's expository technique; rather, the organizing *structure* of the opening narrative is a function of the narrative's *theme*. To this end, it will be necessary to evaluate an additional contrast introduced in the divine assembly between Aigisthos and Odysseus. For the present, note that in the finely wrought passage comprising the Odyssean prologue, the differing fates of Odysseus and his comrades at Troy are balanced by the contrasting attitudes of Poseidon and the other Olympian gods.

Aigisthos and Odyssean Thematic Structures

The divine assembly reintroduces the themes of the exposition in a series of speeches which observes the same organizing principles found the prologue. Moreover, the assembly restates and elaborates on the contrasts in the prologue. The relationship between the two narratives can be observed from the following outline:[14]

B) The Divine Assembly	*Corresponds to*
4) Poseidon is absent, the other gods are on Olympos	3
5) Aigisthos dies by his own reckless acts	1b & 2b (the crew)
6) But Odysseus suffers	1a & 2a
7) Poseidon versus the other gods regarding Odysseus	3

Zeus begins the assembly by objecting to the claim that the gods are responsible for human suffering. He substantiates his objection by observing that the gods had sent Hermes to Aigisthos with an explicit warning not to court Clytemnestra or kill Agamemnon (5). Far from inflicting pain, the gods of this story actively seek to prevent mortals from bringing pain upon themselves. Zeus thus assigns the gods a role analogous to that of Odysseus in the proem, who sought to prevent the destruction of the crew.

Athene seizes the occasion to mention her favorite, Odysseus, whose predicament would seem to challenge the moral that Zeus draws from the story of Aigisthos (6). She thereby reintroduces the contrast between men who die by their own reckless acts and the long-suffering Odysseus that informs the proem. Zeus concedes Odysseus' wisdom and piety and explains the cause of Poseidon's anger. He concludes with a resolution that once again depicts Poseidon in isolation against a united Olympos (7):

ἀλλ᾽ ἄγεθ᾽ ἡμεῖς οἵδε περιφραζώμεθα πάντες
νόστον, ὅπως ἔλθῃσι. Ποσειδάων δὲ μεθήσει
ὃν χόλον· οὐ μὲν γάρ τι δυνήσεται ἀντία πάντων
ἀθανάτων ἀέκητι θεῶν ἐριδαινέμεν οἶος.

(1.76–79)

But come, let all of us who are here give thought
to return, so that he [Odysseus] may go home. Poseidon will release
his anger; for he will not be able in any way to strive in opposition
against the will of all the deathless gods, alone.

[14] Note that the theme of the gods' pity (3a) is present throughout the discussion of Odysseus by Athene and Zeus (6–7) and motivates their resolve to bring him home. Their decision reintroduces the opposition of Poseidon to the will of the other gods (3b).

The divine assembly is framed, not by Poseidon's hatred for Odysseus, but by his isolation and opposition to the collective will of the other gods.

In retrospect, it is clear that Orestes offers a paradigm of behavior for both Odysseus and Telemachos.[15] In the divine assembly, however, this story of a son's vengeance on behalf of his father is followed by a complementary account of a father's vengeance on behalf of his son: Odysseus, Zeus explains, is languishing on Ogygie because Poseidon is angry with him for blinding Polyphemos. The analogy in the two situations calls attention to a basic difference between them that reflects on the character and outlook of Poseidon. By having the god act on behalf of a cannibal who is not killed but blinded in self-defence, the poem shows that for Poseidon no moral justification whatever can take precedence over a family's right to avenge itself on behalf of kin. The vengeance of Orestes, by contrast, is drawn into a moral pattern of divine warning, criminal folly, and punishment with important theological consequences that we shall consider below.

Conversely, the fate of Aigisthos foreshadows that of the suitors. In its immediate context, however, his fate also comments on that of the crew. Homer emphasizes the latter parallel with close repetition of a weighty and significant word in the dative plural, "through reckless acts" (*atasthaliēsin*). In verse 7 the word assigns responsibility to the crew for their demise off Thrinakie. Its recurrence in verse 34 links the story of Aigisthos—and its moral—to the fate of the crew. Like Aigisthos, the crew die before their time by their own reckless acts, and Odysseus, like Hermes, attempted to warn them, but they ignored his warning. The audience, alerted to the parallel through verbal echo, is invited to infer Odysseus' own role by verses 5–6: "striving to win . . . the homecoming of his companions. But not even so did he save his companions eager though he was."

The Aigisthos paradigm supplements the reference to the crew in the proem, which for the sake of proportion had to remain elliptical. In their immediate context, then, Zeus's opening remarks provide a com-

[15] For the analogy between Aigisthos and the suitors see Hommel. The roles of Orestes and Agamemnon are repeatedly reassigned to Odysseus and Telemachos throughout the opening books. For detailed analysis see Olson, with whose findings I generally agree, although I believe that to an audience familiar with the basic story line of our poem the analogy between Telemachos and Orestes would have been immediately apparent in the speech of Zeus. I also feel that the comparison between Agamemnon and Odysseus begins as early as the proem, where the audience could have well assumed from the first five verses that they were about to hear the story of Agamemnon's return "after he sacked the sacred citadel of Troy" (compare 9.263–66).

mentary on the behavior of Poseidon and the crew, and of Odysseus, whose attempts to save the crew relate him to the gods in the story of Aigisthos. The contrast in the proem between a clever, long-suffering man who survives and reckless men who perish continues in the divine assembly as a contrast between the just and the unjust, in which justice is revealed to be a criterion of survival. The assembly does not simply reintroduce the themes of the prologue but elaborates on them and helps establish their significance: thematic development through suppletive repetition is an important feature of Homer's narrative technique. Here in the Introduction we can observe a second recurrent feature of that technique: the repetition consists of a story pattern shared by groups of related characters.

The theme of men who perish by their reckless acts prepares for the scene to shift from Olympos to Ithaca, and we should note the care with which Homer prepares for that shift.[16] Repetition of *atasthaliēsin* links the crew to Aigisthos and pulls the word itself into prominence.[17] As the poem continues to unfold, an insistent echoing of words beginning *atasthal-* helps underline the affinity among the crew, Aigisthos, and the suitors. The attentive listener, whose suspicions were alerted as early as verse 18 by "not even there [at home on Ithaca] did he escape from his trials," would have noted the parallel between Aigisthos and the suitors established by "he married the wedded wife of Agamemnon" (*alokhon mnēstēn,* 36), together with "we warned him not to kill him [Agamemnon] or court his wife" (*mnaasthai akoitin,* 39). The brusque, even heated, manner in which Athene draws her own moral from Aigisthos' punishment, "thus may any other man perish who does such deeds [that is, kill the husband and court his wife]" (1.47), indicates that she is thinking of the suitors as she says this. Indeed, Athene makes the first explicit mention of the suitors immediately following the discussion of Odysseus, and her words relate them at once to the paradigm of "men who die through their own reckless acts":

αὐτὰρ ἐγὼν Ἰθάκηνδ᾽ ἐσελεύσομαι, ὄφρα οἱ υἱὸν
μᾶλλον ἐποτρύνω καί οἱ μένος ἐν φρεσὶ θείω,
εἰς ἀγορὴν καλέσαντα κάρη κομόωντας Ἀχαιοὺς

[16] Since the work of Reinhardt (1948–1960), few would argue that the *Telemachy* does not belong to our *Odyssey,* but the mechanism of the transfer from Olympos to Ithaca has yet to be explained adequately.

[17] For the word, see Jones, 3–10; Andersen (1973) 21–23; Nagy (1979) 162–63; Nagler (1990).

πᾶσι μνηστήρεσσιν ἀπειπέμεν, οἵ τέ οἱ αἰεὶ
μῆλ' ἀδινὰ σφάζουσι καὶ εἰλίποδας ἕλικας βοῦς.

(1.88–92)

But I shall go to Ithaca to rouse his son
the more, and put force in his mind,
to call the long-haired Achaioi to assembly
and denounce all the suitors who slaughter without cease
his thronging sheep and crumpled cows with swinging feet.[18]

Upon reaching Ithaca, Athene encounters not a host prepared to fulfill the all-important obligations of hospitality, or *xenia,* but the suitors, who render the proper fulfillment of those obligations impossible:[19]

εὗρε δ' ἄρα μνηστῆρας ἀγήνορας· οἳ μὲν ἔπειτα
πεσσοῖσι προπάροιθε θυράων θυμὸν ἔτερπον,
ἥμενοι ἐν ῥινοῖσι βοῶν, οὓς ἔκτανον αὐτοί.

(1.106–8)

And now she came upon the haughty suitors, who at the time
were amusing themselves with dice before the doors,
sitting on the hides of cattle which they themselves had slain.

These verses echo Athene's earlier remark that the suitors are plundering Odysseus' herds, and thus reinforce the connection between the suitors and the crew. Indeed, throughout the poem and especially here in the programmatic first scene of the Ithacan narrative, the improper feasting of the suitors (which links them to the crew) is no less emphasized than their courtship of Penelope (which links them to Aigisthos).[20]

Athene rouses Telemachos to call an assembly (1.272–73) in which he takes on the monitory function of Hermes in the Aigisthos paradigm.[21] The events of 1.102 to 2.259 thus initiate a third repetition of the scenario "men who die by their own reckless acts," as it dramatizes the situation to which Odysseus will return and what that return will mean to his family and to Ithacan society. The absence of the king has resulted

[18] For my translation of verse 92 see *IC* at *Il.* 9.466.

[19] For Homeric *xenia* see below, Chapter 3.

[20] See *Od.* 1.160, which becomes emblematic of the suitors, and 1.225–29. Leokritos, one of the suitors, lays stress on feasting, not courting, as the central activity (2.242–56). The suitors' preference for food is not lost on Horace, *S.* 2.5.79–80.

[21] Odysseus later appropriates this function himself (16.278–80). For his similar role in the Thrinakian episode, see Chapter 4 below.

in the collapse of social order on the island. The collapse is represented chiefly by the suitors' violations of the laws of hospitality, including their improper feasting and courtship. Whereas the proem introduces Odysseus as the wandering hero who conquered Troy, his son's maturation in the *Telemachy* culminates in a journey to meet the cause of the war, Helen, whose story graphically illustrates the social upheavals that can result from courting another man's wife. Appropriately, our first image of Telemachos, in which "he sits among the suitors grieving at heart" (1.114), echoes the contrast between a good man who suffers and reckless men who eat the cattle of another in the proem.

The parallel among the crew, Aigisthos, and the suitors is not confined to the repetition of a single—albeit tagged and prominent—word, but insisted upon throughout the narrative that follows. The relationship among these stories is brought out by the following outline based on the information provided up to 2.259:

A) Proem
Odysseus tried to save his crew,
but they died by their own reckless acts;
they ate the cattle of the sun
but Helios killed them in revenge.

B) Divine Assembly
Hermes, sent by Zeus, tried to warn Aigisthos,
but he died by his own reckless acts;
he married Clytemnestra and killed Agamemnon
but Orestes returned and killed him in revenge.

C) *Telemachy*
Telemachos tried to warn the suitors and Zeus sent an omen,
but they continued to court Penelope and eat Odysseus' cattle . . .

Each repetition of the story expands upon the one before it, and the situation on Ithaca combines elements of both the Thrinakian episode and the story of Aigisthos. The human assembly of Book 2, in which Telemachos denounces the suitors, has served a very important function indeed, and this explains the stress laid upon it by Athene.[22]

[22] For Athene's emphasis of the *agora,* see *Od.* 1.88–92. See also Chapter 3 below. The *agora* has been a favorite point of attack for the Analysts, and Unitarian defenses generally center on the fact that Telemachos defines the suitors' presence in the house as a communal problem and makes it a matter of public record that they are not welcome. Note that in 5.23–24 Zeus makes Odysseus' return contingent on the events of Books 1–4; he

Let us apply our initial findings to Analytic readings of the Introduction.[23] The proem mentions two events from the past—the sack of Troy and the loss of the crew—which constitute the temporal boundaries of the *Apologoi*.[24] Verses 11–21 indicate the initial situation on earth and among the gods (Odysseus alone on an island, the gods assembled on Olympos) and allude to the future course of events (Odysseus' struggles on Ithaca). The first twenty-one verses thus refer to the three principal narrative sequences devoted to Odysseus, although they observe the temporal rather than the narrative order of events: Odysseus' wanderings since the Trojan war (Books 9–12), his return from Ogygie (Books 5–8), and the Revenge (Books 13–24). Homer links the demise of the crew to the Aigisthos paradigm in the divine assembly, and in so doing reveals the significance of Thrinakie in the proem. Immediately afterwards, the *Telemachy* introduces the suitors in a manner that emphasizes their conformity to the same paradigm.

The first hundred verses provide an invaluable insight into Homer's compositional technique: structural and verbal parallels allow the fate of one character or group to provide tacit commentary on that of another. The Introduction simultaneously develops the theme of "men who die by their reckless acts," and uses that theme to ease the transition from the proem to the divine assembly, and from the assembly to Ithaca. Similarity in the fates of the crew and the suitors helps unify a narrative consisting of two Ithacan sections, between which an account of Odysseus' wanderings is interposed.

The claim that men die by their own reckless acts emerges as a central theme of the poem. Alternatively and, as I shall presently argue, more accurately, the fates of Odysseus and the groups to which he is related illustrate complementary aspects of a single theme: people like Odysseus survive, people like the crew do not. The Thrinakian episode was singled out for mention in the proem because it is a vehicle for introducing that theme.[25] The fact that theme, rather than event or character, organizes the narrative helps explain the prominence of Thrinakie in

---

must be referring chiefly to the situation created by the assembly and by Telemachos' subsequent journey.

[23] I rehearse Analytic attacks on and Unitarian defenses of the Introduction below, Appendix 1.

[24] See Bassett (1923) 341–42.

[25] Rüter, 77, concludes from his comparative study of epic introductions that "it is precisely in its opening sections that epic customarily announces its purpose and defines the perspective [Aspekt] from which the narrative events are to be considered."

the Introduction and shows the *Telemachy* to be fully integrated into the poem.

The Odyssean proem was conceived for the kind of story our *Odyssey* tells. It was not created for a "core" poem or Urtext devoted to the wanderings of Odysseus. This leaves unresolved for the time being: 1) whether reference to Thrinakie in the proem fairly represents the actual events on the island, and 2) whether and in what sense the Thrinakian episode stands for the collective experience of the crew. Formal analysis has shown, however, that there is nothing in the composition of the prologue that betrays "incompetence" or "haste." The material has been organized with care by a poet in full control of his craft who has employed an identifiable narrative technique.

Intertextual Beginnings

Iliadic parallels corroborate my reading of the Introduction, which has thus far been based on internal evidence. The proems of the two epics resemble one another so closely that a number of scholars working solely from the strength of the structural parallels have concluded that the *Odyssey* imitates its predecessor:

> The proems of the *Iliad* and *Odyssey* are strikingly similar, particularly at the beginning. The theme comes first (ἄνδρα/μῆνιν . . .), next the invocation (μοι ἔννεπε, Μοῦσα/ἄειδε, θεά), then a four-syllable adjective characterizing the theme (πολύτροπον/οὐλομένην), expanded by a relative clause (ὃς μάλα πολλὰ πλάγχθη/ἣ μυρί' Ἀχαιοῖς ἄλγε' ἔθηκε), further elaborated by two δέ-clauses (πολλῶν δ', πολλὰ δ'/πολλὰς δ', αὐτοὺς δέ). In both the poet refers to the vast possibilities of the theme (μάλα πολλά, πολλῶν δ', πολλὰ δ'/μυρί') and sorrows to be described (πάθεν ἄλγεα/ἄλγε' ἔθηκε). . . . The resemblance between the two proems may partly reflect a traditional pattern for beginning a long heroic narrative, but the parallelism is so close as to suggest that the poet of the *Odyssey* modelled his opening on that of the *Iliad*.[26]

More revealing is the contrast between the protagonists, Achilleus and Odysseus. Although treated separately in the secondary literature it is, I submit, precisely this contrast which explains the structural parallels.[27]

[26] *CHO* at 1.1–10. See Bassett (1923) 340–41; Groningen; Rüter, 28–39; A. Lenz, 21–22, 49–56; Pucci (1982).

[27] On the contrast between the two heroes, see Nagy (1979) 42–58; Pucci (1982) 40–53; Clay (1983) 96–112; Rubin, 103–4.

In the second verse of the *Odyssey,* the poet announces that "the *polútropos* 'man,' not the quick-footed Achilleus, son of Peleus, sacked the city of Troy."[28] Odysseus' conquest demonstrates the superiority of *mētis* over *biē,* intelligence over force, as do his later conflicts with the crew, Polyphemos, and the suitors within the *Odyssey* itself.

The contrast extends beyond their relative success at conquering Troy: the destructive hatred of Achilleus, announced with the first word of the *Iliad* and elaborated by its proem, caused untold suffering and the death of countless Greeks, including his own best friend, and ultimately himself (*muri' alge' ethēke, Il.* 1.2). Achilleus eventually describes himself as *atasthalos* for causing such pain (*Il.* 22.418).[29] Odysseus, on the other hand, suffered greatly (*polla . . . pathen algea, Od.* 1.4) and tried to save his men who, however, died by their own *atasthaliai.* The relationship between Odysseus and Achilleus thus mirrors the relationship between Odysseus and his crew within the Odyssean proem.

Both proems refer to the death of many Greeks. Yet herein lies a fundamental difference of outlook: while the army at Troy suffers due to the wrath of Achilleus, the crew of Odysseus bring suffering on themselves. The *Odyssey* represents the destruction of the crew as punishment for crime by displacing the *atasthaliai* that typifies the epic hero onto his men. The situation changes somewhat on Ithaca where Odysseus kills the suitors of Penelope. Yet by making the suitors rather than Odysseus guilty of *atasthaliai,* Homer reconciles the theme of the hero as a source of pain with the fact that Zeus and Athene both support Odysseus and identify themselves as patrons of justice in the divine assembly. Conversely, Achilleus, like the crew, perishes because he ignores a divine warning, but the reentry of Achilleus into battle in the face of certain death defines his heroism, whereas in the *Odyssey* the motif of the divine warning that goes unheeded contributes to the guilt of the crew.

The introductory verses of both epics find meaning in the names of Achilleus and Odysseus that reinforces the contrast in their character. The word Achilleus has been plausibly derived from *Akhí-lāu̯s meaning "whose *laós* [host of fighting men] has *ákhos* [grief]."[30] The proem would seem to acknowledge this etymology by deriving a collective designation for the Greek *laos,* the *Akhaioi,* from the *akhos* caused by

[28] Pucci (1982) 46. The scholia to *Od.* 7.77 interpret the quarrel between Achilleus and Odysseus in the first song of Demodokos as over whether Troy would be taken by force or by guile. See Rüter, 249–51; Thornton, 43–45; Nagy (1979) 22–25.

[29] Nagy (1990) 13–14.

[30] Nagy (1979) 69. Holland offers an up-to-date review of previous scholarship and proposes a new etymology.

Akhilleus: "sing about hatred, goddess, the deadly hatred of Peleus' son, *Akhilleus, which brought the Akhaioi many woes.*" (*Il.* 1.1–2)[31] Odysseus, by contrast, is introduced in the Odyssean proem as a man who suffers (*pathen algea*) and is hated (*meneainen . . . Odusēi*) rather than as one who hates (*mēnin . . . Akhilēos*) and causes suffering (*alge' ethēke*). Thus, the derivation of Odysseus' name becomes the subject of a famous pun in the divine assembly, when Athene asks Zeus "why do you find him [Odysseus] so odious?" (*Od.* 1.62)[32] The Odyssean proem would also seem to exploit the semantic polyvalence of the epithet *polutropos,* which can refer to Odysseus' many travels (verses 1–2) and to his many wiles (verse 2), thus bringing us back to the contrast between the *biē* of Achilleus who did not return and the *mētis* of Odysseus who will.[33]

Two further points of contact between Odysseus and Achilleus are relevant to my larger argument: both poems contain scenes in which the protagonist chooses the equivalent of *kleos aphthiton,* 'unwithering fame', over an alternate destiny. In Book 9 of the *Iliad,* Achilleus declares that he can win unwithering fame at the cost of his homecoming, *nostos,* or he can return to Phthia, where his fame will indeed wither, but he will enjoy a long life (*Il.* 9.412–16). The latter alternative corresponds to the destiny of the average man, if he is lucky; the first constitutes the destiny of Achilleus, who, however, initially rejects this alternative after concluding that fame provides inadequate compensation for death. Achilleus ultimately returns to battle, where he does win *kleos aphthiton,* although his choice is motivated by a desire not for fame but for revenge.

The *Iliad* thus offers a paradigm of the heroic warrior in which *kleos aphthiton* is purchased with an early death.[34] In the *Odyssey,* by contrast, Odysseus must choose between a long life with fame and eternal obscurity as the husband of Calypso, 'The Concealer'.[35] Like Achilleus, Odysseus chooses fame over obscurity; he does so, however, not because of a desire for revenge but for *nostos,* 'homecoming', although his choice does include vengeance on the suitors. The first of Odysseus' choices recombines the elements of the destinies available to Achilleus

31 See Peradotto, 114–15. For an Odyssean example, see 11.486.

32 I appropriate the word "odious" from Stanford (1954) 11.

33 On the epithet see Pucci (1987) 16–17, 24–25; Peradotto, 115–16.

34 Nagy (1979) 36–41; Pucci (1982) 56; Clay (1983) 106–12. Pucci (1982) 47, sees the suppression of Odysseus' name in the proem as a bow to the Iliadic view of *kleos,* even though he recognizes the "consistent anti-Iliadic point of view" of the Odyssean proem.

35 The complaint is constantly made in the *Odyssey* that Odysseus lost his fame together with his return (for which, see Chapter 2 below).

to produce a third destiny vastly superior to either: return with a long life and fame. "The alternative" immortality with "The Concealer," is a hyperbolic version of the long life that awaited Achilleus in "Phthia."

From the perspective of the *Odyssey*'s human actors, however, Odysseus' apparent fate as the poem begins is as inferior to the choices available to Achilleus as his eventual fate is superior: loss of life and return without *kleos*. Moreover, the fate actually offered him by Calypso corresponds to the immortality offered by hero cult, in which the hero was thought of as continuing his physical existence on Elysium or the Islands of the Blessed.[36] Whereas the *Iliad* denies its heroes the possibility of personal immortality as an alternative to the undying fame granted by epic, the *Odyssey* makes this possibility available to Odysseus so that he can refuse it; his longing to return home dramatizes as it were the superiority of epic immortality to that offered by cult.

Finally, self-restraint is the key to the success and survival of each hero. In the *Odyssey*, self-restraint regularly involves subordinating desire to reason, and as such belongs to the subordination of *biē* to *mētis* in the successful hero (in Chapter 2 we shall also see that self-restraint bridges the themes of intelligence and suffering). In the embassy scene of *Iliad* 9 it is ironically Odysseus himself, together with Phoinix and Aias, who counsels the importance of self-restraint to an unheeding Achilleus.[37] Achilleus' inability to govern his emotions results in Patroklos' death and ultimately in his own. Odysseus' own powers of self-restraint, by contrast, ensure his continued survival, eventual return, and revenge on Polyphemos and the suitors.

The sort of intertextual reading in which I am engaged has often carried with it the assumption that the Odyssean poet was satisfied with mere imitation, or at most competition.[38] I have argued instead that structural parallels between the proems reinforce a contrast in the character and destiny of Achilleus and Odysseus. Both heroes suffer and inflict suffering, but Odysseus survives whereas Achilleus does not, and in the *Odyssey* it is the hero's *laoi*—both the crew and the suitors—who

[36] Nagy (1990b) 272, 421. Note that in cult the immortalized hero was also thought of as a present and beneficent force at his center of worship.

[37] *Il*. 9.252–61; for the self-restraint of Odysseus, see Chapter 2 below.

[38] For imitation, see *CHO* at 1.1–10, and the sources cited there. Jacoby (1933) 161, offers rivalry as a motive, on which see also A. Edwards (1985); Martin, 227–39; Ford, 94–95, 114–118. The agonistic model developed by Edwards (1990), Martin, Griffith and Ford dovetails with my own position that the Homeric poems achieved their written form in a festival context. It also conforms to the agonistic model of Homeric society formulated by scholars such as Beidelman, thus corroborating the argument of I. Morris (1986) that Homer belongs to the cultural system that he is describing.

bring suffering on themselves by their own reckless acts. The contrast between Achilleus and Odysseus thus contributes to a larger pattern of opposition introduced in the proem by the fate of Odysseus and his crew and points to a fundamental difference in the portrayal of human suffering in the two epics.

It is thus highly significant for my interpretation that the terms in which I have discussed Achilleus and his relationship to Odysseus apply equally to Agamemnon. In the *Iliad,* Agamemnon forcibly deprives Achilleus of his spear bride Briseis; in the *Odyssey* he foolishly returns home without taking precautions, and as a consequence is murdered while feasting.[39] The two Iliadic heroes to whom Odysseus is contrasted throughout the *Odyssey* cause their own destruction and the loss of men under their command by a lack of *mētis* manifested in unrestrained behavior and in reliance on *biē*. Achilleus supplies a negative foil for Odysseus' martial exploits, Agamemnon for his domestic relationships. The poem dramatizes the need for and the virtual impossibility of successfully integrating wisdom and force in the person of the king: this Achilleus and Agamemnon are never able to manage, Odysseus just barely. Zeus alone unites *mētis* and *biē* in the person of a ruler who moderates the behavior of others.

We shall now consider how the transfer of *atasthaliai* from the protagonist onto his *laos* in the *Odyssey* conforms to the themes of the divine assembly. The assembly has the purpose of announcing that in this poem humans are responsible for their actions and that suffering is punishment for crime. That announcement, delivered by Zeus at the beginning of the assembly, points to a fundamental difference in the gods of the *Iliad* and *Odyssey,* one that has been explained in diachronic terms as a record of Greek intellectual progress.[40] I suggest instead that we account for these theological differences in synchronic terms with the polarity between *mētis* and *biē*. The relationship between the gods of the two Homeric epics is analogous to that between the protagonists.

Intertextual Justice

The plot function served by the first divine assembly is to initiate the return of Odysseus; yet the scene begins with a discourse by Zeus on the nature of human suffering. Werner Jaeger, who dismissed the pas-

[39] Felson-Rubin 97–98; Segal (1994) 78–79, 107.
[40] See below, Appendix 1.

sage as an interpolation influenced by later philosophical speculation, demonstrated that it became something of a fixed reference point for Attic political writers of the sixth and fifth centuries B.C.E.:[41]

> ὢ πόποι, οἷον δή νυ θεοὺς βροτοὶ αἰτιόωνται.
> ἐξ ἡμέων γάρ φασι κάκ' ἔμμεναι· οἱ δὲ καὶ αὐτοὶ
> σφῇσιν ἀτασθαλίῃσιν ὑπὲρ μόρον ἄλγε' ἔχουσιν,
> ὡς καὶ νῦν Αἴγισθος· ὑπὲρ μόρον Ἀτρεΐδαο
> γῆμ' ἄλοχον μνηστήν, τὸν δ' ἔκτανε νοστήσαντα,
> εἰδὼς αἰπὺν ὄλεθρον, ἐπεὶ πρό οἱ εἴπομεν ἡμεῖς,
> Ἑρμείαν πέμψαντες, ἐύσκοπον Ἀργειφόντην,
> μήτ' αὐτὸν κτείνειν μήτε μνάασθαι ἄκοιτιν·
>
> (1.32–39)

> My now, how these mortals blame the gods,
> for they say that evils are from us; but of themselves
> by their very own reckless acts they get pains beyond their share,
> as even now Aigisthos has got; beyond his share he married
> the wedded wife of Agamemnon, and killed him on his return
> though he knew of his sheer destruction, since we told him earlier
> —having sent Hermes, the sharp-sighted killer of Argos—
> not to kill him and not to court his wife.

Jaeger attached great importance to the idea that individuals who have been forewarned deserve the consequences of their actions.[42] Such knowledge becomes significant for assessing guilt when humans are felt to be responsible for their behavior. Thus, in the assembly Zeus insists that humans bring sufferings on themselves. And it is no coincidence that as early Greek political philosophers pondered the emergence of the *polis* they repeatedly turned to the *Odyssey* to express their views.[43] In the *Odyssey*, Olympian justice is civic justice; in the mouth of Solon, the themes of the divine assembly became political propaganda (fr. 4 West). Athens, says Solon in an elegy to his fellow citizens, will never

[41] Jaeger (1926). See Pfeiffer (1928) 2364–66; Pfeiffer (1935) 2133–34; Focke, 27–31.

[42] The importance of the warning is acknowledged by Jacoby (1933) 186–87, and denied by Focke, 249, and his followers. For the motif see, in particular, Whitman, 225; Schadewaldt (1958, 1960); Lloyd-Jones (1971) 28–32; Kullmann (1977/8, 1985); Nagy (1990b) 241–42. Further bibliography in Heubeck (1954) 72, note 107; Lesky (1961) 1, note 4; Kullmann (1985) 1, note 1.

[43] For the rise of the *polis* as a principal formative influence on Homeric poetry, see Nagy (1979) 115–17; Nagy (1990) 9–11, with further bibliography. I find Meier's remarks on Solon, 45–46, especially cogent in this context; McGlew, 88–91, stresses Solon's affinity to Hesiod.

perish from a Zeus-sent fate or from the anger of the gods, for Athene protects us. But the citizens themselves in their folly (*aphradiēsin*) choose to destroy a great city, because they are ruled by greed. The mind of their leaders is unjust, and they are sure to suffer many pains for their hybris, for they do not know how to hold down their excess (*katekhein koron*) nor to show good order in the present merriment of a quiet feast.

The gods of Solon, like those of the *Odyssey,* mean well by the city. By making humans responsible for their suffering, Solon does not simply exculpate the gods, but he suggests that humans have some measure of control over their destiny. The continued well-being of Athens—for better or worse—is in the hands of its leaders and citizens. The well-governed *polis,* Solon's *eunomiē,* thus becomes a way of ensuring the continued prosperity of its citizens by restraining immoderate behavior. In the generation before Solon, Athenian legal reforms attributed to Draco addressed the issue of intent, in some circumstances allowing the community to pardon a man who had killed unintentionally. The divinely sanctioned warnings given the crew, Aigisthos, and the suitors remove the plea of ignorance from their defense. Moreover, in the first Athenian legal code of which we have any knowledge, we see the state asserting itself at the expense of a family's right to vengeance. For this, too, the divine assembly offers a parallel, when the gods agree to secure Odysseus' return despite the wrath of Poseidon at the blinding of his son. Over a century before Aeschylus composed the *Oresteia,* the Odyssean assembly could furnish the Greeks with a metaphysics for social law.[44] Yet Poseidon's hatred of Odysseus frames that assembly. As in the *Oresteia,* Olympian justice is opposed by a system of blood vengeance that refuses to acknowledge any challenge to its prerogatives.

The assembly proceeds by a series of implied logical inferences from the premise that humans bring sufferings on themselves to the conclusion that Odysseus should be allowed to return to Ithaca. The development of the argument can be schematized as follows:

B.5) Zeus: Men blame the gods for suffering;
but men bring suffering on themselves.
Illustration: Aigisthos brought suffering on himself;
although the gods tried to prevent him from suffering.

[44] The word "moral" has become controversial, although I will register my belief that rumors of Homer's otherness have been greatly exaggerated. For the state of the discussion, see Long; Adkins (1971, 1972, 1987); Lloyd-Jones (1971, 1987); Gagarin.

6) Athene: Men who behave like that should suffer
(suffering is punishment for crime);
but Odysseus suffers
(Odysseus is not a criminal and should not suffer).

7) Zeus: He suffers because of Poseidon.
Resolution: let us bring Odysseus home
(Odysseus should not suffer).

In his account of Aigisthos, Zeus tacitly assumes a causal link between human suffering and crime. By his words, and subsequently by his actions, Zeus establishes the role of the gods as patrons of that justice. He begins by correcting the widely held belief that evils come from the gods, a belief that he must correct if there is to be such a thing as universal justice. Zeus makes the counterclaim that humans bring troubles on themselves. Far from causing pain, the gods actively seek to prevent it. Homer prepares us to see the gods of the *Odyssey* in just these terms as early as verse 19 with the declaration: "the gods all pitied [Odysseus]." The statement and its implications are arresting, since it is customary in the opening verses of archaic epic to ascribe the miseries suffered in the poem to divine will.[45]

Athene responds by drawing the moral from Aigisthos' fate that wrongdoers should pay for their crimes. The optatival form of her expression, "may anyone who behaves like that perish," clearly implies a readiness to see that justice is served. Athene's desire to bring about the return of Odysseus is here as elsewhere inseparable from her desire to punish the suitors.[46] From the outset, the *Mnesterophonia* remains her plan. It is appropriate to Zeus' own characterization of the gods, and a mark of Athene's tact, that the assembly contains no direct mention of the gods' punitive role; Zeus, however, demonstrates his commitment to the principle by sending a favorable omen when Telemachos appeals for retribution on the suitors in the human assembly of Book 2.[47]

Athene next uses the actions undertaken by the gods on behalf of Aigisthos to dictate their response to the undeserved sufferings of Odysseus. The resolution to bring Odysseus home is an inverse correlate of the moral that transgressors should pay for their crimes: if suffering is to

[45] Rüter, chap. 1, especially 45, whose survey includes non-Greek epics.

[46] See also *Od.* 13.189–93, 24.479–80; note that the only mention of Athene in the *Apologoi* occurs in the context of Odysseus' vengeance on Polyphemos for eating six of the companions.

[47] *Od.* 2.143–76; see also 20.98–121, 21.413–15.

be understood as punishment, then the good should not suffer. The role that Zeus here ascribes to the gods in the Aigisthos paradigm is clearly valid as it applies to Odysseus and the suitors.[48] In fact, throughout the *Odyssey* survival and successful return are made to depend on the justness of the individual.[49] The opposed fates of Odysseus and the crew in the proem thus illustrate complementary aspects of a code of justice announced in the divine assembly. At the same time, in his efforts to save his crew and to punish the suitors, Odysseus emerges as the human counterpart to the gods of that assembly.[50]

The speech in which Zeus announces the metaphysics of his rule takes the form of a polemic.[51] Rüter believes that Zeus directs his remarks against claims made by the human actors in the *Iliad,* such as Agamemnon's in the opening scene of Book 19.[52] One may fairly ask, however, whether the audience had to turn to the *Iliad* for examples of men who blame the gods for their troubles; indeed, as Jenny Strauss Clay observes, Odyssean characters regularly level such accusations at the gods, especially Zeus.[53] Our earliest example comes from the second scene of the poem, in which Telemachos complains of the cruelty of the gods to none other than Athene disguised as Mentes. In keeping with the themes of the divine assembly, Athene urges Telemachos to take responsibility for his own destiny rather than to dream idly of his father's return (1.267–305). But perhaps the most striking example comes from Book 20, in which the neatherd Philoitios inveighs against Zeus for the loss of his master while standing before the disguised Odysseus himself:

> Ζεῦ πάτερ, οὔ τις σεῖο θεῶν ὀλοώτερος ἄλλος·
> οὐκ ἐλεαίρεις ἄνδρας, ἐπὴν δὴ γείνεαι αὐτός,
> μισγέμεναι κακότητι καὶ ἄλγεσι λευγαλέοισιν.
> ἴδιον, ὡς ἐνόησα, δεδάκρυνται δέ μοι ὄσσε
> μνησαμένῳ Ὀδυσῆος, ἐπεὶ καὶ κεῖνον ὀίω

48 Focke, 25–31; see Jones, 16. One is obliged, however, to take seriously the instincts of two of this century's most learned students of the history of ideas, Jacoby and Jaeger, when they sense a philosophical flavor to the text.

49 *Od.* 3.132–34, 4.499–511, 5.108–9. This link between success and justice elucidates the sense of Athene's assurances to Penelope at 4.806–7. Laertes takes the punishment of the suitors for their *atasthalos hubris* as proof of the gods' existence (24.351–52).

50 Kullmann (1985) 10; Rutherford. See also Whitman, 175; Fränkel, 96–98; Erbse (1972) 157.

51 Jacoby (1933) 186; Dodds (1951) 32; Rüter 64–82; Lloyd-Jones (1971) 29.

52 Rüter concluded from his study of archaic epic openings that Iliadic cosmology was unique (see esp. 64–68).

53 See below, Appendix 1.

τοιάδε λαίφε' ἔχοντα κατ' ἀνθρώπους ἀλάλησθαι,
εἴ που ἔτι ζώει καὶ ὁρᾷ φάος ἠελίοιο.

(20.201–7)

Father Zeus, there is no other god more deadly than you.
You do not pity men, even when you yourself produced them,
and permit them to consort with evil and grievous pain.
I began to sweat as I saw you, and my eyes filled with tears
as I remembered Odysseus, for I believe that he too,
with rags such as these, wanders among men,
if he still lives somewhere and sees the light of the sun.

The poetic irony of this scene prefaces the *Mnesterophonia* with an emphatic restatement of the themes of the divine assembly: Zeus *is* merciful, he *is* just, Odysseus *has* returned, the suitors *will* be punished, justice *does* exist. Odysseus is guilty of making similar accusations, although his knowledge of Olympos has generally been excused from any human limitation when he does so.[54]

Zeus' polemic in the divine assembly is directed against the very premise of Iliadic cosmology; if we are meant to recall a specific statement from the *Iliad* it is surely the poet's own assessment of the disasters that befell the Greek army at Troy: "and the plan of Zeus was being brought to completion" (*Dios d'eteleieto boulē,* 1.5).[55] The contrast between sufferings that fulfilled a plan of Zeus and those that men bring on themselves (*Od.* 1.7) encapsulates the theological difference between the two epics. The Odyssean proem announces the difference in a verse structurally parallel to the Iliadic declaration that Zeus was ultimately responsible for "countless woes" suffered by the Greeks at Troy. It is reintroduced by Zeus himself when he sets forth the principles of a rule based on justice and compassion for human suffering (*Od.* 1.32–34). When so understood, Zeus's words in the Odyssean assembly acquire a thematic significance in keeping with the prominence of their position. The *Iliad* provided a convenient text against which the *Odyssey* could react in order to emphasize the nature of its own cosmology.

The divine assembly of *Odyssey* 1 initiates a so-called double embassy which is completed in Book 5. It seems likely that the double embassy

[54] *Od.* 9.38, 550–55 (for which see below, Chapter 4). At *Od.* 6.324–26 Odysseus' charge against Athene is clearly ironic and the irony belongs to the poet.

[55] Note that the Iliadic proem simultaneously views Achilleus and Zeus as the cause of suffering. The expression *Dios d' eteleieto boulē* occurs at *Od.* 11.297 (compare *Od.* 13.127; for the sentiment, see also *Od.* 8.82 and *Il.* 16.684–91). See also Nagy (1979) 113, note 3.

was a standard compositional device in archaic Greek epic, since the *Iliad* provides two further examples, one in Book 15, the other in Book 24. Yet the embassies of *Odyssey* 1 and 5 and *Iliad* 24 are not only formally cognate, but the situations closely resemble one another as well.[56] Once again, these parallels serve to underscore the theological differences between the two poems. Both embassies belong to an assembly of the gods, are motivated by a hero's suffering indignities, and occur at a time when corrective action by the gods is long overdue. A divine advocate rouses the gods to effect the hero's return to family and home. The hero's antagonists, Poseidon and Achilleus, rage unceasingly in their desire to avenge another for whom they care deeply, and both have carried their anger too far. Finally, in the *Odyssey* as in the *Iliad,* Poseidon's attitude is opposed to that of Zeus and the other gods (in the *Iliad,* to be sure, he is joined by Hera and Athene).

The parallel between the two scenes is announced by the verse that bridges the Odyssean prologue and divine assembly:

> . . . θεοὶ δ' ἐλέαιρον ἅπαντες
>
> *Od.* 1.19)
>
> . . . but the gods all pitied him

which corresponds to:

> τὸν δ' ἐλεαίρεσκον μάκαρες θεοὶ εἰσορόωντες
>
> *Il.* 24.23)
>
> but the blessed gods ever pitied him as they looked

In the *Iliad,* the pity of the gods motivates the events of the entire twenty-fourth book, in the *Odyssey,* those of the entire poem. There follows in both scenes an immediate qualification of the gods' pity:

> νόσφι Ποσειδάωνος· ὁ δ' ἀσπερχὲς μενέαινεν
> ἀντιθέῳ Ὀδυσῆι . . .
>
> *Od.* 1.20–21)

[56] *Il.* 24.23ff. Discussion in Groeger, 1–21; Arend, 57–63; Reinhardt (1961) 469–505; Müller, 15–22. Heubeck (1954) 40–54, however, argues that the Odyssean embassy is modeled on *Il.* 15.157ff.

apart from Poseidon, who raged incessantly
against godlike Odysseus . . .

This corresponds to:

ἔνθ' ἄλλοις μὲν πᾶσιν ἑήνδανεν, οὐδέ ποθ' Ἥρῃ
οὐδὲ Ποσειδάων' οὐδὲ γλαυκώπιδι κούρῃ,
ἀλλ' ἔχον ὥς σφιν πρῶτον ἀπήχθετο Ἴλιος ἱρὴ

Il. 24.25–27)

Then all the other gods wanted to [steal away Hektor's corpse],
except for Hera, Poseidon and the grey-eyed maiden,
whose hatred for sacred Ilion continued unabated.

Next, a god acts as an advocate before Zeus, and bases his or her plea on the hero's sacrifices. Athene asks:

. . . οὔ νύ τ' Ὀδυσσεὺς
Ἀργείων παρὰ νηυσὶ χαρίζετο ἱερὰ ῥέζων;

Od. 1.60–61)

. . . did Odysseus not
please you as he sacrificed by the Argive ships?

just as Apollo asks:

. . . οὔ νύ ποθ' ὑμῖν
Ἕκτωρ μηρί' ἔκηε βοῶν αἰγῶν τε τελείων;

(*Il.* 24.33–34)

. . . did Hektor
never burn the thighs of cows and perfect goats for you?

Zeus responds to Apollo's outburst with the declaration that Hektor was dearest to him of all Trojans. He offers a similar assurance to Athene in the *Odyssey* and employs the words with which Diomedes praises Odysseus at the beginning of the *Doloneia*.[57] The parallel does nothing to further the contrast between the two assemblies, but it does continue the pattern of allusion in evidence throughout the Odyssean Introduc-

[57] *Il.* 10.243–44a = *Odyssey* 1.65–66a.

tion. Interestingly, Diomedes' further remark clearly refers to Odyssean tradition:

> . . . φιλεῖ δέ ἑ Παλλὰς Ἀθήνη.
> τούτου γ' ἑσπομένοιο καὶ ἐκ πυρὸς αἰθομένοιο
> ἄμφω νοστήσαιμεν, ἐπεὶ περίοιδε νοῆσαι.
>
> (*Il.* 10. 245–47)

> . . . And Pallas Athene loves him [Odysseus].
> With him along we could even return (*nostēsaimen*)
> from blazing fire, for he knows well how to think (*noēsai*)

Odysseus will have a homecoming, a *nostos,* because of his surpassing intelligence, his *noos.*[58] When Zeus grants Athene's request to give Odysseus a homecoming, he likewise singles out the hero's surpassing intelligence (*peri men noon esti, Od.* 1.66) and his ritually correct behavior towards the gods as the two qualities that endear Odysseus to him.

In the *Iliad,* Zeus sends Hermes to the Greek camp to secure the release of Hektor's corpse from Achilleus so that it can be returned home for burial. In the *Odyssey,* Athene instructs Zeus to send Hermes to secure the release of Odysseus from Calypso so that he may return to his home on Ithaca. Zeus also sends Iris to Priam, whom she finds mourning his dead son; Athene herself journeys to Ithaca, where she finds Telemachos pining for his absent father. Iris rouses Priam to retrieve his son for burial, and Athene rouses Telemachos to search for his father and to offer funeral rites should he prove to be dead. Priam's journey to the hut of Achilleus is a multiform of the journey to the Underworld, or *Catabasis,* while Odysseus finds himself on an Island of the Blessed.[59]

Before his departure, Priam goes to the storeroom to collect ransoms for his son. When he summons Hecuba and announces his decision to venture out to the Greek camp, she cries out in distress and attempts to dissuade him from undertaking such a dangerous journey. Telemachos encounters similar resistance from Eurykleia when he asks her to gather provisions from the storeroom for his journey to Pylos. Telemachos departs from Ithaca at night, and is accompanied on the first leg of his travels by Athene disguised as Mentor, who puts the suitors in the palace to sleep. Priam too sets out at night, and meets Hermes disguised as a Myrmidon who escorts the king on the latter half of his mission and puts the soldiers guarding the camp to sleep.

58 On the association of intelligence and return in the *Odyssey* see Frame.
59 See Nagler (1974) chap. 6, especially 184–86; Crane 36–38.

The embassies of *Odyssey* 5 and *Iliad* 24 are the only two occasions in which Hermes performs the function of messenger-god in Homer. These two passages share seven *versus iterati* that are virtually unique to them.[60] Of particular interest is the staff with which Hermes "charms the eyes of whomever he wishes, while others he rouses even from their slumber" (*Il.* 24.344). Whereas Hermes puts the soldiers guarding the Greek camp to sleep in the *Iliad,* he performs the complementary function in the *Odyssey* of rousing Odysseus from his torpor.[61] The verbal parallels between these passages reach something of a climax with Calypso's angry:

> *σχέτλιοί ἐστε, θεοί, ζηλήμονες*
>
> (*Od.* 5.118)
>
> Merciless you are, you gods, and jealous (*zēlēmones*)

just as Apollo scolds the gods for neglecting Hektor:

> *Σχέτλιοί ἐστε, θεοί, δηλήμονες·*
>
> (*Il.* 24.33)
>
> Merciless you are, you gods, and deadly (*dēlēmones*).

Zēlēmones is unique to this one verse in extent Greek literature except for passages based on the *Odyssey.* It clearly echoes *dēlēmones,* which occurs only here in the *Iliad.*[62]

In comparing these two scenes, Karl Reinhardt observed that "Apollo's rebuke of the *theoi dēlēmones* is the most forceful protest against the Olympian gods to be found in the *Iliad,* and there can be no question that every word of it strikes directly home."[63] When Calypso, with an all-important modification, employs the very words with which Apollo

[60] *Od.* 5.43–49 = *Il.* 24.339–45 (the first three verses are shared by Athene in the context of the same embassy at *Od.* 1.96–99); *Od.* 5.28–29 ~ *Il.* 24.333–34. Note the depiction of Hermes as a youth at *Od.* 10.279 and *Il.* 24.347–48, which is not typical of archaic artistic representations of the god (Leaf at *Il.* 24.348; Jörgensen, 374; Reinhardt (1961) 479).

[61] Against Reinhardt (1961) 479, and Macleod at *Il.* 24.339–48 that Hermes' wand serves no purpose in the *Odyssey* and has been mechanically taken over from the *Iliad.* Pucci (1987) 23, note 14, and Crane, 36, offer other explanations.

[62] Groeger, 21; Reinhardt (1961) 471–473; K. Usener, 148–55. Δηλήμων occurs three times in the *Odyssey* in the line: *εἰς Ἔχετον βασιλῆα, βροτῶν δηλήμονα πάντων* (18.85, 116, 21.308; see 12.286).

[63] Reinhardt (1961) 471.

launches into his own tirade, the audience is reminded that a very different view of Olympos is here being presented. Hera's savage and sarcastic reply to Apollo's scolding in the *Iliad* forcefully corroborates his charge. In the *Odyssey* Poseidon is absent, with the result that ugly scenes are avoided. Poseidon's absence from the Odyssean assembly has as much significance for the portrayal of the gods in that poem as does the presence of Hera, Athene, and Poseidon in the *Iliad*.[64]

The unity and harmony of the Olympians in the *Odyssey* is not a simple reflection of the peace on earth that followed the Trojan war, but the necessary result of the justice of heaven.[65] It stands in direct contrast to the rancor and apparent success of injustice in the human assembly that begins the Book 2. In that assembly, Olympian justice is opposed by a competing policy of might makes right: when Mentor scolds the Ithacan elders for allowing the suitors to use *biē* against Telemachos (*erdein erga biaia,* 2.236), Leokritos replies that he does not speak in a manner appropriate to the situation (*kata moiran,* 2.251) because the suitors are more numerous.[66] Telemachos' attempt to assert control over his household, as Athene-Mentes suggested, forces the suitors to align themselves openly with *biē.* The actions of Telemachos in the assembly serve to thematize the situation on Ithaca as a conflict between representatives of *biē* and *mētis.*

Odysseus' eventual return and victory over the suitors show the potency of his values and qualities in the face of superior physical force. It is the same battle he fought, and won, against Polyphemos. The *Odyssey* polemicizes against two of the most flagrant examples of divine injustice in the *Iliad,* the embassy scene of Book 24 and the synoptic statement that "the plan of Zeus was being brought to fulfillment" in the Iliadic proem. In so doing, the *Odyssey* advertises a theodicy conditioned by the needs of political life that emerges within the first hundred verses as the central theme of the poem. The polemic is the metaphysical component of a contrast in ideologies introduced with the declaration in verse 1 that it was Odysseus—rather than Achilleus—who sacked Troy, suffered greatly, and reached his home.

Scholarship on the divine assembly has long been dominated by a teleological approach to intellectual history. Jaeger dismissed the scene

64 Rüter, 56–63; Eisenberger, 2–3.

65 Against Rüter, 56–63.

66 See also 2.191 and 198–202. Telemachos openly accuses them of *huperbios hubris* 'exceedingly violent hubris,' at 1.368. *Od.* 22.33–40 explicitly equates *biē* with unjust behavior. Compare in this context the remarks of Long, 137; Adkins (1971) 13–14.

as an interpolation because he found that its concerns and sensibilities were those of the sixth century B.C.E. rather than the eighth century. Hermann Fränkel and his followers have focused on supposed developments in the Greek concept of fate and free will—and so avoid reaching Analytic conclusions—but often at the cost of ignoring or even failing to recognize that in the *Odyssey* these issues are subordinated to the concept of human responsibility.[67] Either approach assumes that the cosmologies of the Homeric epics naively reflect the *Zeitgeist* in which they were composed. If valid, this assumption would greatly weaken the argument that the contrasts which I have found between the *Iliad* and *Odyssey* are purposeful. However, as Klaus Rüter has shown, from what can be gathered about Greek epics of the archaic period, the Iliadic vision of human destiny is unique.[68] To be sure, Rüter was no less prepared than Fränkel to account for the different aspects under which the *Iliad* and *Odyssey* were formulated in terms of historical evolution. Yet are we to posit another phase in the development of Greek religious thought to account for the *Aithiopis,* which bears not the slightest resemblance to the *Iliad* or *Odyssey* in its portrayal of the relationship between man, god, and fate? In fact, the polemical model that I am proposing for interaction between the two Homeric traditions could easily be applied to cases in which the *Iliad* draws on episodes from the *Aithiopis*.

It seems more productive to treat the differing theological outlooks of the Homeric poems in terms of their differing objectives.[69] The Iliadic poet created a descriptive model that could account for why things happen as they do. Odyssean cosmology, on the other hand, prescribes a code of human behavior; and its chief bow to "realism" is in fact the theme of Poseidon's wrath, by which the justice of Zeus, although realized in the end, is seen as the distant goal of a frequently arduous process. In the world of the *Iliad* it is therefore a given that the Fates are all-powerful and distribute their favors and afflictions at random.[70] The gods' sometimes comical, sometimes horrifying, behavior and favoritism based on parentage and petty grudges seems designed to answer the question why there is no justice. In the *Iliad,* the complaints of mortals are warranted; the gods, sometimes out of simple spite, inspire men to

[67] Heubeck (1954) 83; Lesky (1961) 35; Eisenberger, 6–7; Rüter, 69–70; Andersen (1973) 16. As an important exception to this tendency I cite the work of Segal (1994) chap. 10.

[68] Rüter, 67–68. See also A. Edwards (1985b).

[69] Scholarship on the gods in Homer is vast. Relevant works include Heubeck (1954); Lesky (1961); Fränkel (1962), 58–83; Rüter, 66–82; *GR* 119–25; Kullmann (1965, 1977/8, 1985); Erbse (1986); Janko (1992) 1–7.

[70] See *Il.* 24.525–26, 6.487–89.

their ruin.[71] This is not to imply that the gods of the *Iliad* have no concept of justice, but that they feel less bound to it than the human actors of the poem.

Arthur Adkins has shown that divine behavior "is governed by the same values as human behaviour in the poems."[72] Yet our assessment of Iliadic characters in terms of that value system remains deeply ambivalent. No one may properly be said to be evil, but the position of virtually every major character in the poem, divine or human, is compromised. Ambivalence is not, or need not be, lacking from our reception of the *Odyssey;* Odysseus is not a simple embodiment of Olympian values and the suitors are not uniformly wicked, yet the story still affirms the existence of justice in this world.[73] Homer, then, destabilizes the polarities introduced in the Introduction, but he does not utterly subvert them. His expository method of introducing his characters by mapping them onto a system of oppositions with an ethical component can in fact be seen as a solution to a technical challenge, since it allows him to avoid an overly schematized presentation of character in a story designed to illustrate a moral theme. Against the tragic sense of life that lies at the heart of the *Iliad* stands the fundamental idealism of Odyssean cosmology and the optimism of its denouement. That optimism is to be sure chastened by realism: suffering is in the *Odyssey* no less than in the *Iliad* a fact of life, even the way of life.

In short, the tragic vision of the *Iliad* and its realism are predicated on the willingness of the forces governing the *kosmos* to tolerate the suffering of the innocent and support, even valorize, those guilty of *atasthaliai*. If a poem is to celebrate a character of *biē* who is a favorite among the gods, then "Iliadic" theology is a natural—though by no means necessary—result. In the *Odyssey,* however, the gods have become the guardians of justice rather than of the Fates, and with one notable exception no one has a mortal child to defend or avenge.[74] The *Odyssey* offers new scenario for human suffering and with it a new relationship between gods and humans. The death of Aigisthos, which

[71] *Il.* 13.631–35; compare in this context *Il.* 3.365–68.

[72] Adkins (1972) 1.

[73] My argument here is directed in part against the view that the *Mnesterophonia* has developed out of a tale of revenge that has successfully resisted the poet's efforts to moralize it (for which see Appendix 1).

[74] On the relationship of the gods, fate and justice in the Homeric epics see the works on the gods in Homer cited above. See also Jacoby (1933) 184–92; Pötscher, 12 and note 21; Rüter, 58–59; Dihle (1970) 169–71 (rebutted by Eisenberger, 7, note 23). *Il.* 20.296–308 is telling, for which see Whitman, 348–49, note 37. See also *Il.* 2.155–56, 6.73–76, 17.319–25.

serves as a paradigm for the deaths of the crew and suitors, is presented as punishment for crime; such men have no right to complain to the gods, who in all three instances tried vainly to warn them. As a result, the gods may no longer be seen as instruments of Fate, just as suffering itself is no longer invariably predestined. It is the purpose of the divine assembly to announce the Odyssean view of human destiny in the programmatic first scene of the poem. The rhetorical request at verse 10, "of these things, from whatever point, divine daughter of Zeus, tell us also," emphasizes the responsibility of the Muse in selecting the divine assembly as the starting point of the narrative.

Yet it is not new to the *Odyssey* that the gods warn those about to transgress the boundaries assigned them or punish those who have done so, that the boundaries of Fate can be transgressed, or that mortals are responsible for their actions.[75] There is no need to explain these features of Odyssean cosmology in terms of intellectual progress. The fact that each of these ideas finds expression in the *Iliad,* if only on rare occasions, indicates that they formed part of the common thematic stock of archaic Greek epic and were thus known to Iliadic tradition, but that they were suppressed in favor of the poem's unique tragic vision. What is distinct to the *Odyssey* is that divinity absolves itself from responsibility for evil and hence from suffering: in as much as the gods now champion justice, they can no longer be seen as the inspiration for all human impulses.[76] Much the same could be said of the gods' decreased role in the *Odyssey* as opposed to the *Iliad:* it has nothing to say about an evolution in Greek thinking to an increasingly secular outlook. The polarization of Ithacan society into good and bad characters leaves little room for gods who are good to dart back and forth from Olympos promoting conflict on the island. There is then little reason to suppose that the contrasting views of the two epics are the coincidental artifacts of development from a more "primitive" to a more "advanced" way of thought. That the code of justice presented in the *Odyssey* is opposed to that of the *Iliad* is clear, and to the extent that the Iliadic view is unique the contrast must be specific to it.

Poseidon's hatred, with its significance for the moral program outlined in the assembly, is regularly dismissed as belonging to a primitive

75 Warning: *Il.* 1.194–214; punishment: *Il.* 16.384–93; transgressing the boundaries of Fate: *Il.* 16.780. For responsibility, see Lesky (1961) 38; see also Kullman (1985) 14, 18; Kullmann (1993) 136–37. In drawing this comparison I have greatly benefited from the spoken and written comments of Richard Janko.

76 Heubeck (1954) 83; Lloyd-Jones (1971) 31; Eisenberger, 7, with further bibliography.

stratum of the poem, praised as a remnant of the Urtext, or simply ignored. Rüter declares, for example; "If Zeus here dismisses the notion that evils come from the gods as an undeserved accusation and says rather that through their own fault humans suffer beyond what is destined, then he wishes to reject not just a portion of the responsibility for suffering, but is at pains to dismiss the entire reproach. If humans suffer what Fate has determined for them, then they have no right to reproach the gods as well."[77] I am in full agreement that Zeus takes no responsibility for suffering, whether sent by the Fates or otherwise; the scene would border on the comic if Zeus professed indignation that mortals blame the gods for their sufferings, yet rebutted the charge by observing that mortals bring grief on themselves *in addition to those* for which the gods are responsible.[78] Yet the assembly shows that Athene, with the endorsement of Zeus, is ultimately responsible for the *Mnesterophonia*. Poseidon's responsibility for sufferings—which move the other gods to pity and which Zeus himself finds unwarranted—frames the very scene in which Zeus sets forth the principles of his rule.

The introductory scenes do not allow us to minimize the theme of Poseidon's wrath or the significance of his outlook. The divine assembly presents an image of the Olympians that cannot easily admit of their nursing private grudges. Yet the vengeance of Poseidon on behalf of a murderous cannibal and his opposition to the plans of the Olympians to bring Odysseus home are both in direct contrast to Olympian pity and Olympian justice. If a teleological approach to these issues were correct, our poet would be guilty of some singularly peculiar methods of composition. Structural and thematic analysis would show Homer to have employed an expository technique that highlights an element in the *Odyssey* at variance with the program of justice that the poem illustrates. And Homer does this in the very scene in which he announces that program.

Detailed structural and thematic analysis has shown that the divergent views of Poseidon and the other Olympian gods belong to a larger pattern of oppositions that organize the introductory narrative. This pattern is not simply a convenient narrative device used to introduce the central characters of the poem. Rather, the narrative structure of the Introduction is itself thematically significant. The antithetical pairs Odysseus-crew and Poseidon-Olympians are not simply the products

[77] Rüter, 70 (see also 61). See also Kullmann (1985) 5–7.

[78] The text can be taken to support either interpretation. For the view that Zeus absolves the gods of responsibility for human suffering see Dawe, and Ameis and Hentze, and for the contrary view see Stanford and *CHO*, all ad loc.

of a single narrative technique, but they instantiate analogous oppositions on the divine and human level. In the chapters that follow, we shall find that the struggles of Odysseus with Polyphemos and the suitors can be similarly understood.

Poseidon's character, then, does not reflect a more primitive stage of Greek religious thought but the forces he represents. A diachronic explanation for the theme of Poseidon's wrath is at least irrelevant to understanding how Homer uses that theme, and is almost certainly incorrect, as are more traditional Analytic reconstructions of the Odysean proem.

As the poem begins, Odysseus finds himself within the realm, the *Machtbereich,* of the sea god Poseidon, in a world beyond Greek culture and the justice of Zeus. Zeus concedes as much when he protests to Athene that he is not responsible for the detention of Odysseus on Ogygie, and that Poseidon is the one who hates Odysseus, for blinding Polyphemos (1.65–75). The autonomy of Poseidon, which Zeus and Athene respect both here and throughout the poem, solves the problem of the god's significance. Poseidon is both physically and spiritually absent from the divine assembly, just as the Olympians and their values are conspicuously absent from the world in which Odysseus has wandered these last ten years. Poseidon is portrayed in the *Odyssey* as a god of the *Iliad,* and he stubbornly retains that character throughout the evolution of Greek thought. In the same scene we see a united Olympos motivated to act by pity and a sense of justice, and Poseidon moved by a desire for vengeance.

Let me conclude by summarizing the development of the introductory narrative. The proem contrasts the fate of a clever man with that of his foolish companions who perish by *atasthaliai.* Structural and thematic parallels between the Odyssean and Iliadic proems invite us to compare the character and destiny of Odysseus with that of Achilleus. This comparison reproduces the contrast between Odysseus and the crew that informs the Odyssean proem. At the same time, it broadens that contrast to include the polarity between *mētis* and *biē.*

The divine assembly reveals that the contrasting fates of Odysseus and the crew illustrate a code of justice authorized by Zeus. The gods of the *Odyssey* contrast sharply with those of the *Iliad,* and once again the contrast is reinforced by comparing the Odyssean assembly to a parallel scene at the beginning of *Iliad* 24. On the other hand, the divine assembly is framed by a contrast between Poseidon and his fellow Olympians which corresponds to the theological differences between the two epics, just as the opposed fates of Achilleus and Odysseus correspond to those of Odysseus and the crew in the Odyssean proem. Thus, the series of antithetical statements comprising the Introduction distinguish between characters who participate in the justice of Zeus and those who do not. In the human sphere, justice emerges as a criterion of survival and return, and it is to be found in characters distinguished by their intelligence (*mētis* and *noos*) and self-restraint. Unjust characters are distinguished by their unrestrained behavior and reliance on *biē,* for which they are eventually punished after failing to heed the warnings of the gods.

In the chapter that follows we shall see that in the enchanted realm characters of *mētis* become aligned with Greek culture and cultural values, those of *biē* with more primitive beings. Odysseus' adventures thus supply an added perspective on his later conflicts with the suitors, one that ultimately prepares us to see Odysseus' punishment of the suitors, the *Mnesterophonia,* as a foundation myth. Homer did not cast the *Apologoi* of Odysseus in Books 9–12 in the form of a first person narrative because he found it impossible to incorporate the adventures into his cosmology;[79] rather he set two very different worlds in apposition. Only a mediator capable of bridging the gap between these worlds will be able to return home to Ithaca.

[79] See Rüter, 77–78; Fenik (1974) 226–27; *CHO* 2:7.

CHAPTER 2

The World of Poseidon

Where has Odysseus been these past ten years? Scholars of a conservative bent assign the *Apologoi* to the world of fantasy, an enchanted realm located in the far distant east or west. Others speak of journeys through the subconscious, of ritual purification, symbolic death, and rebirth. In a sense all this is true. Yet Homer speaks of the sea, and though his words may seem too simple to satisfy, it is worth considering how far they can take us. We shall see that the polarities organizing the *Odyssey*'s introductory verses are operative in the *Apologoi* as well: Poseidon's more primitive outlook in the divine assembly is reflected in the "character" of his realm. Whereas the divine assembly invests these polarities with a theological aspect unavailable to the poem's human actors, Odysseus as narrator of the *Apologoi* re-presents them as a conflict between worlds.

The Topography of Dissipation

The prologue states that, excepting Odysseus, "as many as escaped sheer destruction were home, having escaped both war and the sea" (1.11–12).[1] This neatly divides the events of the last twenty years into two theaters of activity and awards equal significance to each. In Book 8, Odysseus declares to the Phaiakian Euryalos that he had suffered greatly

[1] For the collocation of sea and war see *Od.* 3.90–91, 3.192, 5.224, and for the hostility of the sea 8.138–39.

"cleaving wars and the grievous waves of the sea" (8.182–83), and his words are later repeated verbatim in the authorial voice (13.91; see 13.264). Elsewhere, Odysseus describes his efforts to reach home as *porous halos exereeinōn* (12.259), or as Michael Nagler has suggestively rendered, "investigating ways [to get] through the sea."[2] The sea is at once a path and an obstacle; to Odysseus, as to so many Greeks on their return from Troy, it is essentially hostile.

The disasters suffered by Odysseus and his men occur not only in the course of a sea voyage, but while they are on board their ships: when Odysseus falls asleep while piloting his ship, the crew open the bag of winds entrusted him by Aiolos. The Laistrygones then destroy the flotilla in their harbor, albeit after eating two men in the palace, and Scylla snatches six men from the ship that remains as it sails on to Thrinakie. Zeus punishes the crew for eating the cattle of Helios, but he does so by raising a storm at sea. Had Zeus dispatched them on the island, Odysseus could have taken up with Phaethousa or Lampetie and the story line would have remained the same. Finally, in a programmatic episode from Book 5, Poseidon destroys Odysseus' raft as it approaches Scherie. The only disaster to occur on land does so in the sea-side cave of Polyphemos, the son of Poseidon. Two of the four episodes in which disaster is averted, the Sirens and Charybdis, take place at sea. Of the remaining two episodes Odysseus encounters the Lotophagoi before he earns the wrath of Poseidon, while Circe becomes his faithful companion.

For the last seven years, and for over a quarter of the poem, Odysseus is stranded on an island, Ogygie.[3] Athene introduces the island with the remark that Ogygie is "girded by waves and located at the navel of the sea" (1.50). Calypso, 'The Concealer', personifies the threat of the sea, as does her "destructive thinking" father Atlas (1.52).[4] The threat is oblivion, the oblivion of forgetting to return or of being forgotten.[5] Thus, when Poseidon raises the storm in Book 5, Odysseus cries out: "Would that I had died at Troy . . . since I would have received

[2] Nagler (1977) 77.

[3] Odysseus uses the Calypso episode to tell Arete who he is (7.241–66). For Calypso and the sea, see Wilamowitz (1927) 177; Segal (1994) 15. On the motif of concealment, note that the pens of Circe are called *keuthmōnas* (10.283). Odysseus describes his encounter with Polyphemos as the time when "Polyphemos shut us up in the cave" (12.209–10), for which see below.

[4] Atlas is a pre-Olympian Titan associated with the Paradise of the Hesperides (for the enchanted realm as an ambivalent Paradise, see below). Like Proteus the sea god, Atlas "knows the depths of the sea" (1.52–53; compare 4.385–86, 460). Further on the maritime connection in *CHO* at 1.52–54.

[5] Dimock, 15: "By choosing to begin her story with the image of Odysseus's captivity to Calypso, the Muse identifies obscurity as Odysseus's prime enemy."

my share of funeral rites, and the Achaioi would have maintained my *kleos*" (5.308–11). Similar thinking lies behind Telemachos' complaint to Athene-Mentes in the poem's second scene: Had Odysseus perished at Troy, he would have received the lasting memorial of a funeral mound, and for his son as well he would have won great *kleos* in days to come (1.236–40).[6] To be lost at sea is to lose one's *kleos,* that is, one's heroic identity, either as a subject of song or as an object of cult veneration.[7] As long as Odysseus remains within the cave of Polyphemos he is who he claims to be, "Nobody." The *Odyssey* projects the traditional opposition between *lēthē* and *kleos,* oblivion and the unwithering fame bestowed by epic, onto the larger categories of nature and Greek culture as signified by the enchanted realm and Ithaca.

A world that denies *kleos* is opposed to the very concept of heroism. In the *Cyclopeia* as nowhere else in the enchanted world Odysseus plays the hero; and as Robert Schröter has shown, the scene in which Odysseus blinds Polyphemos is organized as an *aristeia.*[8] Yet Odysseus owes his success to the fact that he temporarily suppresses his name. Emerging from the cave thus becomes functionally equivalent to recovering his identity. In the scene that follows Nobody identifies himself as a hero when in typically Iliadic fashion he boasts to his victim: "If some mortal man asks you about the unseemly blindness of your eye, tell him that Odysseus the city-sacker blinded you" (9.502–4). Odysseus also owes his prolonged sufferings to this act of self-disclosure. Undying fame brings suffering on those who win it, yet had Odysseus not revealed himself to Polyphemos, "Nobody" would have gotten the *kleos.*[9] In this scene, Odysseus is unable to master his anger; laying claim to heroic identity thus becomes an act of unrestrained behavior.[10]

In each of the episodes following the *Cyclopeia,* Odysseus must control his passions, or *thumos,* in order to survive and return to civilization.[11] This condition of his return becomes an explicit test on Thrinakie, as we shall see below. For characters of *biē* such as the Cyclops,

[6] His words are echoed by Eumaios at 14.366–71. Compare Penelope's fears concerning Telemachos' voyage at 4.722–28.

[7] For Odyssean *kleos* see Chapter 1 and 5; see also A. Edwards (1985) 71–93; Segal (1994) chap. 5.

[8] Schröter, 98ff. (approved by *CHO* at 9.375–94). For the *Mnesterophonia* as an *aristeia,* see Chapter 5 below.

[9] Nagy (1979) 36–41; Pucci (1982) 47, 56; Clay (1983) 106–12.

[10] Attempts to find Odysseus guilty of a more severe crime are misguided, I feel. See Merry and Ridell at *Od.* 9.231; Focke, 168; Germain, 68–70; Bona, 45–46; *CHO* at 9.231.

[11] For the *thumos* as the seat of passion, see Bremmer (1983) 54–56; for the partially overlapping concept of *menos* see Bremmer (1983) 57–61.

yielding to *thumos* and using *biē* against others are coincident acts. If he were to yield to his *thumos,* Odysseus would assimilate himself to the world in which he travels. Yet we have also seen that Achilles is distinguished by his lack of restraint and his *biē;* in fact, these very qualities typify the heroic persona. To return home from the martial world of Troy, to have an identity outside the *Iliad,* Odysseus must suppress the destructive aspect of the generic hero, who "endures great suffering and performs many reckless acts" and thereby causes suffering to those around him.[12] The enchanted realm is his testing ground. Like the world of Troy it is characterized by and elicits in others *biē* and unrestrained behavior. If Odysseus identifies with these qualities he will not return, just as Achilleus did not. The enchanted realm only permits Odysseus to identify with the aspect of the heroic persona that defines his character: return to civilization depends on his capacity to endure suffering.

The Scylla episode dramatizes the impotence of Iliadic heroism in the enchanted realm. Although he is warned by Circe not to oppose the daughter of Krataiis, 'Ineluctable Force', Odysseus arms himself for combat, only to watch as six of his men are devoured by the monster. As Reinhardt remarks; "Nowhere is heroic behavior so out of place as here. . . . The hero is sacrificed to the contrast between two worlds; there are horrors that can only be suffered."[13] Appropriately, combat with a polycephalic, serpentine monster such as Scylla is a typical ordeal in the initiation of the heroic warrior.[14]

The enchanted realm is intimately associated with the sea, and is hostile to Odysseus and his fellow Greeks. In other words, we can retrieve the theme of the sea god's wrath from the "character" of his domain.[15] The Olympians, moreover, respect Poseidon's prerogatives so long as Odysseus remains within the enchanted realm. Zeus himself waits until Poseidon is absent from Olympos to effect the return of Odysseus. Similar thinking lies behind Athene's statement to Odysseus that she did not help him during his wanderings because she did not wish to fight with her uncle (13.341–42). Her explanation echoes the poet's own remark that Athene heard Odysseus' prayers to her on

[12] The phrase is from *h. Hom.* 15.5–6; discussion in Nagy (1990) 13–14.

[13] Reinhardt (1960) 59–60.

[14] Lincoln (1976) 62, remarks that the monster is often three-headed, as in fact Scylla was sometimes said to have been.

[15] Segal (1994) 204: "Through his siring of Polyphemos and his association with the Giants (7.56–59) . . . Poseidon is . . . displaced into an older world order. By making him the father of Polyphemos . . . Homer virtually makes Poseidon one of the deities of primordial creation."

Scherie, but did not yet appear to him face-to-face out of respect for Poseidon (6.328–30).

By associating the enchanted realm with the sea, Poseidon, the hero's antagonist, becomes an inscrutable force behind the events that occur there. The hostility of the god and of the enchanted realm are somehow related. In our first account of the hero's misfortunes, and the only one narrated in the authorial voice, Homer identifies the god responsible: Poseidon raises a storm which destroys Odysseus' raft. By making Odysseus the narrator of his other adventures, the poet absolves himself from the task of describing the god's influence. Was Poseidon somehow responsible for the behavior of the crew in the Aiolian episode? Odysseus cannot tell us, but he is able to report that Aiolos recognized in the mishap the wrath of the gods. Poseidon's influence is meant to be mysterious, and the effect is achieved in part by having the narrative reflect the human limitations of the protagonist.

In the preceding chapter I argued that the physical absence of Poseidon from the divine assembly of Book 1 points to an underlying difference of outlook between him and the other Olympian gods. Corresponding to his own absence from the assembly is that of the other Olympians from the enchanted realm, a fact carefully registered by Athene's assistance to Odysseus in the course of the poem. Before Odysseus sets out from Ogygie, her influence is only felt through Hermes, an intermediary capable of crossing between worlds.[16] As Odysseus approaches the border realm of Scherie, Athene offers anonymous assistance, and after he arrives there she twice appears in disguise.[17] Only when Odysseus reaches Ithaca does she reveal herself to him in manifest form.

Athene, the patron deity of Mycenaean kings and of the *polis,* is absent from the enchanted realm; yet her powers become increasingly available to Odysseus as he approaches his homeland.[18] Her aid to Telemachos likewise diminishes as he journeys from Ithaca to Sparta, with the result that his homecoming too is delayed.[19] Conversely, Poseidon's control over Odysseus leaves off as the assistance of Athene begins.

[16] Not only on Ogygie but Aiaie as well, where the god's appearance presupposes an assembly like that which begins Book 5.

[17] On Scherie as a border realm see, for example, Segal (1994) especially 14–20; Vidal-Naquet 26–29.

[18] Reinhardt (1960) 70–71; Erbse (1972) 17–19, 144; Nagler (1977) 80; Segal (1994) 39.

[19] This lends additional force to the simile comparing Eumaios as he greets Telemachos at 16.17–21 to a father whose son has returned after a ten-year absence.

When Poseidon departs after raising the storm in Book 5, Athene sends a countervailing wind that drives Odysseus to Scherie. Poseidon strikes on Scherie, but his anger is redirected against the Phaiakes, and he ceases his persecution altogether when Odysseus arrives at Ithaca. The potencies of Odysseus' antagonist and patron are inversely related; physical and spiritual topographies converge in a map whose poles are marked by Ogygie and Ithaca, Poseidon and Athene.

The absence of the Olympians from the enchanted realm is explained by its physical remoteness from civilization. When Hermes arrives at Ogygie, he declares that he came reluctantly: "For who would willingly cross such an unspeakable expanse of water? There aren't any cities nearby to offer sacrifices and choice hecatombs to the gods" (5.100–2). The voyage of Odysseus from Ogygie to the border realm of Scherie lasts twenty days, by far the longest voyage of the adventures and in fact the longest uninterrupted voyage in Greek or Latin literature before Lucian (5.278–79, 388–89).[20] Yet Scherie is also so remote from Greece that Euboea, at the center of Homer's Greece, lies at the edge of their own experience (7.321–23; see also 6.203–5).[21]

Not only the Olympians but their values are absent from the enchanted realm, and it is for his efforts to insist on those values that Odysseus ultimately incurs the hatred of Poseidon. The isolation of the enchanted realm, from both Greece and Olympos, belongs to a more comprehensive typology: the enchanted realm is set in Paradise.[22] The Greeks did not have a collective expression for Paradise—which is frankly a modern hermeneutic construct—but they did have a common way of describing places remote from the here and now. In Paradise there is no need to practice agriculture, since the earth spontaneously produces a never-ending supply of food. In Greece, by contrast, culture and agriculture were made necessary by the poverty of the soil, as we see most clearly in Hesiod's *Works and Days*. Greek culture is thus superfluous in Paradise, as are the laws on which Greek society is based and the gods who validate those laws. Paradise is a place before or beyond Greek culture and the reign of Zeus.

The Greeks entertained a deeply ambivalent view of temporal Para-

[20] Lucian, *VH* 1.6; noted by Bassett (1938) 44.

[21] M. West (1988) 166–67; Burkert (1984) 16.

[22] The locus classicus is Hesiod, *Works and Days* 106–201, for which see Nagy (1979) chap. 9 and 213–16. M. West ad loc. and E. Cook (1992) treat the Near Eastern parallels. Gatz and *RE* S15 (1978) 783–850, provide the most helpful comprehensive treatment of the Golden Age.

dise.[23] The myth of the "Five Ages of Man" preserved in Hesiod treats the rise of culture as a process of degeneration, a fall from an initial state of grace. By a second and competing view, which we may call the "cultural foundation model," humankind once lived like wild beasts (the *thēriōdēs bios*).[24] Civilization raised us from this savage existence and is thus recognized as a good. The Greeks' view of geographic Paradise is similarly ambivalent: Elysium or the Islands of the Blessed satisfied their need for a positive image of the afterlife. Ogygie, and perhaps Aiaie, correspond to this type of Paradise, although in the former case the ambivalence of Homeric poetry towards hero cult tarnishes the image somewhat.[25] As befits the status of Scherie as a border realm, the Phaiakes are a hybrid, resembling the Golden Race in some respects, Elysium-dwellers in others, and in still others a community of Ionian colonists. The cultural foundation model could also be evoked to describe the conditions encountered by Greek explorers as they ventured beyond their native culture. In such a world one might find Cyclopes, Laistrygones, and forbidden herds of cattle. Scylla and Charybdis illustrate the monsters thought to inhabit the world beyond the Greek cultural horizon—be that horizon geographic or temporal—and which culture-heroes such as Herakles were obliged to destroy. Indeed, in flagrant violation of Homeric chronology, Herakles is said to have killed Scylla for eating six of the cows of Geryon.[26]

These observations resolve a question already voiced in antiquity: how could Polyphemos, the offspring of Poseidon and an Okeanid nymph, properly be called a Cyclops? Polyphemos' character and his paternity are conceptually equivalent.[27] The *Cyclopeia* rationalizes the theme of Poseidon's wrath with the epic paradigm of the hero and his divine antagonist. Thus, our sense that Poseidon is the invisible force behind events comes from the rationalized text. At another level, Posei-

[23] Van der Valk, 5–6, argues for a similarly ambivalent attitude towards Kronos. In support of Van der Valk note that divination by dice distinguished between the good and the child-eating Kronos (see Frazer at Pausanias 7.25.10).

[24] I here translate Gatz's "Kulturentstehungslehre."

[25] Crane, 15–18, 34–44. I treat the affinity between Aiolie and Scherie below. The liminal status of Scherie helps explain the inhabitants' unfriendliness to strangers, although the episode also serves to foreshadow events on Ithaca (on which see Lang).

[26] For Scylla see the Scholia to Lycophron 46, 651. Pindar, *N.* 1.62–63, declares that Herakles killed countless beasts on land and sea who had no knowledge of *dikē;* Sophocles, *Tr.* 1012, describes such labors as a "purification" of land and sea (see also Euripides, *HF* 225–26).

[27] By way of parallels note that the Chimaira was the progeny of the sea god Phorkys, and the Centaurs were born to an *eidōlon* of Hera by Ixion.

don is not the cause of Odysseus' misfortunes so much as the hostile aspect of nature manifesting itself in the character of both Poseidon and the inhabitants of the enchanted realm. Poseidon, the god of the sea, earthquakes, and horses, reifies the *biē* of nature, a *biē* no less ambivalent than that of heroes. At the same time, his son Polyphemos has been rightly described in these same terms, as could several other inhabitants of the enchanted realm.[28]

The crew succumb to the temptations of Paradise, and in so doing regress to a precivilized condition. To elucidate this point, we must address the topics of food and self-restraint in the *Apologoi*.[29] In Greek myth, the dietary code is used to explain the origin of culture in an act of violence and an ancient crime: the first sacrifice. In so doing it also creates a cosmic hierarchy that defines civilized humans in contrast to the gods and animals, and a cultural hierarchy in which savages are characterized by eating food raw (*ōmophagia*) either as vegetarians or as cannibals (*allēlophagia*).[30] Thus, while Polyphemos' diet characterizes him as savage, improper eating by the crew assimilates them to the enchanted realm. For this reason they will not be allowed to leave it. As in the Netherworld, food binds those who consume it to the place. While the enchanted world repeatedly attempts to deprive Odysseus of his heroic identity, it successfully undermines the identity of the crew as civilized, even as human.

The Kikonian episode introduces the crew in the *image fixe* of the suitors, feasting on boundless meat and wine (9.45–46). As on Thrinakie, they ignore Odysseus' warnings to press on, and for this many lose their homecoming. While in the enchanted realm, the crew eat the lotus and the drugs of Circe, and Elpenor falls to his death from the roof of Circe's home after drinking Pramnian wine. When Odysseus falls asleep in the Aiolian episode, the crew open the bag of winds thinking they will find riches. In what proves to be their final adventure, the crew in their weariness put in at Thrinakie, again despite Odysseus' warnings, and later eat the cattle of the sun.

28 Segal (1962) 34; for Poseidon see also *GR* 219.

29 My discussion of food and self-restraint dovetails with Svenbro's analysis of *gastēr*, 'belly', and related terms: the narrative employs this system of relations to mark the crew's alienation from the human condition. The *gastēr* that marks their bestial nature becomes the *gastēr* of a beast. Note, however, the qualifications of Svenbro's theory in Arthur (1983) 100–104. See also recent discussion of the thematic overlap between *gastēr*/ food and self-restraint by Pucci (1987) 157–87; Segal (1994) 154–57.

30 Svenbro; Arthur (1982); Arthur (1983); Vidal-Naquet, 1–38; Burkert (1987) 163–68, 175–76; Rosaldo, 240–41; Detienne and Vernant (1979–1989) chap. 1.

The crew are repeatedly tested by their physical appetites and succumb to them; the most important is hunger. On the other hand, Polyphemos, the Laistrygones, Scylla, and Charybdis attempt to eat Odysseus and the crew. The adventures are a series of forbidden banquets that follow an alternating pattern of eating or being eaten.[31] The effect of either banquet is assimilation, with the result that the crew will not return home.

The connection between improper feasting and loss of return, which remains latent in the Kikonian episode, becomes explicit in the land of the Lotophagoi, the first of the adventures to take place in the enchanted realm. Odysseus relates that "whoever ate the sweet fruit of the lotus had no desire to report back or return, but wished to remain there among the Lotophagoi munching on the lotus" (9.94–97).[32] The verb *ereptomai,* which I have rendered with 'munching', is elsewhere used only of cattle and implies that the plants are eaten without preparation. In the *Iliad,* the verb occurs once more in conjunction with the lotus, where the horses of the Myrmidons are tethered beside the chariots "munching on lotus and parsley" (*Il.* 2.776).

Scholars have been anxious to distinguish the lotus consumed by the Lotophagoi from that of the Iliadic passage. Stanford calls the Odyssean verse "a good example of the adaptability of a *Formula:* the phrase is used of horses grazing on trefoil . . . in *Il.* 2.776, and the verb is better suited to that."[33] Of course, the Odyssean lotus is a plant with special properties, whatever its appearance. Yet Glaukos of Anthedon is said to have become immortal by eating grass; as Emily Vermeule remarks, "It was his *pharmakon.*"[34] In the Lotophagian episode, the formula *ereptesthai lotou* has not been extended infelicitously to human subjects; rather, it indicates that by eating the lotus Odysseus' companions are reduced to a subhuman state. Their implied, or metaphorical, transformation into animals returns at the close of the episode when Odysseus compels his men to return to the ships and binds them *hupo zuga,* which can mean either "under the benches" or "beneath their yokes" (9.99).

The effect of the lotus consists chiefly in its mind-altering properties,

31 Exceptions are the *Nekyia* and the Aiolian and Siren episodes. The *Nekyia* should, however, be treated as a single narrative unit with the Circe episode, and the crew's release of the winds from the cow hide may be seen as a kind of perverted sacrifice. For the food theme in the Siren episode see Vidal-Naquet, 23.

32 With *Od.* 9.97 compare *h.Merc.* 107. Vidal-Naquet, 21, notes that the lotus is eaten raw.

33 Stanford at 9.97; *CHO* at 9.97 labels the usage "catachrestic."

34 Vermeule (1979) 189; see Apollodorus 3.3.1 and Hyginus, *Fab.* 136. Note that by eating the grass Glaukos was transformed into a sea god with a fishtail.

but the drugs of Circe are said to work physical change on the crew while "their *noos* remained sound." In either case, the food makes the crew "forget to return."[35] In the Circe episode, the mental operation of *lēthē* is represented in plastic terms by their transformation into domestic livestock.[36] Whereas the adventures repeatedly alternate between scenes of eating and being eaten, in these episodes the crew become animals that are eaten.

On Thrinakie, the nymphs Lampetie and Phaethousa are, like Circe, daughters of Helios who control foodstuffs that can prevent the homecoming of the crew; in this respect the sacred cattle are like the drugs that turn the crew to swine. This link between the episodes lends special point to the comparison of the crew to sea-crows when Zeus destroys the ship (12.418).[37] By eating the cattle of the sun, the crew lose their identity as civilized beings, which is equivalent to saying that they will not return home to civilization.

A retrograde scale within the Thrinakian episode underscores their loss of humanity: at first, Odysseus and the crew eat the food of civilized men, albeit provided by a goddess. Afterwards, with the ship's stores depleted, they resort to hunting wild fowl and fish.[38] Finally, the crew eat the cattle of the sun, food altogether denied to human use. The lack of provisions compels them to substitute water and grass for the wine and barley required by the sacrificial ritual which they perform: water and grass are not agricultural products, and are inappropriate to the sacrificial act, itself definitive of civilization, in which cultural artifacts are offered by civilized beings to the gods of civilization (see below, Chapter 4). With every step down, and ultimately beyond, the food chain, the crew regress to the status of animals, which they have more than once already become.

Thus, while the dietary code registers the inhabitants of the en-

[35] Frame, 50–53, treats the theme of *noos* as a means of achieving *nostos*. The *lotus* makes the crew "forget their return" (9.102); the drugs of Circe make them "utterly forget their homeland" (10.236). Note that Teiresias' prophecy balances "thinking of return" with abstinence from food (11.104–11).

[36] Compare the Theseus myth in which *lēthē* is represented as a chair with snakes that bind Theseus and Pirithous so that they are unable to return from Hades.

[37] Traditions of the soul-bird (for which see Vermeule [1979] 8, 17–18; Lincoln [1977] 258) may account for the comparison of the crew to birds, although this does not alter the fact that they move down the food chain with each transformation and with each act of eating on Thrinakie. Note that the birds to which the crew are compared live about the cave of Calypso (the word is restricted to these two passages). The other similes devoted to the crew likewise relate them to animals that are eaten: fish (10.124, 12.251–55) and calves (10.410).

[38] Compare Plato, *Lg*. 823d–824b.

chanted realm as civilized, noncivilized, or divine, in the case of Odysseus and the crew it also serves as a mechanism of change. The drugs of Circe transform the crew into swine; Calypso offers Odysseus the ambrosia of the gods which would transform him into an immortal.[39] The threat posed by food to the return of the crew is that they will move down the cosmic hierarchy. The threat for Odysseus is that he will move up the hierarchy to become a deified hero on an Island of the Blessed—albeit without a funeral mound.

We thus return to the point from which we began: the enchanted realm offers oblivion. While it attempts to rob Odysseus of his *kleos,* that is, culture's memory of him, it successfully effaces the crew's memory of culture. The temptations of Paradise subvert the rational faculties that distinguish human from beast, from the inhabitants of the enchanted world. Those who forget to return are lost, precisely as they are lost if forgotten. The threat posed by food is obliviousness; the threat posed by the sea is anonymity. Both threats are aspects of *lēthē,* or 'forgetting'. The oblivion of the crew is permanent, but Odysseus merely sleeps, as humans do.

Epic *kleos* is an antidote to the *lēthē* of the enchanted realm, though only for the hero as the subject of song. Hesiod declares that his poetry offers the listener forgetfulness from pain (*Th.* 94–103). The poet's gift would thus rob "much enduring Odysseus," who "suffered greatly at sea" of his thematic identity. Within the enchanted realm, the Sirens threaten to make Odysseus forget his return by transforming him into an auditor of the *Iliad,* the "other hero's poem." For Odysseus, listening to their song becomes an act of remembering and of forgetting. Whereas the Sirens affirm that their song is true, Odysseus affirms that it is pleasurable, thus creating a nexus of relations analogous to that found in the Hesiodic portrait of the Muses.[40] For Odysseus, the key to surviving the Sirens is to restrain the emotional response roused by the past; *nostos* to civilization becomes aligned with consciousness and pain, the enchanted realm with poetic inspiration and loss of self in a song that is also a memory.

A narrative that condemns yielding to temptation ultimately privileges restraint. As we have seen, self-restraint is a condition of return

[39]For Calypso's offer see Crane, 18–21. An obvious parallel from Greek myth and ritual in which violations of the food code result in a loss of human identity is cannibalism, where, however, the cannibal is transformed into a predator (see Chapter 3 below).

[40]Nagy (1989) 30–31; Segal (1994) 100–106, 134. For the relationship between epic and *lēthē* see also Nagy (1979) 96–97, 113. For *lēthē* as the antonym of *noos* and *nostos,* see Frame 210–11; Nagy (1990) 218.

for both Odysseus and Achilleus in their respective epics. Thus, Teiresias warns Odysseus that return to Ithaca depends on his capacity to restrain his own *thumos* and that of his companions when they reach Thrinakie:

> ἀλλ' ἔτι μέν κε καὶ ὥς, κακά περ πάσχοντες, ἵκοισθε,
> αἴ κ' ἐθέλῃς σὸν θυμὸν ἐρυκακέειν καὶ ἑταίρων,
> ὁππότε δὴ πρῶτον πελάσῃς εὐεργέα νῆα
> Θρινακίῃ νήσῳ, προφυγὼν ἰοειδέα πόντον,
> βοσκομένας δ' εὕρητε βόας καὶ ἴφια μῆλα
> Ἠελίου, ὃς πάντ' ἐφορᾷ καὶ πάντ' ἐπακούει.
> τὰς εἰ μέν κ' ἀσινέας ἐάᾳς νόστου τε μέδηαι,
> καί κεν ἔτ' εἰς Ἰθάκην, κακά περ πάσχοντες, ἵκοισθε·
>
> (11.104–11)

> But even so you may yet return home, for all that you suffer evils,
> if you are willing to restrain your *thumos* and your companions',
> when first you approach the Thrinakian isle
> in your well-built ship, escaping the violet-faced sea.
> You will find there the pasturing cows and stout sheep
> of Helios, who looks on all things and hears all.
> As to these, if you let them go unharmed and think of your return,
> you may even yet reach Ithaca, for all that you suffer evils.

The prophecy of Teiresias gives a new perspective to the threat posed by food: because the crew are warned, the issue of whether or not to eat the cattle becomes an explicit test of self-restraint. Thus, from the perspective offered by Teiresias, Odysseus will survive and return because he is able to control his *thumos,* but the crew are punished because they cannot, even when they are warned by the gods through Teiresias and the nymph Circe. Polyphemos, by contrast, declares that fear of the gods will not prevent him from harming Odysseus and the crew unless his own *thumos* bids him (9.272–78). Polyphemos' own words make his cannibalism an act of unrestrained behavior for which he is likewise punished. If justice is a condition of return, then restraint is a condition of justice.

The prophecy of Teiresias also points to the affinity between self-restraint and endurance, the latter forming part of Odysseus' personal nomenclature in the epithet *polutlas,* or 'much enduring'.[41] Thus, Odys-

[41] For Odysseus' epithets in *tlē-, tla-,* and *tala-,* see Pucci (1987) 44–49. Odysseus' endurance is also known to Iliadic tradition (see *Il.* 5.670, 8.97) and was appreciated by later authors. For this reason Odysseus becomes a paradigm of ethical excellence in Antisthe-

seus urges the crew to sail past Thrinakie despite their weariness and the apparent safety of its harbor. When they are later faced with starvation on the island, Odysseus withdraws to pray to the gods while the crew yield to the temptation posed by the cattle of Helios. Odysseus undergoes further endurance trials on his own: in the Charybdis episode, he hangs from a fig tree for an entire day to avoid being swallowed by the goddess, and afterwards rides for nine days astride the ship's mast to Ogygie. Odysseus sails from Ogygie for seventeen days without sleep, and when he again suffers shipwreck he must swim for three more days and two nights in order to reach Scherie. In the palace of Alkinoos, Odysseus must also "endure" to narrate the story of his sufferings through the night (11.375–76).[42]

As Odysseus hangs from the fig tree and as he swims to Scherie, his alternative to endurance is sleep—a sleep that differs from the oblivion offered by the lotus or by the drugs of Circe only in its fully rationalized equation of loss of *noos* with death. These endurance trials are another manifestation of the attacks on consciousness endemic to the enchanted realm. When Circe realizes that Odysseus has not been transformed into a pig, she says: "I am amazed that you were not charmed although you drank my drugs; for no other man has endured (*anetlē*) them" (10.326–27). The apotropaic drug *mōlu,* with which Odysseus fortifies himself against Circe, rationalizes his superhuman powers of endurance.[43]

Although a temporary loss of self-restraint after blinding Polyphemos condemns Odysseus to ten years of wandering, his ability to restrain his *thumos* and endure suffering while in the cave ensures his survival and revenge:

τὸν μὲν ἐγὼ βούλευσα κατὰ μεγαλήτορα θυμὸν
ἆσσον ἰών, ξίφος ὀξὺ ἐρυσσάμενος παρὰ μηροῦ,
οὐτάμεναι πρὸς στῆθος, ὅθι φρένες ἧπαρ ἔχουσι,
χείρ᾽ ἐπιμασσάμενος· ἕτερος δέ με θυμὸς ἔρυκεν.
αὐτοῦ γάρ κε καὶ ἄμμες ἀπωλόμεθ᾽ αἰπὺν ὄλεθρον·

---

nes and Stoicism. Richardson, *IC* at *Il.* 24.49 remarks that the *Iliad,* unlike the *Odyssey* and later poetry, rarely places a high value on endurance.

[42] Although the Intermezzo of Book 11 in which Alkinoos requests more stories marks the midpoint in the series of Odysseus' adventures, in terms of performance time, the *Apologoi* are at this point two-thirds complete. The poet observes this in the narrative frame: Odysseus begins before sundown, but ends at dawn. By both reckonings he finds himself in Hades at midnight, at which point Odysseus expresses a powerful urge to sleep. Alkinoos requests that Odysseus return narratologically from Hades, just as he will himself provide, and in this scene offers, conveyance from Scherie to Ithaca.

[43] For *mōlu* as a symbol of endurance, see Reinhardt (1960) 81–82; Nagler (1977) 80.

οὐ γάρ κεν δυνάμεσθα θυράων ὑψηλάων
χερσὶν ἀπώσασθαι λίθον ὄβριμον, ὃν προσέθηκεν.

(9.299–305)

I devised a plan in my greathearted *thumos*
to go nearer, draw the sharp sword from beside my thigh,
and strike him on the chest, where the midriff contains the liver,
having felt for it with my hand. But another *thumos* checked me,
for there we too would have suffered sheer destruction.
For we would not have been able with our hands to push away
from the high door the mighty stone which he had set there.

Odysseus must endure a similar test of self-control on the night before his revenge on the suitors, the *Mnesterophonia,* as his own words remind us:[44]

τέτλαθι δή, κραδίη· καὶ κύντερον ἄλλο ποτ' ἔτλης,
ἤματι τῷ, ὅτε μοι μένος ἄσχετος ἤσθιε Κύκλωψ
ἰφθίμους ἑτάρους· σὺ δ' ἐτόλμας, ὄφρα σε μῆτις
ἐξάγαγ' ἐξ ἄντροιο διόμενον θανέεσθαι.

(20.18–21)

Endure now my heart; once you endured a thing even more doglike
on that day when the unstoppable might, the Cyclops,
ate your valiant companions. But you endured until *mētis*
led you forth from the cave, though you thought you were going to die.

Endurance is again equated with self-restraint in that it involves mastering the desire to avenge himself on the suitors and the disloyal servant girls. These verses associate the struggles of Odysseus with Polyphemos and the suitors even as they emphasize the significance of restraint and endurance as a condition of his success. Restraint and endurance are essential aspects of the *mētis* that secures his victory over vastly superior physical force.

The *Cyclopeia* and the *Mnesterophonia* are unified by the theme of Odysseus' successful return and revenge through his ability to restrain

[44] In the programmatic opening scenes of the Revenge, Homer has already announced that Odysseus' success at home will require self-restraint and endurance (see especially 13.306–36, where note that the *allos anēr* at verse 333 alludes to Agamemnon). The first test occurs four books later at 17.235–38, when Odysseus is mistreated by Melanthios. This scene is of particular interest in that it offers a further parallel to 9.299–305.

his *thumos* and to endure mistreatment at the hands of Polyphemos and the suitors. Conversely, both Polyphemos and the suitors are punished for unrestrained behavior emblematized by their improper feasting. The Thrinakian episode tests the self-restraint of the crew and of Odysseus by requiring them to endure hunger while surrounded by cattle.

Odysseus is at his least successful when it comes to sexual self-restraint.[45] As in the *Cyclopeia,* gratifying his desires delays his return but does not prevent it. Thus, after his year of cohabitation with Circe, it is the crew who must remind Odysseus of home (10.467–74). Less than two months later he begins a seven-year relationship with Calypso. In Book 5, the poet indicates that Odysseus' longing for Ithaca is comparatively recent: "Calypso found him sitting on the headland; nor were his eyes ever dry of tears, but his sweet life was shed forth continuously as he lamented his return, since the nymph no longer pleased him" (5.151–53). His encounter with Nausikaa on Scherie thus serves an important narrative function, for it shows him to be impervious to the temptation posed by sex rather than simply bored with Calypso. Odysseus demonstrates his resolve during their first meeting when he compares Nausikaa to the virgin goddess Artemis, thus suggesting the role he wishes her to adopt in response to his supplications (6.149–52).[46] The last obstacle to Odysseus' return has been removed.

Whereas restraint is an aspect of *mētis* and as such distinguishes characters of *mētis* from those of *biē,* the importance of restraint for social order returns us to the polarity between Greek culture and the enchanted realm. The leader of any group controls the behavior of its members both in the positive sense of directing them in collective enterprises and in the negative sense of restraining or punishing improper behavior. In the latter case, the leader adopts the role of parent, or in Freudian terms the superego, of the group.[47] As leader of the crew,

45 Crane, 42–44; Nagy (1990) 234. Note that Calypso attempts to "bewitch [Odysseus] with words so that he will forget Ithaca" (1.56–57).

46 The scene presents something of a dilemma for Odysseus, who must simultaneously win the girl over and keep her at a distance. With typical resourcefulness Odysseus solves his dilemma by defining their relationship as that between a mortal and Artemis, a goddess who is moreover a virgin. Note the poet's ironic evocation of the folk-tale motif of the goddess disturbed at her bath. The motif adds an ominous tone to the scene, yet the threat posed by Nausikaa consists precisely in the fact that she is nubile. The comparison of Nausikaa to Artemis, the Mistress of the Animals, lends further point to the simile which likens Odysseus to a ravening lion in the same episode. Further on the scene in Goldhill (1988) 24–26; Ford, 118–20; Felson-Rubin, 8.

47 Freud develops his theory in *Das Unbehagen in der Kultur,* commonly translated as

Odysseus objectifies their self-restraint, just as the mast to which he is tied in the Siren episode objectifies his own, or the drug *mōlu* his endurance. On one level, then, the sleep that comes over Odysseus in the Aiolian and Thrinakian episodes represents the crew's own loss of self-restraint even as it provides them with an opportunity to indulge in unrestrained behavior. Odysseus is the knot that ties shut the bag of winds—to fall asleep is to untie it.

The effect of Odysseus' narcolepsy for the behavior of the crew is analogous to that of his absence for Ithacan society: the social order breaks down and men under his leadership eat the cattle of the island's ruler. Because the crew sacrifice the cattle of Helios in the enchanted realm, the suitors arrive to create a false Paradise on Ithaca by plundering the exhaustible resources of Odysseus' estate. The return of Odysseus from the enchanted realm to civilization marks the return of Ithaca from the conditions that reign in the enchanted realm. And he employs the very strategies against the suitors that ensured his success over Polyphemos. In the enchanted realm, such strategies result in his continued persecution by Poseidon. On Ithaca, however, Zeus calls an end to the conflict when the parents of the suitors attempt to avenge their sons.

As I have intimated, the *Odyssey* anticipates Freud's political writing in several respects. The repression of physical appetites, which becomes a cultural symbol in the *Odyssey,* creates for Freud the fund of psychic energy that makes civilization possible. Thus, squandering one's spiritual economy through licentious behavior is reflected within Ithacan society in the plundering of another's estate. Conversely, self-restraint and preservation of the physical economy of the *oikos* serve to define just behavior. The lack of a restraining force on Ithaca results in the degeneration of its society, manifested in the suitors' disrespect for social law (*themis*), in particular the laws of hospitality (*xenia*), and in the promiscuity of the disloyal maidservants.

Odysseus' defenses against forgetting to return to Ithaca are self-restraint and endurance, which in turn bridge the concepts of *mētis* and suffering. Intelligence and endurance are a collective definition of civilized humanity, as they are of the *polutropos* 'man' who is the subject of the poem. The epithets *polutlas* and *polumētis* are coextensive expressions

Civilization and its Discontents. We may reject or at least modify Freud's hydraulic model of the human psyche and still appreciate its striking affinities with Homeric man. In this context note the remarks of Vernant (1982) 63, 83.

for the psychic economy by which Odysseus survives the hostility of the enchanted realm and returns to the world of Greece. Without cunning intelligence (*mētis* and *noos*) there can be no return (*nostos*) from the cave of Polyphemos. Because he is *polutropos,* Odysseus will eventually 'make it back' to Ithaca (*hupotropos hikesthai;* See *Od.* 20.332, 21.211 and 22.35).[48]

Structural Fabulation

The first two books of the *Apologoi* observe an "anapestic" pattern of two short accounts followed by one narrated at greater length. The Kikones and Lotophagoi are followed by the Cyclops, Aiolos and the Laistrygones by Circe. The entire third book of the *Apologoi* is devoted to a single adventure known as the *Nekyia,* in which Odysseus journeys to the underworld to consult the seer Teiresias. A fourth and final book contains six episodes, of which Thrinakie, the fourth, is awarded the greatest amount of performance time.[49] The adventures following the *Nekyia* thus equal the combined number of those related in the books preceding.

The relative positions of the *Nekyia* after the long narrative devoted to Circe, and of Thrinakie, which follows three short accounts, fail to observe the anapestic pattern of the first two books. These apparent inconcinnities may be resolved, however, by treating the two Circe episodes as a narrative frame for the *Nekyia.* This is the approach taken by Cedric Whitman, who argues that the *Apologoi* exhibit a "geometric" pattern of organization characteristic of the *Iliad:*

> The Adventures are [a] particularly elegant [example of geometric design], grouped as they are around the supreme adventure, the Journey to the Dead. This central episode . . . is carefully framed, first by the two Elpenor episodes and then by the two scenes with Circe. For the rest, the poet summarizes two out of every three adventures rather briefly, and dramatizes one at greater length, so that the pattern of Odysseus' narrative is as follows:

48 Whitman, 300. Frame, 65, and Pucci (1987) 14–17, 150, treat the theme of intelligence and return, and its opposition to death and loss of identity. For restraint and intelligence see Thornton, 81–84.

49 The pioneering work of Lord reveals that in oral poetry performance-time marks the significance of both speaker and speech. See further in Martin, especially 50.

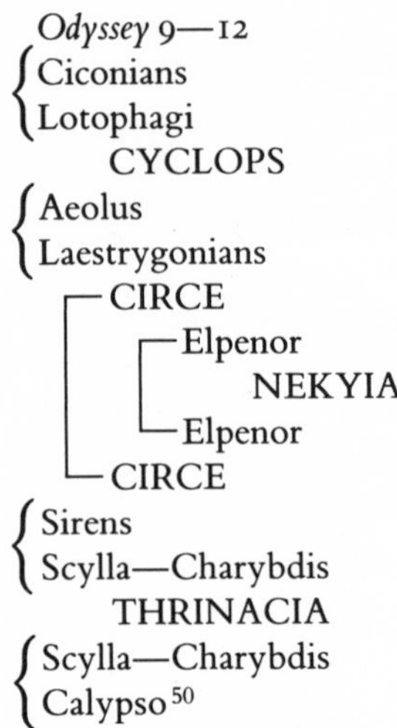

Whitman's analysis is attractive, since it observes both the central position of the *Nekyia* and the organization of the *Apologoi* into an alternating pattern of short and long episodes. Thus, the *Cyclopeia,* the triad Circe-*Nekyia*-Circe, and Thrinakie are the third element of a series. Alternatively, and perhaps more accurately, each of the larger narrative sequences is bracketed by pairs of shorter tales.

The structural link assumed by Whitman's analysis between Circe and the *Nekyia* is confirmed by the mythic tradition to which the stories belong. Nagler, enlarging on the work of Franz Dirlmeier, has shown that Circe belongs to a class of littoral goddesses who assist the hero in his quest, often by facilitating an interview with a mantic figure.[51] The sequence Calypso-Scherie belongs to this pattern as does the interview of Menelaos with Proteus in Book 4.[52] Return to the littoral figure after the journey does not, however, appear to be a common feature of such accounts. The inclusion of a second Circe episode is structurally moti-

[50] Whitman, 288. See also Woodhouse, 43–44.

[51] Dirlmeier (1970) 79–84; Nagler (1977). See also Germain, 417–29; Reinhardt (1960) 98–99; Damon (1969, 1974). For parallels between Proteus and Teiresias in the *Odyssey* see Lord, 165–69; Hansen, 8–19; Peradotto, 34–41. The Herakles cycle supplies a close parallel to this pattern: nymphean daughters of Zeus and Themis who lived in a cave on the banks of the Eridanos suggested to Herakles that he learn from Nereus how to obtain the Golden Apples of the Hesperides. Nereus, like Proteus, could assume all manner of shapes, and had to be overpowered before he would divulge his knowledge. *MMR* 627–28 and Fontenrose, 345–46, identify the myth as a Catabasis.

[52] If I am right to argue that the Phaiakes owe something to traditions involving otherworldly ferrymen (E. Cook [1992]), then both legs of Odysseus' travels end with a nymph who facilitates such a journey, to Hades and Elysium respectively.

vated: it frames the *Nekyia* as well as the second half of the adventures which thereby begin and end with an island nymph.

The *Nekyia* triad divides the adventures into two distinct groups. Before the *Nekyia,* Odysseus has dealings with males who are mortal, while after it he encounters isolated, divine females. The *Nekyia* is organized in turn by catalogues of women and men, separated by an Intermezzo between Odysseus and his Phaiakian hosts. This arrangement creates an alternating pattern within the *Apologoi* of male, female, male and female: that is, encounters with societies, the Catalogue of Women (where note the sexual ambiguity of Teiresias), the Catalogue of Men, and encounters with goddesses. Even Thrinakie is given a pair of nymphs, Phaethousa and Lampetie, to guard the cattle of Helios. They prove rather ineffectual custodians, and the fact that they must report the mischief of the crew contradicts both the typical Greek conception of Helios as all-seeing and Helios' own claim that he looked on his cattle each day at sunrise and sunset (12.379–81).[53] Their presence may be explained in terms of a normative influence exerted by the centrality of divine females in the adventures following the *Nekyia.* The actual focal point of the story, however, is a herd of 350 immortal heifers.

Whereas the first group of adventures begins with the city of the Kikones and ends with that of the Kimmerioi, the second begins and ends with the nymphs Circe and Calypso (the symmetry is imperfect due to the position of the first Circe episode which precedes the *Nekyia,* but as we have seen this finds its explanation in the traditional elements of heroic quest and consultation). In fact, all of the stories before the *Nekyia* triad concern alternative societies: the Kimmerioi, Kikones, Laistrygones, and even the floating island of Aiolie are each given a *polis.*[54] Yet within the enchanted world only the border realms of Scherie and Aiolie approximate the status of normal Greek societies. The Laistrygones have many of the institutions of Greek culture but pervert its customs, while the Cyclopes are described with a "negative catalogue" of Greek cultural institutions (see below, Chapter 3).

During the first leg of his adventures, Odysseus commands twelve ships with approximately six hundred men (9.159); he is the leader of one type of social unit investigating others. Afterwards, as Odysseus

[53] For Helios as all-seeing in Homer, see *Od.* 8.270–71, 12.322–23; *Il.* 14.344–45.

[54] For the Homeric *polis* see Luce; Quiller, 112–13; Scully (1981, 1991); I. Morris (1986) 104; Nagy (1979) 115–17; Nagy (1990) 9–11 with additional bibliography. For the archaeological evidence, see Snodgrass (1991); I. Morris (1991); J. Lenz, especially 177–207; Seaford (1994) 1–10.

ventures on to encounter solitary females, his command is reduced to a single ship.[55] In the first adventure, the Kikonian, the Greeks are the aggressors, in the Aiolian and Lotophagian episodes they are hosted, and they themselves suffer aggression from Polyphemos and the Laistrygones. Representative levels of culture are depicted in these encounters, as well as a variety of social relationships, so that Odysseus receives a kind of hands-on course in comparative civilizations before the *Nekyia*.

We may then dismiss the claim that verse 3 of the proem, which states that Odysseus "saw the cities of many men," inaccurately summarizes his years of wandering (for the claim see Appendix 1). The poet's further remark that "he came to know their way of thought" in the same verse indicates that the societies which Odysseus encountered differed from his own. There is no need to avail ourselves of the argument that verse 3 also holds true as a general characterization of Odysseus and of heroes generally, although this doubtless colored the audience's reception of the statement.[56] Moreover, Odysseus provides a concise account of his travels, and the temporal breaks at which further adventures could have been omitted all occur between the stories preceding the *Nekyia*.[57] Indeed, the rhetorical question with which Odysseus begins the *Apologoi* represents the selection and disposition of the episodes as his own conscious decision: "What then shall I tell you first, and what last?" (9.14).

The amount of time covered by the adventures as narrated leaves the better part of two years unexplained: Odysseus spends eight years with the nymphs Circe and Calypso.[58] Of the adventures preceding the *Nekyia,* Odysseus indicates that the journey from the Kikones to the Lotophagoi lasted twelve days, from Aiolie to Ithaca nine (plus a month on the island and presumably another nine or so days to return), and from Aiolie to the Laistrygones another seven. The total amount of time that transpires after the *Nekyia* is less than a month and a half, to which should be added the month it requires Odysseus to build a ship, journey to Scherie, and secure his passage home. The *Apologoi* thus require approximately eight years and three months.

[55] For just how dispensable the flotilla is see Reinhardt (1960) 53–58.

[56] Everyone in the poem, it seems, remarks at how well-traveled Odysseus was (beginning with Telemachos at 1.177).

[57] At 11.328–29 Odysseus implies that we also receive an abbreviated version of his encounters with the women in Hades.

[58] It may fairly be questioned whether the audience would have noticed the discrepancy, and my broader argument does not depend on it. The better part of two years is, however, a fairly egregious margin of error and on the strength of the other evidence I feel that it is significant.

There is no room for omitted stories in Book 12. Upon leaving Aiaie, Odysseus encounters the Sirens and Scylla and reaches Thrinakie on the same day. After a month on Thrinakie, Zeus destroys the ship as soon as it sets sail, and twelve days later Odysseus arrives at Ogygie. Odysseus thus provides exact figures for both the duration of the stays and the length of the voyages in the adventures following the *Nekyia*. He fails, however, to indicate the length of his journeys from Troy to the Kikones, from the Lotophagoi to the Cyclopes, from the Cyclopes to Aiolie, or from the Laistrygones to Circe. And in Book 3 Nestor informs Telemachos that Odysseus had already embarked on an aborted attempt to return home before the Kikonian episode (3.130–200).

We have then a significant amount of time that remains unexplained, some four junctures at which additional adventures could have been omitted, and direct evidence that at one of those junctures Odysseus has failed to render a full account of his activities.[59] If Odysseus has shortened or "arranged" his story, then he has done so with the adventures preceding the *Nekyia*. This is relevant for assessing the accuracy of the proem, since each of the temporal breaks in the adventures occurs between the episodes in which Odysseus was still "wandering among the cities of men." Are we to see Odysseus as editing his early adventures so as to bring them into some sort of relationship with one another? Does Aiolie follow the Cyclopes in order to reveal that Poseidon had heard the curse of Polyphemos, and do the Laistrygones follow Aiolie in order to validate Aiolos' claim that Odysseus was hated by the gods?

Of course, we need hardly assume that the *Apologoi* are a concise account of the adventures, or that Odysseus is responsible for their arrangement, to maintain that the Laistrygones illustrate the effect of Polyphemos' curse. However we account for its position, the Aiolian episode would also tend to undermine the claim that the role of Poseidon in the *Apologoi* disappoints the expectations raised by the prologue. Like any human actor, Aiolos cannot supply the name of Odysseus' adversary, but he does recognize and is able to announce in the episode following the *Cyclopeia* that divine anger is responsible for his misfortunes.[60] Yet the audience would naturally assign greater interpretive value to the order of events if they felt that the internal narrator were himself arranging the episodes rather than simply reporting them as they were supposed to have occurred.

[59] See Goldhill (1991) 48–49, who compares the *Apologoi* with Odysseus' later account of the adventures to Penelope.

[60] For Aiolos' human identity, see below. Reinhardt (1960) 74–76, and *CHO* at 10.1–79 relate the Aiolian episode to the theme of Poseidon's wrath.

Narrative Structure and Hierarchies of Culture

Within the adventures preceding the *Nekyia,* the Cyclopes most closely resemble the Laistrygones, and the ethical norms of both groups contrast with those of the Phaiakes to whom these stories are told. Odysseus can thus be seen as ingratiating himself with his hosts by relating them favorably to other peoples whose "way of thought" he had come to know. Arete's offer of gifts during the Intermezzo demonstrates his success in this regard. At the same time, these peoples are related to one another largely in terms of their relative affinity to Greek culture. The compliment that Odysseus hands the Phaiakes thus consists of their "Greekness," while the ongoing comparison between them and the Cyclopes and Laistrygones emphasizes the ethnographic focus of the narrative.

To map out the relationship among these groups I will start by comparing the Cyclopes and Laistrygones. The episodes share a number of narrative motifs, and these common elements are all the more striking because the episodes are separated by a mere eighty verses. They begin with a catalogue of civic institutions that the Cyclopes lack and the Laistrygones—for the most part—enjoy, thus introducing a point-by-point contrast between them even as it positions them within a hierarchy defined by Greek culture.[61] Parallels extend to the story line: both episodes are devoted to cannibals of giant stature who herd flocks. Both Polyphemos and the Laistrygones pursue and attack the Greeks in their ship(s) by hurling large rocks from above.[62] The Laistrygonian harbor, in which the flotilla with the exception of Odysseus' own ship is trapped, corresponds both typologically and in its physical description to the sea-side cave in which Polyphemos traps Odysseus and his men.

As noted above, the cultural institutions that distinguish the Laistrygones from the Cyclopes also relate the Laistrygones to the Phaiakes.[63] This emphasis on the civic life of the Laistrygones is striking and seems more than a little incongruous with their dietary habits. Yet, like the Phaiakes, they are politically organized, with a king and queen who reside in a high-roofed palace, and an *agora* at which the people regularly assemble. It is, moreover, precisely their capacity for organized activity that makes the Laistrygones more deadly as adversaries than the Cyclopes: while Polyphemos eats six of Odysseus' companions, for which he is blinded, the Laistrygones eat over five hundred and escape punishment.

[61] Compare 9.112–15, 125–29 with 10.103–20.
[62] Page (1973) 27–28; Frame, 57; *CHO* at 10.112–16.
[63] Crane, 139–40.

Parallels extend once more to the story line. In both accounts a girl fetching water shows the stranger(s) to the palace of the king; in Laistrygonie it is the daughter of the queen, while on Scherie Athene substitutes for Nausikaa, the daughter of queen Arete (compare 7.19–20 with 10.105–6). Athene, repeating the prior instructions of Nausikaa, tells Odysseus to supplicate queen Arete, and shows Odysseus to the palace. On Laistrygonie, the princess herself leads the delegation sent by Odysseus to her father's palace, where they first encounter the queen. Instead of hospitality, however, the delegation meets with cannibalism. The Laistrygonian adventure begins as if it were going to be another *Phaiakis*, but transforms itself unexpectedly and horrifically into another *Cyclopeia*.

The relationship among the Laistrygones, Cyclopes, and Phaiakes is expressed geographically and genealogically. Homer remarks that the Phaiakes had once lived in Hypereie, but that due to constant harassment by the Cyclopes they emigrated under Nausithoos to Scherie (6.4–8).[64] Nausithoos, moreover, was son to Poseidon by Periboia (7.56–57), just as Polyphemos was son to Poseidon by another nymph, Thoosa (1.71–73), so that the royal line of the Phaiakes and the mightiest of the Cyclopes have a common divine ancestor in their immediate past. The pattern of associations between all three groups made Poseidon's paternity of the Laistrygones inevitable, just as the entire race of the Cyclopes could be said to be the offspring of the god.[65]

Alkinoos explains the frequent appearance of the gods on Scherie with the boast: "For we are close to the gods, like the Cyclopes and the savage race of Giants" (7.205–6). The Phaiakes are in fact descended from the Giants (7.59). Thus, when Odysseus likens the Laistrygones to the Giants (10.120), he also strengthens the correlation between the Laistrygones and the Phaiakes. The comparison is substantiated by his own remark a dozen verses earlier that his companions met the Laistrygonian princess at Artakie (10.108), a spring associated with a race of earth-born creatures who figure prominently in the Argonautic Saga.[66] In Apollonius' version of the story, a band of Gegeneis near Kyzikos hurled rocks from cliff tops to trap the Argo in the harbor below, and were for this summarily dispatched by Herakles (A.R. 1.936–1011).

[64] Thornton, 20; Segal (1994) 30–32.

[65] Aulus Gellius 15.21; see the Scholia to *Od.* 10.81, Eustathius 1649.10 and *RE,* s.v. "Lamos 5."

[66] For the connection between the Laistrygones and the Gegeneis of the Argonautic Saga, see Meuli, 91; Vian (1951); *CHO* at 10.108. For the contrary view, see Eisenberger, 149–51; Hölscher, 171ff. Apollonius 1.1047 attests to a character named Artakeus. Note that Odysseus' next destination, Aiaie, also plays a role in the Argonautic Saga, and that

By associating the Cyclopes and Laistrygones with the Giants, archetypal opponents of the Olympian order, Odysseus makes his encounters with these groups represent their hostility to the ethical norms of the Greeks and to the Olympian gods who validate those norms. This theme receives its most developed treatment in the *Cyclopeia* and needs little more than tags—"they looked like Giants" and cannibalism—to evoke it in the Laistrygonian episode.[67] The ancestry of the Phaiakes represents the same opposition in diachronic terms. Alkinoos is a third-generation descendant from the giant Eurymedon "who destroyed his reckless people, and was himself destroyed" (7.60; compare 1.7).

The depiction of these closely related peoples articulates the history of human cultural evolution into three distinct stages. The Cyclopes occupy the first rung on this evolutionary ladder, with the Phaiakes at the other extreme and the Laistrygones somewhere in between them. The intermediate position held by the Laistrygones is carefully registered by the admixture of civic institutions such as the *agora* with their cannibalism and the fact that they apparently do not practice agriculture.[68] The ongoing contrast among the Phaiakes, the Laistrygones, and the Cyclopes contributes to the ethnographic program of the *Apologoi* by representing Greek civilization as the goal of this evolutionary process.

The relationship between the Phaiakes and the Aiolians is one of affinity rather than contrast. As if to mark the spot vacated by the Phaiakes, Aiolie is located in the narrative between the Cyclopes and Laistrygones. Both Aiolos and Alkinoos are "dear to the immortals" (6.203, 10.2; see also 7.199–206), from whom they enjoy special dispensations that permit them to assist Odysseus in his return. The intermarried twelve children of Aiolos reflect the traditional division of the winds

---

Kirchhoff, 287ff., argued for a Circe episode in the Argonautica. See Meuli, 54, 97–114; *CHO* at 10.133–574.

67 For the cannibalism of Giants, see Ephorus, *FHG* 1.255.70; Nonnos, *D.* 45.174–83. The opposition between the Giants and the Olympians recurs in the *Odyssey*'s Catalogue of Women: Heubeck (1954) 33–35, demonstrates that the Catalogue frames Otos and Ephialtes, Giant sons of Poseidon who attempted to storm Olympos, with the contrasting pair of Castor and Pollux, sons of Zeus.

68 Their lack of farming is noted by Vidal-Naquet, 19–20. Another scale is provided by the motif of physical strength: the stones used by the Laistrygones to attack the Greek ships, *andrakhthea* (10.121), 'burdens for a man', or stones a man could lift but not use as weapons, elicit comparison to the "mountain peak" hurled by Polyphemos some two hundred verses before (9.481–82); similarly, Antiphates' appetite is satisfied with one of Odysseus' men as compared to Polyphemos' two. The Phaiakes, on the other hand, are not even a match for a Greek hero in throwing the discus (8.186–98). Diminished physical strength belongs to the degeneration motif in mythic traditions of the Golden Age. This reveals the full significance of the poet's remark that the Phaiakes are weaker than the Cyclopes (6.6): it is equivalent to saying that they are more civilized.

into male and female pairs, although they are not directly equated with the winds, since Aiolos puts these in a sack.[69] The children of Aiolos correspond in number to the twelve kings of Scherie, and the marriage of Alkinoos and Arete is likewise incestuous.[70] The walls of Alkinoos' house are bronze, as is the wall encompassing the whole of Aiolie, and the silver cord used by Aiolos to secure the bag of winds implies a technical sophistication matched only by the Phaiakes. Within those walls both royal families enjoy a work-free life of plenty characteristic of Paradise and take their delight in perpetual banqueting and in listening to stories, all of which afford Odysseus an ideal setting in which to narrate his adventures.[71]

The Aiolian episode and the *Phaiakis* both contain scenes in which Odysseus must plead to the king in desperate circumstances to help him return to Ithaca. The cause of Odysseus' plight at Aiolie is the greed of his crew. Upon his departure from the island, Aiolos presents Odysseus with a bag of winds. When Odysseus falls asleep during the voyage home, the crew untie the knot to the bag in the belief that it contains gold and silver. On Scherie, Odysseus *does* have gold in a coffer given him by Alkinoos. Arete warns Odysseus to tie the coffer shut lest the Phaiakian crew attempt to steal the treasure while he sleeps. Considering that the description of Aiolos' island is under fifty verses in length, the number of similarities is nothing short of remarkable.

Although I have treated the depiction of Aiolie as a utopian Paradise in terms of its relationship to Scherie, this does not supply a motivation for the depiction. Moreover, the social aspect of the Aiolian episode has no intrinsic plot function, and the harmony that reigns at the court of Aiolos is at odds with the character of the winds themselves.[72] The Homeric formulation of the Aiolian episode thus lends support to my assertion that the adventures preceding the *Nekyia* are designed to offer a sample of representative civilizations. The position of the emigrated Phaiakes in the world of the *Apologoi* is occupied not only topographically but typologically by the Aiolians. It should not surprise us to

[69]Germain, 179, 185, and Page (1973) 76, remark that Aiolos is not the god of the winds but their *tamiēs,* or steward, although it should be observed that Zeus is called the *tamiēs polemoio,* 'steward of war' (*Il.* 4.84 = 19.224). Note the use of *daimōn* by Aiolos and his family at 10.64, which conforms to Jørgensen's law on the naming of divine agents by human characters (for which see below, Appendix 1), and both Aiolos and his children are clearly surprised at Odysseus' sudden reappearance (10.63–66).

[70]Thus Powell (1977) 31; their arrangement corresponds, however, to Greek custom (see Pitt-Rivers, 120–21) and an even stronger parallel can, I believe, be found in the cattle of the sun.

[71]Compare 7.98–99, 8.246–49 with 10.8–9, 14–15, 60–61.

[72]Reinhardt (1960) 74: "What one expects can be seen from Vergil [*A.* 1.50–63]."

learn of reported traditions in which Aiolos is the son-in-law of the Laistrygonian king Lamos.[73]

'Mirroring' in the Tales of Odysseus

Thus far, I have been able to confirm Whitman's analysis of the *Apologoi* by demonstrating that the groups of tales isolated by the *Nekyia* exhibit a number of distinct characteristics. As the *Wendepunkt,* the thematic and structural pivot of the narrative, the *Nekyia* is also the endpoint of the first series of adventures; the pair Circe-*Nekyia* corresponds to the Calypso-*Phaiakis* pair which concludes the second series. It would seem natural, then, to suppose that other episodes in these series are related, perhaps by a comprehensive scheme that could explain the sequence in which the events are presented.[74]

Whitman himself did not find evidence of "mirroring" between the individual episodes of the *Apologoi,* although he did believe that the narrative reflects a tendency of archaic Greek thought to articulate experience in terms of polar opposition. Considered separately, however, the *Nekyia* together with the so-called Intermezzo (11.333–84) exhibit structural symmetries as striking as those found in the arrangement of the other adventures, in which the compositional elements unquestionably mirror one another.

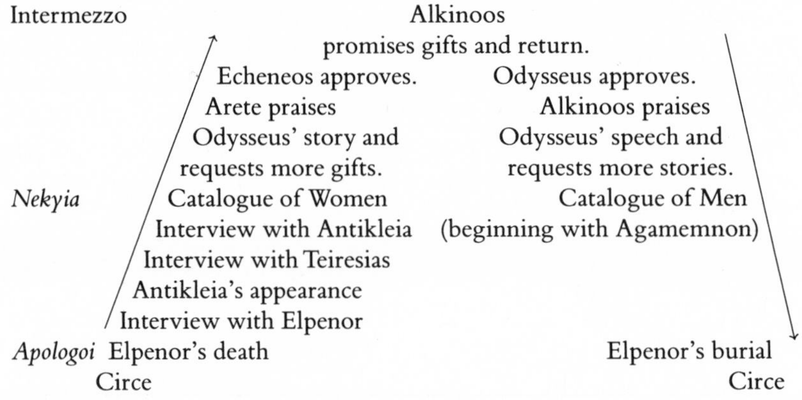

[73] Scholia to *Od.* 10.6; Eustathius 1645.27.

[74] Other attempts to discover a system of correlations between episodes include Germain, 333; Nagler (1977) 79; Niles, 51; Miller, 81; Redfield (1983) 237; Scully (1987) 405; Most, 21.

The advice that Circe offers Odysseus in Book 12 balances her earlier advice in Book 10 and the prophecy of Teiresias in the *Nekyia*.[75] Antikleia serves to introduce the Catalogue of Women, and her appearance and subsequent interview frame the prophecy of Teiresias with a symbol of home, Odysseus' ultimate quest. Antikleia is preceded by Elpenor, whose death and burial frame the entire episode.[76] The unexpected appearance of Elpenor and of Antikleia elicits a surprised and impassioned response from Odysseus, and their juxtaposition before the scene with Teiresias relates Odysseus to the two principal social units, family and fighting band, to which every adult Greek male belongs.[77]

Antikleia, the first of the women encountered by Odysseus, provides her son with news of his family, in particular of his wife's continued fidelity. Antikleia's assurances are balanced in the Catalogue of Men by the comic negativism of Agamemnon, the first of the heroes interviewed, who fulminates against the treachery of his own wife Clytemnestra and her suitor Aigisthos. The structure of the narrative thus draws a comparison between the houses of Agamemnon and Odysseus which Agamemnon's speech makes explicit.

The Intermezzo divides the *Nekyia* into two catalogues, one of women, followed by Arete's request of gifts for Odysseus, and one of men, requested by Alkinoos.[78] William Hansen has shown that Alkinoos' request and the type of story which it elicits are common to three other "conference scenes" of the poem; the interview of Nestor by Telemachos, of Proteus by Menelaos, and of Eumaios by Odysseus. In all cases the request prompts a tale of "sad fates," and in all but one, in which Odysseus asks Eumaios for news of Laertes, the tale concerns the Greek heroes who fought at Troy—allowing the poet to incorporate material from the *Nostoi* tradition—and features the house of Agamemnon.[79]

Arete's request for gifts in the Intermezzo has no part in the narrative pattern analyzed by Hansen. It serves rather to balance the request of Alkinoos for more stories, which is a regular feature of the pattern. At the beginning of Book 13, the Phaiakian counselors each present

[75] On the relationship between Circe's two speeches see Hansen, 20–21.

[76] Crane, 95, suggests a ritual explanation for Elpenor's death.

[77] Note the temporal regression provided by Elpenor, Antikleia, and the Catalogue of Women. The women range from contemporaries of Antikleia to her predecessors by one or more generations; Elpenor is a generation younger than Odysseus. The Catalogue of Men is divided into Iliadic and pre-Iliadic heroes.

[78] The Intermezzo also softens the transition from the *nekuomanteion,* or prophecy of Teiresias, to the *Catabasis* portion of Book 11. 385ff. Further on the organization of the *Nekyia* in Crane, 92–108.

[79] Hansen summarizes his findings at 55–56.

Odysseus with a tripod and a cauldron. As a result, the first half of the *Apologoi* concludes with the promise of gifts, the second half with the actual giving (viewed from another angle, this is an example of ring composition). Odysseus' suggestion at the beginning of the Intermezzo that all retire for the night indicates that the narration has at this point reached a natural conclusion and may thus be treated as a discrete unit.[80]

The reflexive structure of the Intermezzo makes Alkinoos' offer of gifts and return the focal point of the scene. Since the *Nekyia* is similarly structured, Alkinoos' offer serves as the pivot about which the *Nekyia* itself is arranged. And since the *Nekyia* is both the climax of the *Apologoi* and flanked on either side by an equal number of adventures, the internal structure of the episode invites us to relate the stories following to those preceding it. A reconfiguration of Whitman's analysis represents these relationships graphically (see diagram).

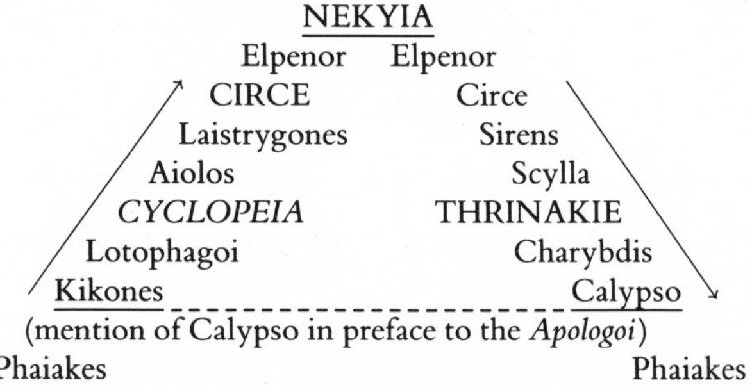

For our purposes, the most important implication of this scheme is that it relates the *Cyclopeia* and the Thrinakian episode, the two long narratives flanking the *Nekyia* triad.[81] While the *Cyclopeia* illustrates Odysseus' polytropic nature as he avenges himself on Polyphemos, Thrinakie provides a scene of similar proportions in which Odysseus suffers hardships while attempting to save his life and win the return of his crew. The complementary nature of these two episodes bears directly on the interpretation of Thrinakie and hence on the description of the crew's demise in the proem. I shall examine this topic at length in Chapter 4.

The organizing pattern that I have proposed for the *Apologoi* is mirrored in the two most important programmatic narratives of the *Odys-*

[80] I do not wish to obscure the fact that this structure emphasizes Alkinoos' offer of escort by making it the *Wendepunkt* of the *Nekyia* and hence the *Odyssey:* a turning-point is also an endpoint.

[81] Frame, 47; Clay (1989) 113–14.

sey, the Introduction in Book I and the prophecy of Teiresias in Book II. In the Introduction, the wrath of Helios concludes the proem and the anger of Poseidon ends the prologue. In the *Nekyia,* the midpoint between the adventures involving those two gods, Teiresias isolates blinding Polyphemos and harming the cattle of the sun as the two events that determine the fate of Odysseus and his men. Together, these episodes illustrate the two sides of the generic hero who both causes pain to others and himself suffers greatly. Most important, however, the *Cyclopeia* and the Thrinakian episode decode the situation on Ithaca even as they create it. Although the *Apologoi* and Revenge are set in antithetical worlds, these worlds are thematically apposite.

By lining up the references to divine interference in the *Apologoi* in accordance with our modified version of Whitman's analysis, we can expose a series of parallels in the reported attitudes and actions of the gods:[82]

NEKYIA

Persephone sends the spirits (11.225–26).
Persephone scatters them (11.385–86).

CIRCE:	CIRCE:
Wine and a *kakos daimōn* kill Elpenor (11.61). Hermes helps Odysseus (10.277ff.). *Theos* sends Odysseus a deer (10.157–59). *Theos* sends the ship to Circe (10.141).	
LAISTRYGONES:	SIRENS: *Daimōn* lulls the waves (12.169).
AIOLOS:	SCYLLA:
CYCLOPEIA:	THRINAKIE:
Zeus thinks of how to destroy .... the fleet (9.554–55).	Zeus destroys the ship (12.405–19; called *theos* 419).

[82]I italicize "Zeus" in accordance with Jørgensen's law in cases where it is unclear whether Odysseus is acting on direct knowledge (again, see below, Appendix 1). The table does not capture the correspondence between Hermes' activities in the Circe and Calypso episodes (the latter not forming a part of the actual *Apologoi*). Parallels between the two goddesses have been discussed above and are easily reconciled with the schematization. For the Sirens and Lotophagoi, see the discussion at the end of this chapter. Other parallels include: 9.67–69 ~ 12.313–15 and 9.158 ~ 10.157–63.

Odysseus sacrifices the sheep of Polyphemos.	The crew sacrifice the cattle of Helios.
Zeus ignores his sacrifice (9.553).	*Theoi* send bad omens following the sacrifice (12.394).
Polyphemos complains to Poseidon.	Helios complains to Zeus.
Poseidon hears the complaint (9.536).	Zeus agrees to punish the crew (12.385–88).
Odysseus boasts to Polyphemos:	Odysseus complains to heaven:
Zeus and the other *theoi* punished you, Polyphemos (9.479).	*Zeus* and the other *theoi* lulled me to sleep for my ruin (12.371–72).
	Theoi send sleep on Odysseus (12.337–38).
	Zeus sends a storm (12.313ff.).
Daimōn gives the crew courage to blind Polyphemos (9.381).	*Daimōn* causes the crew to yield to their weakness (12.295; see 278–93 and 339).
Theos causes Polyphemos to drive the sheep into the cave (9.336–39).	
Theos rewards the hunt (9.158).	
Theos guides the ship into the harbor (9.142–43).	
LOTOPHAGOI:	CHARYBDIS:
	Zeus protects Odysseus (12.445–46).
Zeus sends storm (9.67–73).	*Theoi* lead Odysseus to Ogygie (12.448).
KIKONES:	CALYPSO:
Kakē aisa of Zeus causes defeat (9.52–53).	*Zeus* sends Hermes to Calypso (5.28–42).

At a number of common junctures in the *Cyclopeia* and the Thrinakian episode, similar forms of divine interference are described as determining the course of events, a claim that cannot be made for any of the other pairs of stories so related. Most important, the complaints of Polyphemos and Helios and the punishments meted out by Poseidon and Zeus are thereby related to one another (see Chapter 4).

The references to divine interferences in the *Cyclopeia* and the Thrinakian episode point to an underlying similarity in the story line. On

Thrinakie, Odysseus and his men dock the ship near a cave in the harbor: the setting resembles that of the island adjacent to the Cyclopes. Polyphemos, the progeny of the sea god Poseidon, traps Odysseus and his men in a cave with a flock of sheep, and storms at sea detain them on Thrinakie with the cattle of the sun god in another life-threatening situation. When the storm begins, they draw the ship inside the cave, a measure that would scarcely seem to bode well for the story's outcome.

In both episodes Odysseus holds an assembly, in the *Cyclopeia* to inform the crew of what he intends to do, on Thrinakie to repeat to them what they must not do.[83] When Odysseus comes upon the deserted home of Polyphemos, the crew plead with him to turn the expedition into a cattle raid (9.224–27); on Thrinakie, the crew sacrifice the cattle of Helios in Odysseus' absence. In identical settings, and preceded in both cases with scenes of mourning by the crew, sacrifices are made, in the *Cyclopeia* to Zeus and in the Thrinakian episode to Helios, followed by feasting. On Thrinakie they mourn for the six men eaten by Scylla, on the island adjacent to the land of the Cyclopes for the suspected loss of Odysseus and his companions, where as it turns out six men have been eaten.

The antagonists of both stories are keepers of herds.[84] Polyphemos and Helios each lose part of their herd, which is then sacrificed, and they both appeal to a god to punish the offenders, Polyphemos to Poseidon, Helios to Zeus. Polyphemos complains because Odysseus has blinded him with a fiery stake; Helios threatens to hide his light among the dead, and Zeus destroys the crew with a thunderbolt. Looking beyond the *Cyclopeia,* we should note that the complaints of Polyphemos and Helios are each followed by a storm, caused by the folly of the crew, which results in a "return to point A" and further delays in the quest for home (on the resulting A-B-A pattern, see below). In the *Cyclopeia,* as if to compensate for the theme's displacement, a return to point A also occurs when Polyphemos hurls a rock at the ship. Odysseus' final reconciliation with Poseidon will be achieved when he founds an inland

[83] A third *agora* takes place in the Circe episode, 10.187–88.

[84] Tainaron, the location of a historical herd sacred to Helios (*h.Ap.* 411–13), also contained an oracle of the dead to Poseidon. The temple, in which votive offerings of bronze bulls and horses have been found, was associated with a cave thought to lead to the Underworld. By this cave Theseus was said to have descended into Hades and Herakles to have dragged up the hound Cerberus (Hecataeus, *FGrH* 1.326.15, and Pausanias 3.25.4–5). The latter story is alluded to by Herakles himself as he greets Odysseus in the *Nekyia* (*Od.* 11.623–26). Jacoby, ad loc, argued that Hecataeus' source must have been an epic poem. The analogy of Tainaron to Thrinakie is noted by Wilamowitz (1884) 168; Wide, 216. For further ancient references to cattle of the sun see Crane, 144.

cult to Poseidon. The crew, on the other hand, offer to propitiate Helios by founding a cult to the god on Ithaca.

We have seen that the *Cyclopeia* and the Thrinakian episode are related by our reconfiguration of Whitman's structural analysis of the *Apologoi,* and that they share a number of narrative features, the most striking among them being the instances in which the gods are said to interfere in the course of events. Comparative analysis reveals that the *Cyclopeia* and the Thrinakian episode belong to a common family of myths involving a heroic cattle raid. This gives an added dimension to the prophecy of Teiresias: in order to return home, Odysseus and his men must repeat their Cyclops adventure on Thrinakie, but forego the cattle raid.[85] The Thrinakian episode in effect replays the *Cyclopeia* but at Odysseus' expense: now it is Odysseus who guards the cattle and whose sleep results in losses to the herd, an angry god, and disaster.

Douglas Frame has called attention to the similarity between Polyphemos and the Paṇis of Vedic myth, and his discussion does much to elucidate the significance of the cattle in the Homeric narrative.[86] The Paṇis, or the 'stingy ones', maintain a large herd of cattle which they keep hidden in a cave. The cave, known as Vala or 'Encloser', is sometimes personified as a monster of the same name. In this story, the priests of Indra secure the release of the cattle by singing a hymn that rends the cave in two. The cows are thereby able to emerge from the cave, which allows the sun to shine (in Vedic Sanskrit the word *go,* etymologically cognate with Greek *bous,* has a primary meaning of 'cow' and is also used metaphorically to signify celestial, especially dawn's, light).[87]

In another account, Indra drinks *soma,* the intoxicating milk of these "dawn-cows," to destroy a still more deadly withholder named Vr̥tra or 'Covering'.[88] Vr̥tra is a dragon who obstructs in various ways the

[85] Crane, 147.

[86] Frame, 44–46. See also Lincoln (1976) 44; Nagler (1980) 95. The Minotaur, who bore the name "Asterios" and lived in a cavelike labyrinth, belongs to this family of myths. Note that Pasiphaes is a title of Helios in Orphic *Hymn* 8.14, and that Pasiphae is a cult-title of the moon (Pausanias 3.26.1). A fragmentary Hittite myth, for which see Güterbock, 241, offers an interesting parallel to the story of the Minotaur.

[87] Frame, 66–69, follows Kuhn's interpretation of "circle-eyed" as referring to the sun disk; see also Germain, 72, note 5. A. Cook, 1:302–23, reaches similar conclusions based on his comparative study of the Cyclopes, especially of their portrayal in the visual arts. For the *Cyclopeia* as a solar myth, see Hackman, 3–5. For further references see Glenn (1978) 141–42, who rejects the theory.

[88] Emile Benveniste and Louis Renou have demonstrated in a classic study that the story of Vr̥tra is ultimately based on the combat between the hero Trita and the serpent

primordial waters, which are likewise known as "cows." Indra employs cunning and deceit to split open Vṛtra with his thunderbolt, thereby releasing the secreted waters and allowing the sun to shine. In some versions of the story, Indra narrowly escapes being swallowed by Vṛtra. In others, he suffers various misfortunes for having killed the monster, including a lengthy disappearance accompanied by famine on earth, and must eventually purify himself by horse-sacrifice.

These Indic accounts, like the *Cyclopeia,* depict release from a cave guarded by a monstrous withholding figure as the act on which life generally or particularly depends. Releasing the cattle from the cave, the act necessary for life, becomes in Homer's retelling the means by which Odysseus saves his life—stealing the sheep of the *daimōn* is tantamount to stealing his light.[89] The Indic material helps reveal the central significance of cattle to the tradition preserved in the *Cyclopeia.*

To confirm the correlation between the *Cyclopeia* and the Thrinakian episode I now turn to Thrinakie's filiation within the universe of Greek mythology. Thrinakie belongs to a family of myth devoted to the first sacrifice.[90] The victims are exclusively bovine, with the result that in Greek sacrificial myth, as in the Indic parallels to the *Cyclopeia,* cattle represent the source and essence of life. While Indic myth describes the origins of the universe as the release of cattle from a cave, the sacrifice of cattle in Greek myth creates humankind as beings distinct from the gods and ensures the survival of the race with the introduction of a new source of nourishment.

The *Homeric Hymn to Hermes* provides the most important parallel to Thrinakie.[91] The *Hymn* is likely of Athenian provenience and dates to the sixth century B.C.E.[92] Both the Thrinakian episode and the *Hymn* tell of herds consisting solely of heifers and set off from human use in

---

Ahi. For Vṛtra see also Fontenrose, 194–202; Kirk (1970) 210–11; Lincoln (1976) 46–53; Puhvel, 50–54; Watkins, 272–75.

89 On the solar imagery associated with bulls and rams see also A. Cook, 1:330–665; Germain, 86–114.

90 The Paṇis take their name from the fact that they are stingy in offering sacrifices to the gods. Thus the element of sacrifice is also a part of the Vedic myth.

91 Vernant (1972). A version of the story was to be found in the Hesiodic *Megalai Ehoiai,* for which see Antoninus Liberalis, *fr.* 153, cited by Allen et al., 272.

Lincoln (1975, 1976; see Mallory, 137–38, 140–41) reconstructs a cosmogonic myth from the archaeological and linguistic evidence of Indo-European cultures in which animal and vegetable life come from the body of a sacrificial ox. Although the element of celestial fire is lacking in Lincoln's reconstruction, the ox represents the alimentary source of life, as it does in the myth of Prometheus.

92 Brown, 106–37; Janko, 143. Allen et al., 275–76, argue for a seventh century date.

various ways: the cattle belong to the gods, are themselves immortal, and live in a field that has never been touched by human hand. In the *Hymn,* the depiction is reinforced by the fact that the cattle have never felt the yoke, and in the *Odyssey* they do not reproduce.[93]

The *Hymn* shares with Thrinakie the motifs of the sacrifice of the cattle and the complaint of their owner to Zeus, who then appeases the offended god. The infant Hermes steals fifty heifers from Apollo's herd, sacrifices part of the herd, and hides the rest in a cave. Although Apollo threatens to hurl his brother into Tartaros, Hermes refuses to release the cattle until, at the command of Zeus himself, he relents and "drives them forth into the light of day" (*h.Merc.* 402). Given the strength of the similarity between Thrinakie and the *Hymn* it is important to note that the sacrifice of the cattle and the owner's complaint are motifs that both accounts share with the *Cyclopeia.* Moreover, the *Hymn,* like the *Cyclopeia* and unlike Thrinakie, includes the motif of hiding the cattle in a cave.

For our purposes, the most significant—and controversial—connection between the *Hymn to Hermes* and Thrinakie is the relation of the cattle to the sun. In the *Hymn,* the cattle belong to Apollo, who at some time after his incorporation into the Olympic pantheon came to represent the sun god.[94] On Thrinakie, the cattle belong to Helios, the sun disk, and their numbers correspond to the days of the lunar year.[95] The itinerary of Hermes' journey is also significant in this regard: beginning at dusk, Hermes drives the herd from east to west, specifically from Arcadia to Pylos, a place said to be the gate to the Underworld. There, on his way to fetch the cattle of Geryon in yet another version of the

[93] *Od.* 12.136–37, 262; *h.Merc.* 116–17, 192, 276–77. The cattle are said to belong to "the gods" at *h.Merc.* 71, 276, 310, but elsewhere in the *Hymn* they belong to Apollo. The cattle are explicitly said to be immortal at *Od.* 12.130–31. The point has been debated in the case of the *Hymn:* the adjective *ambrotoi* at *h.Merc.* 71 could mean that they are immortal or merely that they belong to a god. It is taken in the latter sense by Allen et al. For the fields, see *h.Merc.* 72, and for the fact that the cattle had never felt the yoke, see *h.Merc.* 103.

[94] Allen et al. at *h.Merc.* 71: "On the analogy of the Vedic hymns [of Ahi, who steals the cattle of Indra] . . . it might appear probable that in the oldest form of the myth the cattle belonged to the Sun, afterwards to Apollo as Sun-god." The possibility of a connection between the cattle of Helios and of Apollo is rejected by Farnell, *CGS* 4:141, due to his belief that Apollo has no solar characteristics before Euripides. Burkert, *GR* 149, dates the solar cult of Apollo to the fifth century B.C.E., or some fifty years after the composition of the *Homeric Hymn to Hermes.* Aeschylus and Euripides were surely referring to an aspect of the god with which the audience was familiar. It is a pity that we do not possess the Hesiodic version.

[95] Aristotle (as reported by Eustathius, 1717.32–36), who indicates a special affinity of the cows for the sun. See Stanford at *Od.* 12.129–30, and N. Austin (1975) 134.

myth, Herakles himself battled the god Hades. The westward journey of the cattle in the *Hymn* is functionally analogous to the cave in which they are hidden.[96]

The story told in the *Hymn to Hermes* appears to be set in the contemporary world of its poet, while the Thrinakian episode obviously takes place in the heroic period; but closer inspection removes these potential obstacles to treating them as sacrificial myths.[97] We should recall that the enchanted world of the *Apologoi* is located in geographic Paradise, which is conceptually indistinguishable from temporal Paradise in early Greek thought. As if to allow no ambiguity in the Thrinakian episode, Helios places the cattle near his home on the banks of Okeanos, which were regularly identified with Paradise in myth. The sacrifice of the cattle of Helios takes place on the Greek cultural horizon, a horizon created by sacrifice. Hermes was the divine patron of sacrifice, so that it would be natural to conceive of the god's advent and the institution of sacrificial ritual as coincident events.[98] In a manner typical of myths pertaining to divine birth, the infant Hermes defines with his first acts his role as mediator between gods and men.

The *Hymn* relates that Hermes built the first fire using fire sticks in order to cook the cattle which he had killed (108–11). In the *Hymn,* as in the Hesiodic account of Prometheus, the mediator figure responsible for the introduction of animal sacrifice also provides humankind with fire.[99] These myths rationalize the solar cattle known from Indic tradition into celestial fire and sacrificial cattle. In the myth of Prometheus, Zeus takes on the role of the Encloser when he hides the fire; in so doing he simultaneously denies humankind the use of cattle for food. Prometheus' actions overdetermine a single mediation by which the life-force is made available to humans.

As Hermes drives the cows of Apollo to Pylos, he encounters an old man tending a vineyard. The same old man is grazing cattle when

[96]Their journey is answered by Hermes' eastward journey to Olympos, where he becomes an Olympian god (*h.Merc.* 319–23; see Clay [1989] 134–35).

[97]The invention of the lyre precedes the sacrifice of the cattle in the *Homeric Hymn to Hermes,* although if the poet is here depicting the first sacrifice its invention should follow, since the sound board was made of cow hide. This is in fact the order in which the events are narrated in most versions. The changed order was aesthetically motivated since once the *Hymn* came to dramatize the sacrifice at length, the creation of the lyre would have been anticlimactic. For asphodel as pasturage in the Golden Age, see Detienne (1972) 89–90.

[98]Note that Hermes was also thought to have committed the first murder in killing Argos.

[99]Hesiod, *Th.* 533–616. See the discussions in Detienne and Vernant (1974) chap. 2; Nagy (1979) 215–20. For an Indic parallel see Nagy (1990) 103–4.

Apollo later inquires whether he had seen the stolen cows.[100] In *Works and Days,* by contrast, Hesiod indicates that prior to the first sacrifice, there was no need to practice agriculture since the earth produced food spontaneously. Thus, the explicit references to viticulture and herding in the *Hymn* do not belong to the Hesiodic Paradise. The *Odyssey,* however, portrays the Cyclopes as vegetarian shepherds dwelling in geographic Paradise; and accounts set in Athens maintained that men were already practicing agriculture at the time of the first sacrifice.[101] There it was said that a farmer had once killed his own ox, which he had seen impiously eating grain at the altar of "Zeus of the city." The killer fled in horror at the deed, but Zeus commanded that it be repeated. The situation described in the *Homeric Hymn to Hermes* thus corresponds to that in Athenian sacrificial myth. When Apollo first hears the music of the lyre, he addresses Hermes in amazement as *Bouphonos,* or 'ox-killer' (*h.Merc.* 436). This was also the title of the priest who presided over the Bouphonia, a ritual mimesis of the first sacrifice at Athens.[102]

Two further accounts reveal that the solar characteristics of the cattle in such myths are not restricted to Thrinakie even within the Greek sphere. Herodotus tells us that in the territory of Apollonia there was a sacred flock of sheep belonging to Helios which was kept penned in a cave by night.[103] One night Euenios, who had been set over the sheep, fell asleep at his watch, whereupon some wolves made their way into the cave and killed about sixty of the flock. When the townspeople discovered what had happened, they blinded Euenios in punishment. Once the sentence had been carried out, however, the sheep became sterile and the earth ceased to produce normal crops. Delegations sent to the oracles at Dodona and Delphi discovered that the gods themselves had set the wolves upon the sheep.

The local tradition reported in Herodotus shares with the Thrinakian episode the central motifs of livestock owned by Helios, part of which are ravaged, and an ensuing disaster. Parallels to the *Cyclopeia* are still more obvious: the herds consist of sheep, the sheep are kept in a cave, and their guardian is blinded. When Odysseus blinds the Cyclops, Poseidon delays the hero's return, with the eventual result that suitors arrive in the palace and plunder his own herds. In both cases those responsible

100 Vineyards: *h.Merc.* 87; herding: 187–88, 286–88.

101 See the discussions in *HN* 136–43; Durand.

102 The significance of the connection is denied by Allen et al. ad loc. The first inscriptional evidence for the ritual dates to 500 B.C.E., a generation or so after the composition of the *Homeric Hymn to Hermes*.

103 Hdt. 9.92–95. The passage is related to Thrinakie by Frame, 43–44; Nagler (1980).

for blinding the shepherd suffer a curse from the gods that takes the form of an agricultural crisis.

The differences between the two stories are no less revealing: Odysseus and the citizens of Apollonia blind the guardian of the cattle for acts of improper eating—Polyphemos for his cannibalism, Euenios for allowing wolves to plunder the herds. Polyphemos also loses part of his flock to Odysseus and his men who drive them on board their ship later to devour them. Unsurprisingly, Analysts have attacked this detail of the story on grounds that the sheep would have betrayed Odysseus' location and were moreover superfluous on Goat Island.[104] The choice of wolves as predators in the story of Euenios is also significant, since cannibalism was thought to transform humans into werewolves (see below, Chapter 3). Lycanthropy is also characteristic of trickster figures, especially thieves. A famous example from Greek myth is supplied by Odysseus' own grandfather Autolykos, whose name means 'the wolf himself'.[105]

In the myth of Herakles and Geryon, we have the cattle raid denied Odysseus and his men.[106] Like Vr̥tra/Ahi, Geryon is three-headed. Like Helios, he kept a herd of cows at his island home beyond the banks of ocean. In other respects, the herds of Geryon and Helios are mirror opposites: while the cattle of Helios live in the east and neighbor the dawn, those of Geryon live in the west and are associated with the sunset and death. The association can be seen in the name of the island, Erytheia, or 'the Redlands', and in the ruddy complexion of the cattle. In fact, Alkyoneus is said to have caused the war of the gods and Giants when he stole the cattle of *Helios* from Erytheia in what looks to be an inversion of the "good" cattle raid performed by Herakles.[107]

The geographic opposition between Erytheia and Thrinakie has an important thematic echo: the story of Herakles' journey to bring back the cattle of Geryon is a multiform of the *Catabasis* myth, in which the hero conquers death by descending to the Underworld and returning.[108] The conquest may be symbolized in material terms by his retrieval of

104 See Dawe at *Od.* 9.464–65.

105 For the relationship of Autolykos to the trickster Hermes, see *Od.* 19.395ff. In Hesiod, *Catologue Fragment* 64, Autolykos is son to Hermes.

106 Hesiod, *Th.* 287–94; Apollodorus 2.5.10. Discussion with further references and bibliography may be found in Fontenrose, 338–45; Lincoln (1976) 53–57; Burkert (1977); Crane 128, 145–46.

107 See the remarks of Vermeule (1979) 243, note 47.

108 From Hades Odysseus retrieves insight into the forces governing his existence and into his ultimate destiny. His *Catabasis* transforms the heroic conquest of death into a quest for knowledge, and that knowledge affirms the mortality of the hero.

a denizen of Hades such as Cerberus. While Herakles brings the dead back to the world of the living, the crew of Odysseus take the life of immortal cattle; while Herakles drives the cattle of Geryon eastward to Tiryns, Hermes drives those of Apollo westward to Pylos.

In sum, the mythological traditions to which the *Cyclopeia* and the Thrinakian episode belong concern the appropriation of cattle representing the life-force. These traditions share the following motifs: the solar attributes of the cattle, a cave in which they are hidden, the suffering of the hero and the Encloser/Guardian, and an ensuing agricultural crisis. The *Cyclopeia* shares several features with a cosmogonic, or creation, myth preserved in Vedic Sanskrit in which the hero liberates the cattle from a cave by slaying a chaos demon and thereby allows the sun to shine. Greek mythology preserves several accounts, including the Thrinakian episode, in which the cattle belong to the sun god and are sacrificed. Such accounts can be said to be aetiological in that they describe the origins of sacrificial ritual and ultimately of culture itself. The "cattle of life" thus become an alimentary source of life in Greek myth, but they retain their solar characteristics. Whereas Odysseus attempts to establish *xenia* with the savage Polyphemos, the crew import sacrifice into the enchanted realm. As a result of these two events, the return of Odysseus is delayed and the suitors of Penelope arrive to create Paradise on Ithaca.[109]

The *Cyclopeia* and the *Homeric Hymn to Hermes* combine the motif of sacrifice with the release of cattle from the cave in an overdetermined representation of a single process. On the other hand, the release of the cattle from the cave of Polyphemos is functionally analogous to sacrificing them on Thrinakie. Polyphemos' sheep correspond to the herds of Helios in a profound manner indeed. The genetic relationship between the *Cyclopeia* and the Thrinakian episode helps explain the structural and thematic parallels between them. The *Apologoi* have been organized so as to reinforce those parallels by placing them at the same relative position in the tales preceding and following the *Nekyia*. The position of these two episodes within the *Apologoi* restates the contrast between the fates of Odysseus and the crew that informs the structure of the poem's introduction. The prophecy of Teiresias further echoes and reinforces the structural link between these episodes by identifying them

[109] Watkins, 296–97, argues that the punishment of Polyphemos and the suitors illustrates a pair of reciprocal formulas, "anti-hero slay guest (own house)" and "hero slay anti-guest (own house)," which developed out of the theme "hero slay serpent," as reconstructed from cognate Indo-European languages.

as the events responsible for Odysseus' fate in the years following the Trojan war.

A-B-A Structures

My reconfiguration of Whitman's analysis accounts for the internal organization of the *Nekyia* and for the relative positions of the *Cyclopeia* and the Thrinakian episode in the adventures flanking it. Without much effort we could also discover numerous points of contact between the shorter adventures paired by this arrangement, but the relationships so established are rather tenuous.[110] It will be more fruitful to see whether the triadic pattern that organizes the *Nekyia* is also to be found in the series of adventures that precede and follow it.

The Aiolian episode follows the sequence: point A, Odysseus sleeps, an act of folly by the crew, a storm, and return to point A. In the tales following the *Nekyia,* this same pattern occurs in the sequence Scylla, Thrinakie, and Charybdis.[111] Thus, just as the reflexive internal structure of the *Nekyia* also applied to the *Cyclopeia* and the Thrinakian episode, the internal structure of the Aiolian episode anticipates a series of three separate accounts following the *Nekyia.* Moreover, just as Thrinakie is flanked by a pair of adventures, Scylla-Charybdis, representing an initial point of departure and return, Aiolie is itself flanked by the complementary pair Cyclopes-Laistrygones.[112] On the structural level, the folly of the crew "causes" their destruction in the Laistrygonian harbor. As important, this A-B-A pattern also unites the episodes—the *Cyclopeia,* Aiolian and Laistrygonian—that create a hierarchy of culture in the adventures preceding the *Nekyia.*

Thematic parallels between the Aiolian and Thrinakian episodes reinforce the structural parallels.[113] Odysseus and his crew remain idle on both islands for an entire month; on Aiolie they feast continuously, but on Thrinakie they starve although surrounded by cattle. In both accounts they are near home, either literally or metaphorically, and in

[110] For the difficulties inherent in this sort of work, witness the sometimes radically different results achieved in grouping the episodes by Germain; Nagler (1977); Niles; Miller; Scully (1987); Most.

[111] The return in the Aiolian episode is natural since Aiolie is the point of convergence for the released winds, whereas in terms of natural causality the return to Charybdis is coincidental. Charybdis inverts the action of Aiolos' winds by sucking all things to the center rather than pushing them there.

[112] Niles, followed by Most, 21, relates the Cyclopes and Laistrygones to Scylla and Charybdis; see also Scully (1987) 408, with further bibliography.

[113] Germain; Niles; Scully (1987); Most.

both the hero falls asleep from exhaustion at a critical moment (10.31, 12.338). The disobedience of the crew, which is both deliberate and deliberated (10.34–46, 12.339–52), results in disaster. When the bag of winds is opened, the crew and Odysseus are blown back to Aiolie. When the crew kill and eat the cattle of the sun, Zeus raises a storm with the result that Odysseus finds himself once more at the cliffs of Scylla and Charybdis. Finally, these episodes concern elemental nature; winds which must not be released and solar cattle which must not be destroyed. The stability and sterility of Helios' cattle are analogous to that of Aiolos' family: both stand outside the natural life cycle since they embody the eternal resources of nature.

We can take this last point somewhat further: Odysseus relates that Aiolos "flayed and gave me a bag made from the hide of a nine-year-old cow" (10.19). This invites us to think of a bag along the lines of a wine-skin, which reflects the shape of its original occupant. Aiolos inflates the bag with the North, South, and East winds, which are of course immortal, animate beings. Odysseus pilots his ship home as the West wind fills a sail that he controls by two thongs of cow hide. When he falls asleep from exhaustion, the thongs slip from his hands, the West wind escapes from its confinement, and the crew release the winds within the cow hide. The Homeric *psukhē,* or 'spirit', was still a kind of "breath soul": in the Aiolian episode as in the Thrinakian, release of an animate and immortal force consisting of air and contained by a cow hide results in disaster.[114] Not only do both episodes illustrate the theme of "men who bring suffering on themselves," but the crew's acts of folly are essentially the same.

We have already seen that the internal correlation between the Cyclopes and the Laistrygones is as strong as that between Scylla and Charybdis. There is, moreover, an equally compelling correlation between groups: flanking both temptation scenes in which the crew yield to their appetites are beings who would like to eat *them.* Odysseus himself compares Polyphemos to Scylla and Charybdis:

οὐ μὲν δὴ τόδε μεῖζον ἔπι κακόν, ἢ ὅτε Κύκλωψ
εἴλει ἐνὶ σπῆι γλαφυρῷ κρατερῆφι βίηφι·

(12.209–10)

The evil now upon us is no greater than when the Cyclops
shut us up in the hollow cave with his all-powerful *biē.*

[114] For a recent discussion see Bremmer (1983) 21–24, although I distance myself from his treatment of the *psukhē* as a "free-soul."

He is right: Scylla poses no greater a threat than Polyphemos, but precisely the same. Each of these monstrous cave-dwellers of practically invincible strength devours six members of the crew as Odysseus looks on in horror.[115] Both episodes provide tests of leadership and demonstrate the need for a leader, since had Odysseus failed to handle these situations correctly, Scylla and Polyphemos would have eaten the lot of them (for Scylla see 12.201–5, 223–25). Yet these similarities underscore a basic contrast between the episodes: whereas the *Cyclopeia* celebrates the victory of intelligence over brute force, the Scylla episode shows that there are forces over which there can be no triumph. This contrast is reflected in the differing psychological responses of the hero as events unfold: in the *Cyclopeia,* helpless outrage gives way to triumphant self-confidence and boasting; in the Scylla episode, scenes of encouragement and arming are followed by horrified pity and helplessness.

The Charybdis episode reproduces several prominent motifs from the *Cyclopeia*. In the cave of Polyphemos, the instrument of Odysseus' salvation is an olive-wood stake, compared to a ship's mast, around which he wraps a leather thong to fashion an auger (9.384–88). The sound of the stake's sputtering, the screams of Polyphemos, the steam, and even the fire image all have parallels in the boiling surge of Charybdis.[116] After the storm off Thrinakie, it is the mast of his shattered ship, around which a leather thong is wrapped, that saves Odysseus (12.422–23). On that mast he rides for a second time to the whirlpool of Charybdis, where he must hang from the fig tree above her (12.432–33) just as he had hung from the belly of the ram.

Several narrative elements shared by the *Cyclopeia* and the Scylla episode also occur in the Laistrygonian episode, most notably the motif of the cliff-top attack. The name of the Laistrygonian king, Lamos, resembles that of the insatiable man-eating ogres Lamios/Lamia. Scylla, on the other hand, is little more than an embodied appetite, and Lamia is her mother in extra-Homeric tradition.[117] Homer's own name for the

[115] Scully (1987) 402.

[116] Compare 9.389–90, 395 with 12.202, 219, 237–42; see, however, *CHO* at 12.219–21.

[117] Scholia on *Od.* 12.124; Eustathius 1714.33–40; Scholia on Apollonius Rhodius 4.828 (= Stesichorus, *fr.* 43 Page). The Scholia to Apollonius Rhodius report that in Acusilaus (= *FGrH* 2 F 42) Scylla was the daughter of Phorkys and Hekate, and that in Hesiod (= *fr.* 262 Merkelbach and West) she was the daughter of Phorbas and Hekate. Eustathius adds that there were those who made Triton the father. The stories of Lamia and Scylla were similar (for Lamia see the Scholia on Aristophanes, *Pax* 758, *V.* 1035 [= Duris, *FGrH* 76 F 17] and Diodorus Siculus 20.41.3–4, with discussion by Fontenrose, 103–4, 110–11; Burkert [1984] 80ff.). Scylla was transformed into a sailor-devouring hag by Amphitrite on account of Poseidon's love for her (Scholia on Lycophron 46, 650. Ovid, *Met.* 14.1ff., makes Glaukos the lover and Circe the rival). Eustathius says that Scylla was tradition-

mother of Scylla is the significant term Krataiis (12.124–25). The supplied genealogy of Scylla seems expressly designed to reinforce Circe's warning that Odysseus should flee rather than struggle against the monster; yet even if the audience did not know Lamia as the mother of Scylla they would have seen in the Laistrygones the descendants of an equivalent type. Finally, the simile comparing the men caught by Scylla to fish (12.251–55), has a clear echo in the Laistrygonian episode (10.124). The fish simile is, however, later used of the suitors (22.383–89), and certainly one of its functions is to link the crew and suitors with a common symbol.[118]

The parallels adduced between Thrinakie and Aiolie, and between Thrinakie and the *Cyclopeia,* are equally persuasive. Moreover, the Cyclopes and Laistrygones are just as clearly related to Scylla and Charybdis as complementary pairs, thus further reinforcing the link between Aiolie and Thrinakie. Schematizations that assume a one-to-one corresponsion between episodes will thus necessarily distort the interpretation of the *Apologoi*.

Two groups not included thus far in this triadic pattern are the Sirens and the Lotophagoi; these episodes also complement each other.[119] In the Lotophagian episode, Odysseus must physically restrain the crew members who have eaten the lotus by binding them to the benches of the ships. In the Siren episode it is the crew who must restrain Odysseus by binding him to the mast of the ship. The storm off Maleia that precedes the crew's encounter with the Lotophagoi is paralleled by the supernatural calm preceding Odysseus' encounter with the Sirens. Both episodes, which are the second elements in their series and concern temptations directed at the crew and Odysseus respectively, serve as a kind of thematic prelude to the stories that follow. The Lotophagian episode predicts the failure of the crew to refrain from eating foods that threaten their return, while the Siren episode predicts Odysseus' ultimate success at restraining his *thumos*. Before and after the *Nekyia* the same story is told: Odysseus does not retrace his steps working backwards, but begins the same sequence over again.

Both of the above sequences of triads are followed by a nymph and a journey to the death realm or its equivalent. As we have seen, how-

---

ally thought of as having not six but three heads, citing the fourth-century comedian Anaxilas: "three headed Scylla, the sea-dog."

[118] The net image at 22.383–89 also provides a motivic link with the unfaithful maidservants, who are said to be trapped in a bird net at 22.465–73, and with the golden net by which Hephaistos traps Ares in bed with Aphrodite (8.266–366).

[119] Scully (1987) 409–10.

ever, with the inclusion of a second Circe episode Homer provides a narrative frame for both the *Nekyia* and the second group of adventures. It is this third triad, Circe-*Nekyia*-Circe, that explains the significance of the other two. In all three accounts, conditions are placed upon the successful completion of a journey. On Aiolie and Thrinakie the destination is home; on Aiaie it is Hades, across the ultimate distance that could separate one from home. In the Underworld, however, Odysseus does meet his mother, Antikleia, who provides him with news of his family.[120] Odysseus is in a sense as close to Ithaca here as when he falls asleep at the rudder of his ship in the Aiolian episode.

The triads created by Aiolie and Thrinakie resemble each other more closely than they do the *Nekyia* group. In fact, they seem to be an inversion of it. Whereas the *Nekyia* is literally a voyage to the death realm, Aiolie and Thrinakie are bordered by agents of death.[121] The Aiolian and Thrinakian episodes center on the actions of the crew and end with their demise. The *Nekyia* concerns Odysseus alone and ends with his return to the world of the living. In his journey to Hades, Odysseus' *success* at performing an elaborate sacrificial ritual for the dead is followed by his return to his point of departure. In the other two accounts, return is due to the *failure* of the crew to restrain their *thumos*. As we have seen, the failure of the crew on Thrinakie results in their perversion of sacrificial ritual and in the threat of Helios to shine among the dead in Hades.

In sum, the *Apologoi* are arranged by two different but not exclusive patterns of organization. Common to both schemes, the *Nekyia* divides the adventures into distinct groups. By the first arrangement, which can be represented graphically by a modified version of Whitman's analysis, the *Cyclopeia* and the Thrinakian episode balance one another in the narrative just as they complement one another thematically. The stories flanking the *Nekyia* are also organized by a pair of complementary triads observing an A-B-A pattern. These triads comprise Cyclopes-Aiolians-Laistrygones and Scylla-Thrinakie-Charybdis. They are introduced by the Lotophagoi and Sirens, whose temptations of the crew and Odysseus foreshadow the events that follow. The structuring pat-

[120] Antikleia's recognition of Odysseus parallels that by Penelope: after an initial meeting, identification is retarded by an event of central significance. On Scherie, Arete's identification of Odysseus is similarly delayed by an athletic contest, although like Helen in Book 4 she is able to make an initial, albeit incomplete identification based on external appearance. In all three episodes, Odysseus' success is made to depend upon delaying recognition by a woman.

[121] Note, however, that the cattle of the sun, which are eaten by the crew, relate to Odysseus' herds, which are eaten by the suitors; a recognition of sorts does occur in the Aiolos episode, as in Hades and on Ithaca.

tern in which an act of folly results in return to a deathly adversary would seem to invert a third triad in which a successful voyage to the death realm results in return to the nymph Circe. The complex narrative structure of the *Apologoi* causes individual episodes to interact with each other in more than one way. Looking beyond the *Apologoi* proper, we have also observed extensive interaction between the Phaiakes and the elements of the first triad, Cyclopes-Aiolians-Laistrygones. The sheer extent of the cross-influence between tales and groups of tales precludes the explanation that the late insertion of another story has disturbed an "original" structuring pattern.

CHAPTER 3

In the Cave of the Encloser

In a groundbreaking work, Wilhelm Grimm demonstrated that the *Cyclopeia* conflates two folk-tale traditions popular throughout Europe and beyond.[1] The first of these traditions, from which the Homeric account is principally derived, concerns a hero who finds himself trapped in the abode of a giant one-eyed cannibal who roasts his victims on a spit.[2] The hero blinds the ogre with the spit—alternatively, he promises to improve the ogre's eyesight with molten lead—and escapes beneath the ogre's cattle. In the second tradition, the hero subdues a demonic adversary and escapes by means of a trick name, "Myself." In this story, the demon is not a man-eating giant, nor does the hero blind him with a spit, although he often burns or stabs him with a heated metal implement.

[1] It is generally recognized that the *Cyclopeia* depends on the tradition rather than the reverse: Page (1955) 7; Glenn (1971) 135–42; *CHO* at 9.105–566; Röhrich (1962) 60. For the opposed view, see O'Sullivan (1987). Variants are collected by Hackman; Frazer (1965) 2:404–55; Germain; Dawkins; Röhrich (1962); Röhrich (1967) 2:459–60. Possible Near Eastern precedents may be found in Poljakov; Knox; Oberhuber (1965, 1974). For comparative analyses, see Hackman, 157ff.; Page (1955) chap. 1; Glenn (1971); Röhrich (1962, with summary in 1967, 2:447–60); Calame (1986) with an important critique of methodology. Although I remain convinced that the *Odyssey* conflates independent folk-tale traditions, I agree with Calame that the search for "an original version" of the Polyphemos Saga is pointless. For bibliographical surveys see Eisenberger, 130–46; Glenn (1978). Further bibliography may be found in Röhrich (1962) 69–71; Röhrich (1967) 2:448–50, 2:459–60; Glenn (1971) note 1; *HN* 131, note 1.

[2] These are of course generalizations; for much the same analysis, see Page (1955) 4. The Vedic myth of the Paṇis and related accounts (for which see above, Chapter 2) belong to the first tradition.

The Hero as Master of Language

Odysseus manages his own escape by repeatedly outwitting Polyphemos, so that the *Cyclopeia* celebrates the success of intelligence over brute force. This is a theme that the story is well suited to represent, although it is generally not an explicit feature of variants belonging to the first tradition in which the hero blinds the ogre with a spit. The formative influence exerted by this theme accounts for the ruse involving the trick name, which was appropriated from the other folk-tale tradition. On one level, then, the *Cyclopeia* characterizes Odysseus as he is described in the proem: he is a clever man who suffers while trying to save his companions.

Odysseus' self-identification and presentation in the *Cyclopeia* also finds a parallel in the Prologue. Just as verse 2 of the proem identifies him as the man who sacked Troy, Odysseus introduces himself to Polyphemos as one of the host of Agamemnon, "whose *kleos* is the greatest in the world since he destroyed a very great city" (9.264–65). When Polyphemos reveals that heroism and fame are valueless to the Cyclopes, Odysseus adopts an antithetical identity and becomes *Outis,* or 'Nobody'. In the final scene of the episode, Odysseus reclaims his heroic identity by saying "if anyone asks you, tell him that Odysseus the city-sacker blinded you" (9.502–4). As a result of this disclosure Polyphemos is able to curse him to Poseidon, so that the *Cyclopeia,* like the prologue, concludes with the delayed identification of the hero and with the wrath of Poseidon. It is this pervasive contrast between *kleos* and anonymity, together with Odysseus' paradoxical use of anonymity to achieve *kleos* at Troy, in the cave of Polyphemos, and on Ithaca, that explains the change from "Myself" in the folk-tale tradition to "Nobody" in Homer.

There is an obvious irony in the fact that a Cyclops who dismisses the importance of *kleos* and its values is named Polyphemos, or 'Much-Fame'.[3] Odysseus gives that name a transitive force, for Polyphemos more than any other character in the enchanted realm provides Odysseus with *kleos*. Polyphemos' narrative function is thus analogous to the professional function of an epic poet such as Phemios, who is called *poluphēmos aoidos,* or "singer of much-fame" (22.376), or Demodokos, whom the Muse blinded and gave the gift of song (8.62–64). In his moment of triumph Odysseus' own name acquires a passive as well as an active force. Odysseus reveals his name to Polyphemos "with an

[3] Note that Polyphemos' name is likewise delayed to 9.403.

angry *thumos*" (*kekotēoti thumō*, 9.501), and as a consequence is himself hated by Poseidon. The act of reclaiming his personal identity causes a change in that identity. The heroic man of anger who causes suffering becomes also the hated man who suffers. This too is paralleled in the Introduction. Odysseus is introduced as the object of a verb of hatred, thus suggesting a passive meaning for his name (1.20–21). In the divine assembly, Athene uses the verb *odussesthai* in an active sense when she asks Zeus "why do you hate (*odusao*) him so?" (1.62), yet once again Odysseus is the object of that hatred. Zeus responds by affirming that Odysseus is hated (*kekholōtai*) by Poseidon because he blinded Polyphemos (1.69). The *Cyclopeia* reveals that Odysseus is a man of hatred because he is a man of pain, that is, because he is a hero. Yet Odysseus is not simply the "man of hatred" in a generic sense, but is both agent and object of a specific kind of hatred. As the narrator of the story, Odysseus is allowed to define the hatred that defines him.

Odysseus and Polyphemos converse on three occasions during the episode. During these verbal exchanges their relative positions reverse, so that Odysseus, working from a position of "desperate inferiority" in the first scene, emerges in a position of "triumphant superiority" in the third.[4] The theme of piety, which is closely wed to this pattern, reinforces it: Polyphemos' initially superior position is marked by his arrogant disdain for the Olympian gods and the laws of hospitality, or *xenia*.[5] In the final scene of the episode, Odysseus boasts that Zeus and the other gods have punished the Cyclops for violating those same laws.

On each occasion, Polyphemos attempts to outwit Odysseus. In the first two instances Polyphemos mistakenly believes he has succeeded, although he is himself deceived by Odysseus. The battle of wits in which these characters engage develops the themes of piety and *xenia* as the background against which Odysseus demonstrates his mastery of language and Polyphemos his lack of acquaintance with rudimentary human discourse.[6] The difference between them is epitomized in the *outis* trick.

Odysseus creates a new signification for *outis* by adopting it as his

[4] *SH* 33; see also Calame (1986).

[5] I here define piety as "ritual correctness to the gods," following Nagy (1990) 68–71, in his treatment of the conceptual overlap between moral and ritual correctness in Archaic Greek thought. For *xenia* and gift-exchange in Homer and Archaic Greece see M. Edwards (1975); Finley (1979) 95–103; Thornton, chap. 3 and 8; Pitt-Rivers, 94–112; Coldstream (1983); I. Morris (1986b); Herman; Beidelman, especially 242–43; Morgan, 218–20; Kurke, chap. 4; Seaford (1994) 7, 13–25.

[6] N. Austin (1975) 147; *SH* 33.

name. Polyphemos is the only individual to share in this meaning; for the other Cyclopes it is univocal, signifying personal absence. Odysseus owes his salvation to the fact that he is able to exploit an ambiguity for which he is himself responsible. To put his plan of vengeance into effect Odysseus offers an ambiguous gift, the wine of Maron.[7] Wine belongs to the worlds of nature and of culture, both as an agricultural product that is further "denatured" by vinification, and as a drink that must be domesticated with the addition of water. Its effect is likewise ambiguous: for civilized humans wine is a great benefit, but for Polyphemos, as for the Centaurs and the rustic neighbors of Ikarios, it can have deadly consequences. If oblivion is the threat posed by the enchanted world, then anonymity and ambiguity are Odysseus' weapons against that threat.

For using these weapons, Odysseus earns the wrath of Poseidon. Yet the antagonism between them is resolved with their partial identification, as Odysseus founds a cult to the god and thereby serves as its first priest (11.119–37). Ambiguity is his ultimate destiny; the hater becomes united with the hated, *mētis* with *biē,* a civilized mortal with the divine embodiment of natural force. The polyvalence of Odysseus' personal nomenclature thus mirrors the union of the hero with his ritual antagonist in cult. The cult is founded at the place where an oar loses its identity as such and becomes a winnowing shovel. Thus, when Odysseus dedicates an oar to Poseidon, the significance of his act is ambiguous: to a maritime people it would mean "the sailor is finished," to the local inhabitants, "the harvest is complete."[8] As in the cave of Polyphemos, these semantic and ritual ambiguities are available to Odysseus because he is a figure belonging to one system who finds himself in another; since he is *polutropos,* both in the sense of 'clever' and 'much-traveled', he recognizes that the meaning of language, objects, and actions is complex and contextually determined. He survives because he can exploit that knowledge.

[7] Page (1955) 6–8, and Röhrich (1962) 62, both conclude from their review of the comparative material that the wine is likely an Homeric innovation. There are several versions in which wine plays a role—see Frazer (1965) 433–46, variants 21, 23, 26, and 31—but none in which the hero intoxicates his opponent. For the deployment of the motif in the *Cyclopeia* see Meuli, 71–73; Auffarth, 315–27; Segal (1994) 207–9.

[8] Nagy (1990b) 231–32. See also Peradotto, 66, 158; Segal (1994) chap. 9. I use the word "finished" to call attention to a further ambiguity: an oar fixed in the earth can serve as a burial marker, while as a dedication to Poseidon it symbolizes the sailor's renunciation of sailing at the end of his career.

The *Cyclopeia* as Cultural Catalogue

The wealth of comparative material for the *Cyclopeia* provides us with a unique opportunity to observe the relationship of the *Odyssey* to the tradition on which it draws.[9] The Homeric formulation of the tale elaborates the traditional opposition between intelligence and force with a series of related dualities that can be placed under the rubric of Greek culture and its negation in the savage race of the Cyclopes.[10] The opposed attitudes of Poseidon and the Olympians in the first divine assembly are superseded by an actual conflict between Poseidon's son Polyphemos and Odysseus, the protégé of Athene.

Odysseus introduces the Cyclopes in contrast with civilization, and it is in this manner that he will conduct the entire exposition:

> Κυκλώπων δ' ἐς γαῖαν ὑπερφιάλων ἀθεμίστων
> ἱκόμεθ'
>
> (9.106–7)

> we reached the land of the Cyclopes,
> an insolent folk, without social law

The adjectives *huperphialoi,* 'insolent', and *athemistoi,* 'without social law', link the Cyclopes to the suitors, and *huperphialoi* links them to the Phaiakes as well.[11] By describing the Cyclopes as *athemistoi,* Odys-

[9] Glenn (1971) lists twenty or so features of the story which seldom if ever recur in the tradition. I consider Glenn's motifs 1–3, 11–22, and 24 to be unique but dismiss 4, 5, 7, and 9. In 6, 8, 10, and 23, Homer is, if not in the mainstream, at least wading. Röhrich (1962) 60–69, working from the perspective of the non-Homeric variants, offers a somewhat different list.

[10] Kirk (1970) 162–71 (refutation by O'Sullivan [1990]); Calame (1976, 1977, 1986, chap. 6); Clay (1983) 112–32; Vidal-Naquet, 21–22; Segal (1994) 32–33. The only elements unique to the Homeric episode that are not directly explained in terms of this polarity is Odysseus' selection of assistants for blinding Polyphemos by lot. Page (1955) 12 (followed by Eisenberger, 137–38; *CHO* at 9.331–35), proposes that "in some earlier version of this story the drawing of lots decided not who should help Odysseus, but who should be eaten next." However, Glenn (1971) reviewed 125 folk-tale variants and found the evidence to be inconclusive. It seems more likely that Homer's source is not an obscure variant of the Polyphemos Saga but the conventions of heroic narrative. Eisenberger, 138, compares *Il.* 7.170–99; see also *Od.* 10.205–7.

[11] *Themis,* the root word of *athemistoi,* means 'a code of behavior set down by custom'. In the plural, it generally has the sense of 'laws established by custom', laws often specifically said to be sanctioned by the gods and enforced by kings and judges who act as mediators of divine will. It was the personified Themis who called and dissolved assemblies of men and of gods where *themistes* were announced (*Od.* 2.68–69; *Il.* 20.4). The *athemistoi* are people excluded from society (see *Il.* 9.63). For the suitors see *Od.* 17.360–64, 18.141, 20.287.

seus indicates that they are apolitical, while the same term when applied to the suitors reveals that Ithacan society has degenerated to a state of anarchy.

Odysseus associates social law with the *agora,* the public assembly, in the verses that follow:

τοῖσιν δ᾽ οὔτ᾽ ἀγοραὶ βουληφόροι οὔτε θέμιστες,
ἀλλ᾽ οἵ γ᾽ ὑψηλῶν ὀρέων ναίουσι κάρηνα
ἐν σπέσσι γλαφυροῖσι, θεμιστεύει δὲ ἕκαστος
παίδων ἠδ᾽ ἀλόχων, οὐδ᾽ ἀλλήλων ἀλέγουσι.

(9.112–15)

They have no counsel-bearing assemblies, nor social law (*themistes*),
but live on the peaks of lofty mountains,
in hollow caves, and each one sets down the customs (*themisteuei*)
for his children and wife, and they have no concern for one another.

The *agora* functioned as the corporate political memory of preliterate Greek society and preserved its *themistes.*[12] The close association of the *agora* with *themis* reflects its significance as a cultural marker: without it Homeric society could not function.

We have already seen that the Ithacan assembly of Book 2 relates the suitors to the Aigisthos paradigm by the motif of the divinely sanctioned warning left unheeded. Yet the simple fact that Telemachos calls an assembly is significant, for it announces the coming restoration of social order on the island. Just as the Cyclopes have always been, the suitors have become *athemistoi* and hostile to strangers. They have also become godless. The absence of a ruler on Ithaca has led to social conditions analogous to those that reign in the land of the Cyclopes.

The oblique strategy of scene painting in the verses separating these references to *themis* adds a new perspective on the story's cultural theme: the Cyclopes do not farm, since earth freely provides for them barley, wheat, and wine-producing grapes (9.107–11). The Cyclopes live in Paradise, and it is this which explains their savage way of life. In traditions that give a positive valuation to the rise of culture, Earth's spontaneous production of food (the *automatē gē*) produces excess or surfeit (*koros*) which results in hubris.[13] Odysseus punishes this hubris in Poly-

[12] Vernant (1982) 46–48, treats the *agora* as a defining characteristic of the *polis* as opposed to Bronze Age palatial society.

[13] On the relationship between luxuriance, hubris, and savagery see Nagy (1990b) 267–68; see also Nagy (1990) 73, in context of the parallel that I draw below to the suitors.

phemos, and in the suitors who have transformed his own household into a surrogate *automatē gē*. His introductory remark that the Cyclopes are *huperphialoi* immediately locates their Paradise in this tradition, as do Polyphemos' later acts of cannibalism.

Paradise typology also links the second mention of *themis* in verses 112–15 to the description of Goat Island that follows (9.116–51).[14] Reinhardt argues that the island was created as a holding tank for the flotilla while Odysseus ventures off with a single ship to encounter Polyphemos.[15] Yet Homer could have found an isolated cove on the mainland for the purpose, and his concern for this sort of verisimilitude may be measured by the nonchalant manner in which Odysseus leaves his own ship in general proximity of the cave.[16] Moreover, Goat Island serves a narrative function that is of some importance to the larger themes of the *Apologoi,* since it eliminates a common reason for visiting the ogre—the hunger of the hero and his companions. The hero's visit is thus motivated solely by intellectual curiosity and a desire to establish guest-friendship, or *xenia*.

Goat Island continues the exposition under the rubric of navigation. It introduces a further series of negations around the idea of goods and commerce that can be ordered causally: since the Cyclopes dwell in Paradise (9.107–11), they are not organized socially (9.112–15), and therefore lack skilled craftsmen and ships (9.125–27). As a result, they do not engage in commerce or any other kind of exchange between cities (9.127–29). There is, moreover, an important point of contact between navigation and *themis:* with travel and commerce goes the need for *themistes* governing the behavior between guest and host. Hence, Odysseus' premonition that he might be going to face a savage brute would not have appeared as arbitrary to an ancient Greek as it has to some modern scholars.[17] Odysseus knows how to read the signs posted clearly about him.

[14] Glenn (1971) 149–50, remarks that the island is unique to the Homeric version. The island bears a close resemblance to Scherie, and Clay (1980) argues that it was originally inhabited by the Phaiakes. See, however, Bremmer (1986). For more on the uses to which the island is put, see Calame (1976); Nagy (1979) 180–81.

[15] Reinhardt (1960) 55–56, and canonical since.

[16] *Od.* 9.181–82, 193–94, 216.

[17] For example, Page (1955) 8, and Dawe at *Od.* 9.187, 213–15 explain the premonition as a matter of simple plot necessity created when Homer chose to have Odysseus overpower the Cyclops with Ismarian wine. Yet Odysseus could have said "I brought along a skin of my best wine to offer our expected host," and any arbitrariness in the plot would vanish. This interpretation assumes a poet scarcely more resourceful than the Cyclopes. Further on the premonition in Bona, 82–85; my analysis also supplies a motivation for 9.174–76.

Odysseus equates civilized behavior with piety when he announces his plan to cross over the bay and meet with the inhabitants:

> *ἐλθὼν τῶνδ᾽ ἀνδρῶν πειρήσομαι, οἵ τινές εἰσιν,*
> *ἤ ῥ᾽ οἵ γ᾽ ὑβρισταί τε καὶ ἄγριοι οὐδὲ δίκαιοι,*
> *ἠὲ φιλόξεινοι καί σφιν νόος ἐστὶ θεουδής.*
>
> (9.174–76)

> I will go and test these men, to find out who they are,
> whether hubristic, savage (*agrioi*), and lawless (*oude dikaioi*),
> or friendly to strangers (*philoxeinoi*) and godfearing (*theoudēs*).

With *hubristai* and *oude dikaioi* Odysseus restates the themes by which he introduced the Cyclopes, while *agrioi* summarizes the intervening description.[18] Odysseus' premonition upon seeing the dwelling of Polyphemos serves as a refrain to this first alternative (9.213–15). With the second alternative, Odysseus opposes *hubristai, agrioi,* and *oude dikaioi* with *philoxeinoi,* 'friendly to strangers', and *theoudēs,* 'godfearing'. The antithetical form of the expression makes respect for the gods and friendliness to strangers a definition of civilized behavior.[19] The *themistos* and *dikaios* man is also *philoxeinos* in Greek society, which engages in seafaring, aristocratic exchange, and commerce.

In equating piety with justice, Odysseus echoes the themes of the divine assembly from the perspective of social discourse. He thus delimits the opposition between the savage and the civilized with a nexus of associated concepts that will prove central to the rest of the episode. Moreover, the expository narrative would have been impossible without a number of Cyclopes living in the area who could have formed an organized social unit but did not. Although the other Cyclopes were made necessary by the "Nobody" trick, they are not a simple accident of adaptation but play an integral role in articulating the themes of the Homeric account.[20] Odysseus defines his mission as a test: "I shall go to see if they are civilized." If the Cyclopes had been, then Odysseus and his men could have been assured of their escape from the enchanted world.

[18] In Homer, the word *dikē* is still quite close in meaning to *themis,* and like *themis* it was intimately associated with the *agora*. See *Od.* 4.691, 11.569–70, 12.439–40, 14.83–88, with the remarks of Stanford ad loc., of Hoekstra *CHO* at 14.56, 59, and *IC* at 16.387–88. Thus *oude dikaioi* is virtually synonymous with *athemistoi*.

[19] For *xenia* as a cultural marker see also *Od.* 6.119–21, 13.200–202.

[20] Mondi, 23–24, holds that 9.107–15 depicts the Cyclopes as noble savages. The foregoing, I believe, adequately refutes his interpretation of 112–15, so that Mondi's argument is only tenable if verse 107 implies piety (verse 111 implies nothing, Zeus is simply

Antagonism by Theme

Polyphemos instantiates the themes of the exposition. Two of the terms that introduced the Cyclopes, *athemistos* and *agrios,* are later applied directly to him by Odysseus and the crew (9.189, 428, 494). Polyphemos himself informs Odysseus that he is neither *philoxeinos* nor *theoudēs* and later mocks the laws of hospitality with the promise to eat Odysseus last as a guest-gift, *xeinion*. His cannibalism is an archetypal act of hubris in early Greek thought.[21]

Although the other Cyclopes are not socially organized, they live in rough proximity to one another in the mountains. Polyphemos, by contrast, is introduced as dwelling apart from the other Cyclopes, just as Poseidon was introduced in Book 1 as physically and spiritually isolated from his fellow Olympian gods (9.187–92). The aloofness of Polyphemos from the other Cyclopes should not be understood as residue left when a story requiring a social setting was grafted onto another involving a solitary monster.[22] Had Polyphemos been set in the mountains with the other Cyclopes—who after all live apart from one another—Odysseus' escape would appear no less credible than it does in our version of the story. The enormous size and strength of Polyphemos render him self-sufficient. His self-sufficiency results in his hubris and exclusion even from the rudimentary society of the family unit in which the other Cyclopes participate.[23] The Paradisiacal setting of the

personified weather). The verse could indeed be prompted by Golden Age typology, but this suggests nothing about its association with the Cyclopes prior to the *Odyssey*. We may also fairly ask how much piety is implied by the verse. Anyone who does not plant crops is trusting in the gods to see to their needs, and to describe them so could simply be a traditional way of saying that they did not practice agriculture. Thus Stanford, ad loc.; see also O'Sullivan (1990) 10–11. Note that the poet could sing these verses in the same breath as verse 106.

21 His milk-drinking, on the other hand, is characteristic both of the noble savage and of the savage brute. See *Il.* 13.4–6, with which compare Aeschylus, *Prometheus Lyomenos, fr.* xii Griffith; Herodotus 1.216; Strabo 7.3.7–9. See also *Od.* 4.84–89, with which compare Herodotus 4.186; Euripides, *El.* 169; Euripides, *fr.* 146. In the old Babylonian version of the Gilgamesh Epic, Enkidu used to suck the milk of wild animals prior to his domestication.

22 Originally an Analytic argument. Glenn (1971) 147, remarks: "As early as Mülder, analysts seized upon it as an indication of a later re-working of an earlier poem. Page, on the other hand, preferred to conceive of a conflation of two stories by one poet. I incline toward Page's view, but we should realize that we are not dealing here with two extreme poles of opinion: both sides recognize a conflation of traditional material." See also *CHO* at 1.70; Bona, chap. 4.

23 Aristotle, *Pol.* 1252b17, calls the village a colony of the *oikos,* and uses Homer's description of the Cyclopes in 9.114–15 to illustrate the primitive society of former times. See also Plato, *Lg.* 680a–c.

story is an environmental analogue to the physical self-sufficiency of Polyphemos.

The flocks of sheep and goats belonging to Polyphemos further emphasize his isolation. Livestock are an indispensable element of the traditional story. The ogre of the folk tradition, however, usually possesses oxen rather than flocks, so this feature of the Homeric account calls for explanation. Herding flocks, particularly goats, was considered an inherently antisocial occupation.[24] At Athens the marginal nature of goatherding manifests itself in the belief that goats were noxious to olive trees: it was said that the goat rendered sterile any olive tree that it bit, since its spittle poisoned the fruit.[25] For this reason, it was customary not to sacrifice goats to Athene. Goats were thus a natural symbol for the marginalized ephebe and his patron-hero Melanthos.[26] Oxen and swine, on the other hand, belong exclusively to the world of the farm. Thus, Odysseus' chief allies among his own servants are the swineherd Eumaios and the neatherd Philoitios, while the goatherd Melanthios aligns himself with the suitors.[27]

Polyphemos protects his flocks and shuts them away in the cave, but does not consume them. Excepting his weakness for human flesh, Polyphemos is apparently a vegetarian. Homer thus eliminates the spit on which the ogre cooks his food and which typically serves as the instrument of blinding. The image of a vegetarian cannibal may be logically contradictory, but it does make a consistent statement about the relationship of Polyphemos to Greek culture and to the Olympian gods who validated the ethical norms of civilized life. Within the Greek sphere, both types of eating entail rejection or perversion of blood sacrifice and the relationship between god and man that it both creates and defines.[28] On this level of analysis, the discrepancy vanishes.

It is often remarked that the disrespect in which Polyphemos holds the gods is surprising in light of his later prayer to Poseidon and of his father's compliance.[29] His prayer does, however, point to the uniqueness

24 Noted by Segal (1974) 293; Arthur (1983) 101–2.

25 See the discussion with ancient references in *HN* 152–53; Pausanius 2.13.6 refers to the goat's antipathy to the grapevine.

26 Vidal-Naquet, 110–12.

27 The hostility of Melanthios can also be explained in terms of polemic against non-Homeric tradition: in Arcadia, Penelope was said to have given birth to the god Pan after she was seduced by Hermes in the form of a goat (Pindar, *fr.* 100; Servius at Verg. *A.* 2.44).

28 Detienne (1977) 197–98.

29 Predictably, this point has been employed by the Analysts. Bethe, 2:111-ff., was the

of the god's position among the Olympians by begging the question of motivation: following Polyphemos' acts of cannibalism, Odysseus looks to help from Athene for vengeance (9.316–17), and upon his escape shouts out that Zeus and the other gods have punished Polyphemos for his outrages against the laws of hospitality (9.475–79). The curse of Polyphemos obligates Poseidon to prioritize kinship over Olympian values (9.528–35). This he does. No other god is required even to deliberate such a choice in the *Odyssey.*

The initial description of the Cyclopes comprises a series of antitheses generated from a thesis that Odysseus himself represents: it is a "negative catalogue" of Greek culture.[30] The exposition follows a clear though overlapping development which begins with social institutions and social law, continues with travel and technology, and culminates in piety and *xenia,* a species of social law related to travel. Because Paradise is by conception a negation of culture, a catalogue such as this is not surprising or unique. Yet by introducing the Cyclopes in this fashion, Odysseus exposes the thematic relationships that will be fundamental to the story of his revenge on the suitors (see below, Chapter 5).

When he finally steps onto a stage that he himself constructs, Odysseus illustrates in programmatic fashion every facet of civilized life that the Cyclopes lack. On the second morning after their arrival, Odysseus calls an *agora* in which he announces his intention of crossing over to the mainland. After crossing over by ship—another use for the island—and inspecting the home of their would-be host, the crew no less than their leader see where events are likely to lead and plead with him to turn the expedition into a cattle raid (9.224–27). Their plea allows Odysseus to reiterate his desire to establish *xenia* in explicit contrast to the piracy urged by the crew (9.228–29).

When at last they meet, Polyphemos asks after Odysseus' identity before offering him food, in flagrant violation of the laws of *xenia.*[31] Odysseus replies by spelling out the guest-host contract, together with its metaphysical underpinnings:

ἱκόμεθ', εἴ τι πόροις ξεινήιον ἠὲ καὶ ἄλλως
δοίης δωτίνην, ἥ τε ξείνων θέμις ἐστίν.

first to athetize 9.531–5. See the discussions in Focke, 159–60; Eisenberger, 144; Glenn (1971) 174–77.

30 See M. Davies (1987, 1988) whose studies concentrate on the climate of Paradise.

31 Nestle, 58–62; Fenik (1974) 20–21; *CHO* at 9.252–55.

ἀλλ' αἰδεῖο, φέριστε, θεούς· ἱκέται δέ τοί εἰμεν.
Ζεὺς δ' ἐπιτιμήτωρ ἱκετάων τε ξείνων τε,
ξείνιος, ὃς ξείνοισιν ἅμ' αἰδοίοισιν ὀπηδεῖ.

(9.267–71)

We have come to see if you may offer a guest-gift or some other
present, which is the *themis* of guests.
But respect, mightiest one, the gods—we are your suppliants.
And Zeus is the avenger, of suppliants and of guests,
Zeus Xeinios, who attends upon guests deserving of respect.

Polyphemos' reply, like Odysseus' request, equates observing "the *themis* of guests" with piety, and he dismisses both with the claim that the Cyclopes are "far mightier," *polu pherteroi,* than Zeus and the other gods (9.273–78). The suitors assert that their sheer numbers leave them in a position to disregard Telemachos' appeals to Zeus for vengeance. In their courtship of Penelope and depredations on the herds, they flagrantly abuse the *themistes* governing *xenia*. The *Cyclopeia* provides tacit commentary on the suitors' behavior and foreshadows their eventual punishment: self-sufficiency, both physically and in the external environment, leads to a hubris that manifests itself as disregard for the Olympian gods and for social law. Odysseus employs the same tactics against the suitors that he had earlier used against Polyphemos when he insinuates himself into the palace disguised as a nameless beggar. His tactics become those of Polyphemos, however, when he traps the suitors inside the *megaron,* or 'public room', in order to kill them.

The two scenes in which Odysseus deliberates and puts into effect his plan of revenge contain the greatest accumulation of cultural symbols to be found in the *Cyclopeia*. They are introduced chiefly by the olive-wood staff with which Odysseus blinds Polyphemos. Denys Page has argued that the *Odyssey* is unique in employing a staff as the instrument of blinding, dismissing the three parallels in Hackman's collection of variants as "all probably dependent on the *Odyssey* in this respect."[32] He

[32] Page (1955) 19, note 16. The accounts in Hackman which Page dismisses, and their analogues in Frazer (1965), are: H.1 = F.24, H.58 = F.9, H.109. Page (1955) 10–11, believes that there is a subconscious reference to the spit in the verb *diaphainein,* which he translates as 'glow all through terribly'. The word in the sense of 'glow' is rare enough; it is a Homeric hapax and *LSJ* cites only this passage, where it renders the word 'glow red hot'. *Dia-* as a verbal prefix elsewhere in Homer often does little more than intensify the meaning of the verb and may be translated with 'thoroughly'. This sense is guaranteed by Herodotus 2.92, 4.73, 4.75 (compare Pindar, *P.* 3.44). To test the theory one need only sharpen a thick piece of green olive wood and place it in a fire at night to

omits, however, two more of Hackman's examples involving a wooden stake and another two from Frazer's collection in which the hero blinds the ogre with a firebrand.[33] Since Page's work, Gabriel Germain has published three other versions of the folk tale in which a staff is used to blind the giant.[34] There are, then, eleven accounts including the *Odyssey* in which the hero employs the same or a closely similar weapon. The theory that the motif is unattested outside of versions dependent on the *Odyssey* should therefore be considered disproved.[35]

The spit is, however, by far the most commonly employed weapon, occurring in fifty-one of the one hundred twenty-five versions of the myth treated by Glenn.[36] The reason for its popularity is obvious since it is a weapon that the plot itself can be made to supply, so that the element of coincidence appears to be nonexistent.[37] Why, then, did Odysseus blind Polyphemos with a shepherd-staff, since "the change has obvious disadvantages which the poet does his best to gloss over"? According to Page "We can only guess. . . . we may conjecture that the cooking of the human victims, whether alive or dead, was rejected as being a deed of the utmost barbarism, outside the law prescribed by tradition to the Odyssean story-teller."[38]

Seth Schein, in a rebuttal of Page, argues that "Polyphemos' eating his victims raw . . . is, by Homeric standards, a more savage act than eating them cooked."[39] He cites three passages from the *Iliad* (4.34–36, 22.346–48, 24.212–13), in which the image of eating an enemy raw serves to illustrate the extremes to which a character has been driven by his or her hatred. Although I am in basic agreement with Schein's argument, one point requires further clarification. Cannibalism is a common motif of the "cultural foundation model," which views the rise of civilization in a positive light. Yet Greek myth and ritual provide numerous other examples of cannibalism involving both willing and unwilling banqueters, and on every occasion in which the cannibal is civilized the

harden it (9.328), let it cool, preferably in dung, and then reheat it in the fire to see if it glows brightly before catching flame. I conducted this experiment in Ano Glyfada in the summer of 1988 and can attest that olive wood so treated will indeed glow brilliant red.

33 Wooden stake: H.47, H.52; firebrand: F.21, F.28.

34 Glenn (1971) calls them G.a.b.d., following Germain's arrangement.

35 Thus Glenn (1971) 164–66, who does not, however, include the firebrand in his tabulation.

36 Glenn (1971) 164, note 127, lists variants in which the spit is employed.

37 Page (1955) 9.

38 The two quotations are from Page (1955) 9, 11.

39 Schein, 74, followed by Eisenberger, 137, note 25.

flesh is cooked. Eating human flesh dehumanizes the cannibal, and as such it functions in the same manner as the lotus or the drugs of Circe.[40] The loss of humanity can be represented by the prolonged isolation of the cannibal from human society or by his transformation into a man-eating animal, specifically a werewolf.[41] The theme of the "raw and the cooked," be the flesh lamb or human, is employed exclusively as a register of civilization. Two independent markers, *allelōphagia* (cannibalism) and *ōmophagia* (eating raw food), are operative, both of which characterize Polyphemos.[42] Thus, when Zeus pictures Hera as devouring Priam and his children raw, he indicates that his wife has already reverted to a subhuman condition which cannibalism was elsewhere said to cause (*Il.* 4.34–36). It is appropriate that Iliadic characters use the image of eating human flesh raw metaphorically to express an anger that has driven them beyond the human pale, but one need only think of how it would sound, to say nothing of what it would mean, were they to declare "I'd like to cook and eat him I'm so mad."

Although it is clear that Polyphemos eats his victims uncooked, no explicit mention is made of the fact. Our poet would thus seem to be less interested in exploiting the cultural register provided by *ōmophagia* than in avoiding the associations evoked by the spit. As a metal implement the spit implies a technological sophistication patently at odds with the Homeric depiction of the Cyclopes. Yet these problems could have been circumvented by roasting the men on a stick which could then have been used to blind the ogre.[43] Or Odysseus could have used the sword with which he at first meant to kill Polyphemos. These substitutions would not have introduced the slightest element of coincidence into the story.

In Homer, the instrument of blinding is a shepherd-staff, and the question why the spit was eliminated may be restated from this perspective. Odysseus introduces the staff with the remark that it was made of olive wood (9.319–20), and repeats his observation three times in the

[40] For cannibalism, see *HN* chap. 2 with discussion of this episode; Redfield (1975) 196–99; Nagy (1979) 135–37; Nagy (1990) 300–1; Goldhill (1991) 89–90.

[41] In H.18 the cannibal is a werewolf.

[42] It is unclear whether Antiphates eats his victims raw or cooked and unlikely that Homer gave the matter much thought, but the depiction of Laistrygonian society favors the latter. The case of Tydeos is not a genuine act of cannibalism. See Apollodorus 3.6.8 with Frazer's note ad loc.; *CGS* 1:309–10; *GG* 197.

[43] The victims are boiled in a pot in: F.1 = H.20; F.6 = H.21; F.12 = H.30; F.19 = H.19, H.26 (H.69 is close). In H.6 and H.119 a kettle is used to cook the flesh and a skewer to blind the ogre. It is one of the recognized archaizing features of the Homeric epics that meat is always roasted.

scene of blinding (9.378, 382, 394). In Greek mythology and cult, the olive tree is a developed symbol of agriculture, technology, communal life and social stability.[44] It is thus Athene's special tree in her civic cult at Athens and was held to be one of her gifts to the Athenian people and to humankind generally. Odysseus finds the staff upon deliberating how he might avenge himself and "Athene give him the boast" (9.317). The olive is also associated with her favorite in the scene in which he devises his return to Ithaca from the enchanted realm (5.234–36), safely reaches Scherie (5.477), and plots with Athene his vengeance on the suitors (13.372–73). Athene sets each of these events in motion, and through them she puts into effect her plan to bring Odysseus home and to punish the suitors. In Odysseus' own home the marriage bed was built upon the stump of an olive tree. It is for their assault on that tree that the suitors will be punished. Where else but in the shade of an olive tree would Odysseus and Athene plan their revenge? What else would Polyphemos uproot to make a shepherd-staff? With what else would Odysseus punish Polyphemos?

Odysseus immediately compares the staff to the mast of a freighter (9.321–24). The nautical motif picks up one of the themes of the exposition (9.125–30) and returns in the scene of blinding when Odysseus compares the staff to a drill boring the plank of a ship (9.383–86). Ships were another of Athene's gifts, so that the comparison associates her with the instrument of vengeance for a second time by means of a cultural artifact.[45] In Book 5 Odysseus builds the ship on which he escapes from Ogygie. He thereby demonstrates his mastery of *tekhnē*, or 'technology', the means by which civilized humanity controls the forces of nature and renders them useful.[46] When Odysseus compares the staff to a mast and later to steel being quenched he twice echoes the language of Book 5, including the words *skeparnon* and *phortis*, or 'adze' and 'merchant ship', which are restricted to these two passages in Homer.[47] The description of the staff in Book 9 was influenced by a scene some four books earlier in which Odysseus effects his escape from another cave-dwelling encloser through mastery of *tekhnē*.

[44] Powell (1977) 11; Beidelman, 246–47; Segal (1994) 60, with note 31.

[45] Athene oversees the building of the Argo, the first ship (the craft of Deucalion was a *larnax*) at Apollodorus 1.9.16. See also Simon (1965) 78–83, and for the cult of Athene-Iasonia, *RE* 9:1.782–83. Atnene also advises Danaos in the building of his ship at Apollodorus 2.1.4; Hyginus, *Fab*. 168.

[46] For Odysseus as master of *tekhnē* see also 10.161–71.

[47] *Skeparnon:* 5.237, 9.391; *phortis:* 5.250, 9.323. The fact that the two objects are unrelated and occur in close proximity to one another in Book 5 increases the likelihood that the echo is not random.

It is surprising that comparison of an olive-wood staff to the mast of a ship has failed to attract more controversy: olive trees are too short and crooked to serve as masts.[48] The comparison is of course readily explained by Odysseus' insistence on the enormous size of Polyphemos. Yet aside from the indicator of scale provided by the mast—from which it appears that Polyphemos is approximately ten meters tall—his height is only vaguely defined as superhuman.[49] Difficulty arises not so much from making a staff out of olive wood, nor from comparing the staff of Polyphemos to a mast, but from comparing an object made of olive wood to a mast. The fact that Homer was unwilling to do without either image suggests that both the material chosen and the object to which it is compared are thematically motivated.

A shepherd-staff is wood at its least worked and still an implement. When Polyphemos fashions his staff from a mature olive tree he actually renders it less useful than it was as a living plant. Odysseus sees in the staff the mast of a ship, one of the highest technological achievements of ancient man. To put out the eye of Polyphemos, Odysseus turns the staff into the first technological weapon of man, the fire-hardened spear.[50] In the act of blinding he becomes a shipwright drilling the plank to a ship, an invention of the age of heroes. Giant planks require giant augers, so Polyphemos is overcome by the coordinated efforts of a group of men under the leadership of Odysseus.

Odysseus employs a second simile in order to dwell at length on the climax of the story, and in doing so, he brings our gaze to rest on a scene taken from domestic life, the tempering of steel. To work the most useful of metals is an act of violence. In this simile Odysseus becomes a blacksmith fashioning the tools with which he built a ship on Ogygie.

48 Merry and Riddell at *Od.* 9.322.

49 Polyphemos is somewhat over twenty meters tall, if we understand *rhopalon* as a club rather than a staff. Homer regularly distinguishes between two types of ships, one with ten rowers on either side (1.280, 2.212), and a second with twenty-five. From these numbers, the length of the Homeric ship is fixed at eighteen meters for the smaller and thirty for the larger (Torr, 21ff., Gray, 108). This means that the mast of the smaller ship would be approximately ten meters long, so that it could be held by the *histodokē* when lowered (I take the difference between a *phortis* and a conventional twenty-oared ship to be chiefly one of girth and assume that Odysseus' reference to such a ship is due to the stoutness required of its mast). Though these numbers are not very precise for us, they likely approached a unit of measurement for the ancient Greeks. For the Homeric ship generally see Casson, 43–53, and for the merchantman Casson, 65–66. For earlier reconstructions see Torr, pl. W; Merry and Riddell, 1:537ff., app.

50 *HN* 151; *SH* 34. See *CHO* at 9.328. For the fire-hardened spear as a tag of primitive warfare see the Scholia to *Il.* 13.564. For its similar use at Rome see Livy 1.32, where the *hasta praeusta* in the ritual of the Fetiales is also smeared with blood. See also Propertius 4.1.28 and Tacitus, *Ann.* 2.14.

Odysseus first compared the staff to the mast of a vessel used to transport metal; he now compares the stake made from it to a metal tool used in building ships. It is as though his description of the staff defines the absence of the spit from the Homeric version of the folk tale. In the space of twenty verses a shepherd-staff has been made to represent the development of technology from the prehistoric dawn of the human race, which Polyphemos himself represents, to the contemporary society of Homer and his audience.

Ships, agriculture, commerce, social organization and social stability, leadership, piety, and Athene—all the themes of the exposition come together in a staff of olive wood and are brought to bear against Polyphemos. It is with culture that Odysseus blinds Polyphemos, with culture that he protects himself from the progeny of reified natural force. Juxtaposed with these images are the inarticulate screams of the Cyclops and the hiss of steam, the sound of steel being quenched. When his fellow Cyclopes ask, "Surely no one (*mē tis*) kills you by deceit or force (*biēphi*)," Polyphemos answers, "Nobody (*Outis*) kills me by deceit and not by force (*biēphi*)." To which the Cyclopes reply, "Well, if no one (*mē tis*) is doing violence to you (*biazetai*), there is no avoiding a disease from Zeus" (9.406–11). Differently accented, *mētis* signifies 'cunning intelligence' and belongs to the traditional nomenclature of Odysseus in the epithet *polumētis*. For the savage Polyphemos, *mētis* and products of *mētis* are a source of pain, which Odysseus presently affirms has been sent by Zeus. So much is gained by changing the spit into a staff.

To kill Polyphemos would have meant Odysseus' own death. Odysseus must plan his revenge so that it aids his deliverance; he must harness the enormous strength of his adversary to perform a task that he could not. Odysseus escapes into the light of day which he himself creates by robbing Polyphemos of his light; at dawn he rides out hanging from its belly. For one agonized moment in the doorway, all that is interposed between the wrath of Polyphemos and its object is a ram, which Odysseus shall presently sacrifice to Zeus. In all of Greek literature there is no more potent image of expiatory sacrifice than this. Any Greek who had established an outpost on the shores of Paradise with its hostile hinterland would have understood: his city walls were no more secure and served as a daily reminder of the polarities that inform the *Cyclopeia*. The same could be said of any Greek who had been caught in a storm at sea or had survived an earthquake, volcano, or tidal wave. Civilization itself hangs from the belly of a ram. In many versions of the folk tale the sacrifice precedes the escape, and the hero avoids the wrath of the ogre by hiding in the animal's skin. The symbolism may be more explicit, but had Odysseus escaped in this manner it would have been the wrong sacrifice.[51]

Odysseus has insisted on the prerogatives of Greek culture in an antithetical realm, and although the *Cyclopeia* clearly depicts the success of the civilized over the savage, the moral is not so simple as this. Odysseus' position reverses once more, and now Polyphemos is replaced by a more universal threat, his father Poseidon. Now there can be no victory, only propitiation for the temerity of surviving. By his wits man saves himself from the *biē* of a hostile nature, but to do so is an offense, a violation of nature. Odysseus builds ships in the cave of the Encloser and to do so he blinds its owner, an act that must be balanced by dedicating his oar to Poseidon in a land far from the sea, a land whose inhabitants are as primitive as the Cyclopes and like them know nothing of sailing.[52]

Odysseus uses his encounter with Polyphemos to represent an opposition in the external environment, where the hero's adversaries can be human, beast, or nature itself. It is the contemporary fight of the Greek explorer. His encounter can also represent historical dialectic; the triumph of Odysseus—and his pain—is that of every age, every technological advance. This same polarity even informs our internal landscape: Homer sends Odysseus to seek out his opponent and he finds his opposite, that is his complement. Much-Fame dances the oldest dance with Nobody. But Odysseus, thanks in large measure to Polyphemos, is much famed, just as Polyphemos is nobody.[53] Together they are everyone and the world, the dislocations that arise when man organizes into society. The union of hero and god is the ritual solution to the crisis of civilization.

[51] *HN* 148–49. See also the depiction of Odysseus' escape on Paris, Cab. Méd. 280, an Attic black-figure lekythos from the end of the sixth century which Röhrich (1962) 63, believes shows him wearing the ram's skin.

[52] Detienne (1977) 176–77, discusses the use of salt as a cultural marker; see also Germain, 275–84.

[53] N. Austin (1983) 22.

CHAPTER 4

Cattle of the Sun

In Chapter 1 we saw that scholarship on the Introduction to the *Odyssey* has often been guided by a prior interpretation of the *Apologoi.* In particular, members of the Analytic and Unitarian schools have both argued that the Thrinakian episode acquired its present form at a more primitive stage of Greek religious thought than that which produced the first divine assembly. The schools differ chiefly in that Analysts assign Thrinakie to Homer and the divine assembly to a *Bearbeiter,* while Unitarians find the hand of the master in the poem's introductory scenes and argue that Thrinakie was appropriated from some earlier, possibly non-Homeric, source and left largely unaltered.[1] Paradoxically, Unitarians must then assume that the emphasis awarded the episode in the proem betrays signs of "hasty composition" or worse.[2] Either interpretation effectively reverses the contrast between Odysseus and the crew in the Introduction: Odysseus deserved his punishment, the crew did not.

Detailed analysis of the Odyssean prologue, the first divine assembly, the *Apologoi,* and the *Cyclopeia* has shown that the text is subordinated at all levels to a common thematic program. In the *Cyclopeia* that program accounts for significant alterations, expansions, and suppressions of the traditional elements of the folk tale as reconstructed by comparative analysis. Odyssean narrative, then, would appear to be driven coher-

[1] The Analytic position is well articulated by Focke, for which see below. Among Unitarians, Fenik (1974) 208–27, holds that Thrinakie faithfully reflects the religious belief of an earlier period; Rüter, 82, on the other hand, sees in the episode an example of Homer's imperfect adaptation of his material to contemporary belief.

[2] Fenik (1974) 225–26; see my discussion below, Appendix 1.

ently by theme. Is it then possible that Homer—whether we mean by Homer an individual master poet or the sum total of all the poets, occasions, and audiences that produced our written text—failed to recognize that Thrinakie contradicts the very metaphysics which he had elsewhere used to shape his epic? And if it were not possible, would the poet who gave us the *Cyclopeia* have felt obliged for whatever reason to retain or leave unaltered material unsuited to his purpose? In short, if Homer did inherit a version of the Thrinakian episode which undermined the theodicy of the divine assembly—that is, the theological and ethical themes of his *Odyssey*—would he have hesitated to excise, modify, or replace from competing traditions those verses which could not be reconciled with his own portrait of Olympos? Is this the Homer who could make a Cyclops the son of Poseidon and an Okeanid nymph, the kingdom of Aiolos peaceful, the Sirens beautiful, Calypso sympathetic, the Phaiakes civilized?

These questions do not necessarily imply that the Thrinakian episode is consistent with the Introduction or with the other adventures. They merely suggest that it would be difficult to account for major inconsistencies without recourse to the interpolations proposed by Analytic criticism. A strong case for interpreting Thrinakie in accordance with the Introduction can, however, be built using the methods and results of the preceding chapters. The traditional debate among Analysts and Unitarians has nevertheless performed an invaluable service, for it has isolated and subjected to the closest scrutiny those features on which a successful interpretation of the episode must be based.

Events on Thrinakie would seem to confirm the expectations raised by the Introduction. Odysseus warns the crew against putting in at the island on the authority of the prophet Teiresias and of the goddess Circe:

κέκλυτέ μευ μύθων, κακά περ πάσχοντες ἑταῖροι,
ὄφρ' ὕμιν εἴπω μαντήια Τειρεσίαο
Κίρκης τ' Αἰαίης, ἥ μοι μάλα πόλλ' ἐπέτελλε
νῆσον ἀλεύασθαι τερψιμβρότου Ἠελίοιο·
ἔνθα γὰρ αἰνότατον κακὸν ἔμμεναι ἄμμιν ἔφασκεν.
ἀλλὰ παρὲξ τὴν νῆσον ἐλαύνετε νῆα μέλαιναν.

(12.271–76)

Hear my words, companions, for all the evils you have suffered,
so that I may tell you the prophecies of Teiresias
and Aiaian Circe, who bad me most insistently

avoid the island of Helios who gives joy to mortals,
for there she said our danger is most dread.
But drive the black ship along past the island here.

To appreciate the force of "our danger is most dread," we should recall that they arrive at Thrinakie directly after encountering Scylla and Charybdis. Yet the crew, worn out by the day's activities, are crushed. Eurylochos, who had already attempted to mutiny against Odysseus in the Circe episode, acts as their spokesman and urges Odysseus to put in at the island (12.279–93). Odysseus responds by accusing the crew of using *biē* against him in order to land on Thrinakie, and then binds them with an oath lest anyone "in his reckless folly" harm the cattle of the sun (12.297–302). It is only when Odysseus withdraws to pray for deliverance that the crew violate the oath and slaughter "the best of the cows." When Helios complains to Zeus that they have killed his cattle 'with exceeding violence', *huperbion* (12.379), Zeus promises to shatter the ship with a thunderbolt. He fulfills his promise seven days later, once Odysseus and his men depart from the island.

In the divine assembly of Book 1, Zeus lays great emphasis on the fact that Aigisthos yielded to his passion despite the warnings of Hermes. He thus offers a scenario in which human suffering can be seen as fully deserved punishment. The theme of divinely sanctioned warning returns at the beginning of the Thrinakian episode, where it supplies the last element of the Aigisthos paradigm still missing from the story of the crew. As a consequence, the crew knowingly commit a crime in slaughtering the cattle of the sun. Their oath repeats the tagged word *atasthalie,* or 'reckless folly', that had linked them to Aigisthos in the Introduction, and it reminds us of the judgment that the authorial voice had passed there on the crew's actions. By a cleverly ironic twist Odysseus requires the crew to agree on oath that if they kill the cattle of the sun they are guilty of *atasthaliai*.

Homeric scholars have arrayed the following arguments against interpreting Thrinakie in the manner urged by the proem: the gods are responsible for what happens on Thrinakie, and their behavior therefore reflects "primitive" religious belief. The crew for their part are forced to eat the cattle of Helios and are exonerated by their piety. As will be apparent, these scholars have particular difficulty in accounting for Odysseus' warnings and the oath that he extracts from the crew.

The Guilt of the Crew

Eurylochos' reasons in favor of putting in at Thrinakie rests on three points: the crew are tired and hungry, and the winds are dangerous at night. Of these, the first two are clearly unimportant in light of Odysseus' dire warnings about the evils awaiting them on the island. Yet Eurylochos frames his argument with mention of eating, so that his concluding words are "let us be persuaded by black night and prepare our dinner" (12.292). We might have expected him to say "and let us take the gift of sleep." His words remind us of the crew's preoccupation with food and inability to withstand physical hardship even as they foreshadow the disaster that follows.

How hazardous were nocturnal winds? Bernard Fenik claims that it is Homeric practice never to sail at night, by which he means that the threat is both great and respected.[3] Telemachos, however, sails from Ithaca to Pylos and back again at night, while the suitors who set an ambush for his return keep watch from an island lookout during the day and patrol the waters only after dark.[4] The observation that these waters were known if not to Telemachos then at least to his crew is irrelevant since they made their crossing over the high seas where the threat consists of storms rather than hidden shoals. If, on the other hand, the danger was thought to consist of running aground, it failed to deter Odysseus from sailing for ten days and nights over unknown waters from Aiolie to Ithaca, or for seventeen days and nights from Ogygie to Scherie.[5]

In fact, the majority of the voyages in the *Odyssey* take place at night or continue through it. If we are to explain Telemachos' nocturnal sailing on the grounds that he was avoiding real or potential danger, then it would have been no less justifiable for the crew to prefer the uncertainties of the sea to the certain dangers that awaited them on Thrinakie. If, as some have argued, the crew are to be seen as pious in this episode, then what better means could be found to demonstrate their piety than to have them obey the explicit warnings of the gods?

Fenik, who recognizes the difficulties posed by Odysseus' warnings for an Analytical reading of the episode, attempts to neutralize their significance. He begins by relating them to the pleas made by the crew

[3] Fenik (1974) 213; see also *CHO* at 1.7–9.
[4] Telemachos: 2.434 (compare 3.1–5), 15.34; the suitors: 16.364–69.
[5] Aiolie to Ithaca: 10.28; Ogygie to Scherie: 5.278–79.

to Odysseus at the end of the *Cyclopeia* against taunting Polyphemos. From this he argues that the anger of Helios, like that of Poseidon, results from a "failure to follow good advice." Since Poseidon's continued harassment of Odysseus is incompatible with the theodicy of the divine assembly, so is the destruction of the crew. Fenik concludes that the motif of disaster caused by a "failure to follow good advice" is in fact a simple device of composition. Thus, although the motif figures prominently in the divine assembly, we need not attach any special significance to it. "Its multiple uses, chosen sometimes for their short-range functions, sometimes for long-range emphases, are not in perfect internal harmony. The divine wraths [of the *Apologoi*] and Zeus' statement in the Prologue make use of the same motif of prudent warnings left unheeded, but they represent two if not utterly irreconcilable, at least strongly divergent concepts of divine justice."[6] Yet the crew's pleading in the *Cyclopeia* bears little resemblance to the warnings they receive on Thrinakie in either form or function. The crew are not concerned with avoiding the anger of Poseidon, nor do they warn Odysseus against revealing his name, but merely against further provoking Polyphemos. Odysseus ignores their pleas in the knowledge that his opponent is mortal, and one of the effects of that decision is to contrast their cowardice with his heroism. Finally, and this point is decisive, the other warnings are each validated by the gods: Hermes warns Aigisthos directly, the prophets Halitherses and Theoklymenos warn the suitors and their parents, and Odysseus reports the warnings made by the goddess Circe and the prophet Teiresias. The analogy that Fenik draws to the *Cyclopeia,* although structurally valid, does not permit us to see Odysseus' warnings in the Thrinakian episode as a simple narrative device, devoid of thematic significance.

Fenik also argues that the warning is fragmented into three parts so that the nature and scope of the danger is never made clear to the crew.[7] For this objection to carry any force, there would have to be some reason to suppose that the crew failed to comprehend the warning or its gravity. Yet the very words with which Eurylochos justifies his proposal to eat the cattle demonstrate his understanding of the situation (12.348–51). Fenik's objection also ignores the tendency of Homeric narrative to amplify through suppletive repetition of motifs or events.[8] This is

[6] Fenik (1974) 208, 218.

[7] Fenik (1974) 212; see also Dawe at *Od.* 12.294.

[8] See Andersen (1973) 12–14. We may profitably compare the bird omens of Book 15. The first omen indicates that Odysseus has already returned and that the punishment of the suitors is imminent (15.160–81). The second treats the same issue from another angle:

surely the case in the Thrinakian episode. Odysseus' warnings come at intervals of approximately twenty verses and at logically appropriate junctures in the narrative: before they reach the island, after they land, and when it becomes apparent that they will be stranded there for an indefinite period of time. By the time disaster strikes on Thrinakie, the warnings of the gods and the misdeeds of the crew have been rehearsed to the audience on no less than six occasions. The effect is one of emphasis, not obfuscation.

Those who would argue that Thrinakie portrays the gods as the cause of human suffering are undoubtedly right on one important point: the crew have little choice but to eat the cattle of the sun. Odysseus himself does not state with what success he and the crew hunted and fished after the stores on board ship were exhausted, but Eurylochos clearly implies that they were on the verge of starvation. Granted, the audience has been prejudiced by Eurylochos' behavior in the Circe episode, which in fact prepares us for his role on Thrinakie, and some room must be allowed for exaggeration in his speech here. The crew are as always portrayed as weak, a fact underscored by Odysseus' own continued endurance in this episode, but the sleep that overcomes Odysseus when he goes off to pray would attain greater verisimilitude if we imagine him as faint from hunger. It is also somewhat unfair, as both Eurylochos and several Homeric experts remark, to hold the crew to the standards of a hero who enjoyed the epithet *polutlas,* or 'much enduring'. Most important, the gods are clearly responsible for the winds that prevent their departure. The gods, then, compel the crew to kill and eat the cattle of the sun.

We must be careful not to isolate Thrinakie from the larger context of the *Apologoi*. The crew are regularly tested by and yield to various temptations, especially food. This makes the cattle of the sun merely the last in a series of such tests. The crew have always failed; they have always eaten. The equivalence of yielding to physical appetites and of failing to return is announced with the very first of the adventures, in the land of the Kikones.[9] The gods may compel the crew to slaughter the cattle of the sun, but this is merely to seal a fate that they have already earned. In like manner, Athene binds the "good suitor" Amphinomos so that

---

who is best suited on Ithaca to provide *xenia* to the prophet Theoklymenos (15.525–38). In this instance, the omen offers Telemachos the assurance that the house of Laertes will maintain its position on Ithaca.

[9] See above, Chapter 2.

none will escape punishment.[10] These gods are no more primitive, or scrutable, than the gods of Sophocles.

In Book 4 Menelaos relates an episode from his Egyptian adventures in which he interviews the sea god Proteus. The interview belongs to a recurrent story pattern in the *Odyssey* known as the "conference sequence."[11] The narrative frame, however, exactly reproduces the situation on Thrinakie. Menelaos and his crew have been stalled for a month by contrary winds on the island of Pharos. When their supplies are exhausted, they turn to hunting wild fowl and fish. Menelaos leaves his men to pray to the gods for deliverance and is met by Eidothea, who helps arrange an interview with Proteus, her father. Menelaos learns from Proteus that the gods are displeased with his neglect of their sacrifices. In order to placate the gods, Menelaos must return to Egypt and there perform the necessary hecatombs.[12]

The story of Menelaos suggests that the gods are angry with Odysseus' crew before the Thrinakian adventure even begins.[13] In the case of Menelaos, the gods are satisfied with a conventional sacrifice, and the affair has a happy outcome. On Thrinakie, however, divine wrath drives the crew to perform an unholy sacrifice that provides an external verification of their guilt. Yet Odysseus also suffers as a consequence of the crew's destruction, and in the *Nekyia* Teiresias predicts that Poseidon will not soon renounce his anger. Are we to understand that Poseidon raised the storm in the knowledge that the crew will eat the cattle of Helios? If so, his vengeance on Odysseus consists in delaying the hero's return by depriving him of human society. These two lines of interpretation are not mutually exclusive: Poseidon can be seen as doing harm to Odysseus by bringing about the just destruction of the crew. Poseidon would then be far closer to the spirit of the divine assembly than

[10] See Rüter, 78, discussed below, Appendix 1. Fenik (1974) 218 ff., especially 212–22, finds this an example of the more primitive textual strata.

[11] Hansen provides a taxonomy of the narrative pattern.

[12] The parallels, which are more extensive than my brief summary suggests, are discussed by Hansen, 8–19, and Nagler (1980) 98–101; for the Proteus episode, see also Peradotto, 35–40. For the possible significance of Menelaos' return to his point of departure see above, Chapter 2, on A-B-A structures.

[13] The audience doubtless also knew the story of how the expedition of Greek ships bound for Troy had been stalled by the gods at Aulis. Homer apparently alludes to the story at *Il.* 9.145, where he corrects the tradition that Agamemnon sacrificed his daughter, named Iphianassa (note that Iphianassa would be an appropriate cult-title for Artemis). At *Od.* 3.253–75, Nestor does not link Clytemnestra's infidelity to the sacrifice of Iphigenia. This, however, does not prove that Homer was unaware of such a link, and his motive in Book 3 is clearly to evoke the tradition of an unfaithful Penelope through analogy to Clytemnestra.

the Iliadic Achilleus, who caused the death of countless fellow Greeks in order to avenge himself on Agamemnon.

Impious Sacrifice

Friedrich Focke argues that the behavior of the crew in the face of starvation reveals their innocence and the gods' cruelty. His argument, which is accepted by Wolfgang Schadewaldt, Heubeck, and Fenik among others, rests on three points.[14] The crew sacrifice the cattle of Helios, an act that demonstrates their piety. The substitution of leaves and water for the barley and wine of ritual lends the scene a pathetic touch that serves to emphasize the injustice of the crew's predicament. Finally, the crew offer restitution by promising to construct a temple to Helios on their return to Ithaca.

Comparative analysis suggests that the cattle of Helios represent the life-force, which in Greek myth is made available to human use through sacrificial ritual. On this level of analysis, moral concerns are irrelevant to the interpretation of the Thrinakian episode. Such myths are, however, commonly rationalized so as to represent the first sacrifice as a crime. In the *Theogony,* Prometheus is punished for an inequitable distribution of the sacrificial banquet, and for providing the fire that assured the perpetuation of that distribution. In the Bouphonia, a ritualization of the first sacrifice at Athens, the individual who kills the ox vanishes in flight, leaving the carcass for the innocent bystanders to enjoy. The ritual nevertheless insists on assigning guilt. After a ceremonial trial the sacrificial knife is condemned and hidden in the purifying water of the sea.

The first sacrificial act is invariably accompanied by a change in the cosmic order. In Hesiod, sacrifice marks the transition from Paradise to the civilized world. Aratus declares that slaughtering the plow-ox for food marked the beginning of the Age of Bronze; the first such slaughter, commemorated in the Bouphonia, took place on the very altar of deified civilization, that of Zeus Polieus.[15] In the Thrinakian episode, Helios threatens to pass beneath the earth and shine among the dead if he is not avenged on the crew. Helios' threat reveals that a disruption of

[14] Focke, 156–61, 247–54; Heubeck (1954) 85–87; Schadewaldt (1960) 861–876; Fenik (1974) 212–13.

[15] Aratus 131–32, connected to the Bouphonia by Burkert, *HN* 138.

the natural order comparable to that of the Bouphonia and the banquet of Prometheus has taken place on Thrinakie.

The fact that the crew sacrifice the cattle which they consume is a defining feature of the tradition from which the episode is derived. It may not be used to defend their behavior. The normative aspect of the story, which represents the crew's sacrifice as a punishable offense, is a common feature of such accounts. There is, however, an important obstacle to explaining the guilt of the crew in these terms alone: whereas myth uses sacrifice to differentiate man from god and beast and to explain the rise of culture, the crew's eating throughout the adventures is at once cause and emblem of their alienation from culture. The fact that the crew also pervert the sacrificial ritual helps to resolve this potential difficulty.[16] The crew undermine the symbolism of the ritual when they substitute the food of animals—grass and water—for the usual barley and wine. Just as wine and barley are agricultural products, only domestic animals are sacrificed to the gods.[17] Here too, the crew pervert the ritual, since the cattle which they slaughter are not domesticated, but belong to a god, are immortal, and have never been used to plow the soil.

The paradox involved in killing immortal animals is graphically illustrated by the portents that follow, in which the meat lows on the spits and the hides stretched out upon the ground begin to crawl. Even as dismembered corpses the animals refuse to die, refuse their sacrifice, and it was sacrilege to offer unwilling victims to the gods. Cultic parallels help reveal the force of the scene: in the Bouphonia at Athens, the flayed hide of the sacrificial ox is stuffed and yoked to a plow in a transparent attempt to reconstitute the life that was taken.[18] On Thrinakie, the creeping hides of the slain cattle fulfill in a horrifying fashion the vain endeavor of ritual reconstitution. Yet despite these portents the crew persist in slaughtering and in feasting on the "best of the cows of

[16] Vernant (1972). See also Reinhardt (1960) 114–15; Eisenberger, 208; Bergren (1983) 57; Nagler (1990) 339–40. Vernant, however, assumes that the crew "hunted" the cattle, and uses this to argue that the crew confuse hunting with sacrificial ritual. The verb *elaunein* at 12.343, 353, 398 simply refers to the driving of cattle to the district where a sacrifice is to be performed and makes no reference to hunting (the French verb *chasser* means both 'hunt' and 'chase/drive'). For the word's use in the description of an exemplary sacrifice, see *Od.* 3.422.

[17] Note that the rule that only domestic animals are sacrificed may well be universal. See J. Smith, 196–205, but see also Burkert (1987) 167.

[18] Burkert, *HN* 14–15, finds a similar reference in the *Homeric Hymn to Hermes* at v. 404.

Helios" over the next six days, thus compounding their guilt as they call attention to their gluttony.[19]

The crew's perversion of sacrificial ritual is finally reflected in the threat of Helios to shine among the dead. But since the cattle possess solar attributes, the crew have in a sense already sent the sun's light down to Hades by killing them.[20] Helios merely threatens to institutionalize the crew's perversion of the natural order.[21] Homer has evoked the paradigm of an aetiological myth of sacrifice but removed the intercessor; on Thrinakie, nothing mediates between divine prerogative and human need, no god validates the feast.[22]

The Thrinakian episode helps expose the nature and magnitude of the suitors' crimes on Ithaca. Not only are the fates of the crew and suitors parallel, but the episode is responsible for the situation awaiting Odysseus on his return. In the *Nekyia,* Teiresias prophesies that, should the crew harm the cattle of the sun, Odysseus will return home to find arrogant men devouring his own *biotos,* or 'livelihood', and courting Penelope (11.115–17). In other words, violation of a taboo against eating leads to the improper feasting of the suitors and to the disruption of the social order of Ithaca. Depletion of Odysseus' *biotos* results from and mirrors a depletion of life itself in the enchanted realm.[23]

The complementary nature of Thrinakie and the *Cyclopeia* offers a further perspective on the relation of both episodes to the Ithacan narrative. Whereas the crew's sacrifice effaces the distinctions between wild and domestic, cannibalism effaces those between human and nonhuman. Cannibalism, no less than sacrifice, can profoundly alter the natural order: after the banquet of Thyestes the sun was said to have changed its course and adopted its present orbit.[24] Violation of a taboo against eating thus serves as a mechanism of change in the organization of the physical world, just as the crew's sacrifice of forbidden cattle leads to the threat of Helios to shine among the dead. The cannibalism of

19 I here follow van Thiel's reading of *eloōntes* at 12.398.

20 See above, Chapter 2.

21 Note that at Lucretius 5.119–20 the Giants sought to extinguish the sun.

22 The sulfurous smell that fills the ship after Zeus strikes it has connotations of ritual purification. See *CHO* at 22.481; *IC* at *Il.* 16.228–30; Segal (1994) 78.

23 Nagler (1980) 89–106, especially 95–96.

24 References and discussion in *HN* 103–9. Burkert shows that the meal of Thyestes can also be read as a perverted sacrifice. See in particular Plato, *Plt.* 269–71, who suggests a link between the banquet of Thyestes, a change in the sun's course, and the end of the Golden Age of Kronos.

Thyestes, moreover, results in his banishment and a change in the rule of Mycene. Sacrifice accounts for the rise of the political order; cannibalism, a perversion of the dietary code, can bring about change in that order. Should we then connect events on Ithaca with the *Cyclopeia* rather than with Thrinakie? The cannibal of the story is admittedly Polyphemos, not Odysseus, yet few who read Walter Burkert's masterful study will find it entirely fanciful to connect the cannibalism of Polyphemos, Odysseus' lengthy absence from Ithaca, and the political consequences of his absence.[25] It is also important to note that we can arrive at this same interpretation with the rationalized theme of Poseidon's wrath. But surely it would be wrong to insist on exclusive schematizations such as this. Both adventures are in some sense responsible for the disruption of Ithacan society, just as both are reflections of it and of one another. To the extent that we may distinguish between them, the *Cyclopeia* belongs to the social and political aspect of the Revenge, Thrinakie to its religious and economic aspect.

Zeus in the *Cyclopeia* and Thrinakian Episode

In the final scene of the *Cyclopeia* Odysseus claims that Zeus ignored his thank-offerings but was instead devising the destruction of the crew (9.553–55). Heubeck and Fenik seize on Odysseus' reproach to argue that the Zeus of the Thrinakian episode reflects the same cosmology that produced the theme of Poseidon's wrath.[26] Yet granted that Odysseus is here referring to Thrinakie, there is no reason to assume that he is offering a fair and accurate account of events. Moreover, as Ove Jørgensen has shown, the poet carefully distinguishes between his own knowledge of divine affairs and that of the poem's human characters.[27]

The *Cyclopeia* and the Circe and Thrinakian episodes all feature a god who actively interferes in events. On each occasion, Odysseus indicates that he has direct knowledge of the god involved in shaping his destiny: in the *Nekyia* Teiresias informs Odysseus of Poseidon's anger, on Aiaie

[25] Burkert, *HN* Chap. 2, who treats cannibalism, its use as a mechanism of political change, and the possible implications of this for the *Cyclopeia*.

[26] See *CHO* at 9.550–55, 12.260–402; Heubeck (1954) 85. Heubeck argues that Thrinakie recreates the same "inner situation" as reigned in the land of the Cyclopes—that is, Zeus is responsible for the crew's misdeed. Heubeck is followed by Fenik (1974) 208–30, esp. 222–23; see also *CHO* at 1.7–9. Clay (1983) 47, 230.

[27] See below, Appendix 1.

he deals with Hermes directly, and Calypso reveals that Zeus struck the ship with a thunderbolt.[28] The mere fact that Odysseus is made to justify—rather emphatically—his knowledge of Zeus' involvement in the Thrinakian episode demonstrates the poet's concern for maintaining the narrative illusion.[29] Elsewhere Odysseus uses *theos, daimōn,* and Zeus to designate what he understands to be divine interference in events.

This is not to dismiss the reference to Zeus in the *Cyclopeia* as a generic reference to divinity. Odysseus can only be thinking of the personal Zeus when he declares that the god was responsible for the destruction of the crew. So much of his statement is validated by Calypso. We need not, however, imagine Odysseus as having also learned that Zeus was planning their death some two years and six adventures before the fact. Jørgensen has offered a satisfactory interpretation of the passage:

> [Odysseus] is quite certain that Zeus and the other gods were responsible for the punishment of the Cyclops (9.479–80). And if a few verses later he says that Zeus "ignored the sacrifice, but was deliberating how all the well-benched ships would be lost together with my dear companions" (9.553–54), there is no genuine contradiction. After all, it is to be expected that Odysseus would sacrifice to Zeus after his success; and Odysseus, who knows that Zeus later destroyed his ship and killed his friends, was naturally reminded of the catastrophe when he mentioned his sacrifice.[30]

Mention of Zeus at the end of the *Cyclopeia* introduces an important parallel with the Thrinakian episode; yet the reference is not an accident of parallel structure. Odysseus makes the unjustified but psychologically valid accusation of a human narrator laboring under human limitations

[28] On *Od.* 12.389–90 see Erbse (1972) 12–16. Odysseus tells us nothing of the divine assembly that presumably instigated Hermes' assistance in the Circe episode. This can be viewed as another case in which Homer sought to preserve the narrative illusion.

[29] Clay (1983) 24–25. One would like to know whether Calypso also told Odysseus that Zeus had saved him from Scylla. According to Jørgensen's law (again, see below, Appendix 1), 12.445–46 should be translated with "she didn't see me, *thank god.*" This scene, which follows immediately upon the description of Zeus's punishment of the crew, could, however, indicate his desire to prevent Odysseus from paying for the crimes of the crew. The question of the extent of Odysseus's knowledge is also interesting in light of another phenomenon: all references to *theos* in the *Apologoi* occur in the scenes before the *Nekyia* and, excepting Odysseus' taunt of Polyphemos (9.479), all mention of *theoi* occurs afterwards in context of the events explained to him by Calypso (note the parallel between 10.31 and 12.338 where, in the first instance, sleep is said to have "come upon Odysseus" and in the second to have been "sent upon him by the gods").

[30] Jørgensen, 367. See also Bergren (1983) 49–50, whose narratological study of Odysean temporality leads her to reach similar conclusions, and Segal (1994) 212–14. I do not follow the interpretation of Vidal-Naquet, 20, that Zeus rejects the sacrifice because "the sheep belong to Polyphemos, animals not reared by man."

to explain his fate. His words may not be used to argue that the Zeus of the *Apologoi* reflects a more primitive stage in the evolution of Greek religious thought than the Zeus of the divine assembly.[31]

Zeus and Poseidon: The Uses of Parallelism

Fenik also calls attention to the similarity between the punishments inflicted by Zeus and Poseidon in the scenes following Thrinakie.[32] Helios complains bitterly to Zeus against the predations of the crew on his herd of cattle, and Poseidon complains to Zeus that he will cease to be honored if his own grandchildren, the Phaiakes, are allowed to transport Odysseus to Ithaca with impunity. In the former case, Zeus himself destroys the crew, in the latter he authorizes the destruction of Odysseus' ersatz crew of Phaiakes. The parallels between these scenes are the more striking for the fact that they are separated by a mere two hundred verses.

Fenik sees in Poseidon's behavior evidence of an outlook that may fairly be called more primitive than that of the other gods in the first divine assembly.[33] He then uses similarities in the reported attitudes of Zeus and Poseidon in the enchanted realm to argue that the behavior of Zeus in the *Apologoi* belongs to a relatively earlier stage in the development of Greek religious thought.[34] Fenik thus assumes that such parallels point to an affinity of character, and that primitive gods belong to primitive cosmologies. Both assumptions are determined by his reading of the *Apologoi*.

The scenes in which Zeus and Poseidon destroy Odysseus' respective crews are separated by the voyage of Odysseus to Ithaca and an assembly scene between the two gods (13.125–58).[35] This is the only occasion on which we see Poseidon and Zeus together in the *Odyssey:* just as Poseidon's hatred toward Odysseus is reflected in the god's absence from the first divine assembly, his presence on Olympos in Book 13 mirrors the fact that Odysseus is now safely home on Ithaca. Comparison of the gods' deportment within the assembly provides a further indica-

[31] Indeed, if we attribute the authority of the Homeric narrator to both 9.479–80 and 9.553–54 then the Analyst's knife cannot be far away, and as soon as we concede that 479–80 represents Odysseus' subjective speech, it would be perverse not to say the same of 553–54.

[32] *Od.* 12.374–419, 13.125–87; see Fenik (1974) 208–30.

[33] Fenik (1974) 211.

[34] Fenik (1974) 222–23.

[35] On the contrast between the gods in this scene see also Segal (1994) 217–18.

tion of how we are to understand the parallels established by the scenes of punishment.

In the assembly, Poseidon complains of the escort which the Phaiakes had provided to Odysseus. Zeus replies that Poseidon is free to punish anyone who in yielding to *biē* fails to honor him, thus according his brother complete autonomy to deal with the Phaiakes as he chooses (13.143–45). When, however, Poseidon indicates his intention to smash the Phaiakian ship, Zeus suggests that he transform the ship to stone instead.[36] The ship of the Phaiakes represents their excellence at seamanship and hence their hubris; they ignore the prophecy of Nausithoos that Poseidon would one day punish them for offering safe conveyance to all (8.564–66, 13.172–83). The ship becomes at Zeus's suggestion a monument that will serve as an eternal admonition, not only for the Phaiakes, but "so that all men will marvel at it" (13.157–58). While Poseidon's thinking does not extend beyond an immediate act of retribution for an affront to his prerogatives, Zeus demonstrates the same concern to caution mortals against transgression that he demonstrated in the first divine assembly. The admonition itself acquires something of the permanence and immutability of the laws it is made to represent.

Had Poseidon been made the author of the storm that destroyed Odysseus' ship in Book 12, the destruction of the crew would have to be seen as an act of vengeance aimed at Odysseus. With Helios as the offended party, it is at least possible to represent their demise as just, so that it properly illustrates the theodicy of the divine assembly. Those who interpret the crew's demise in the manner urged by the proem have a ready explanation for why Helios rather than Poseidon is responsible for it. The same considerations that made Zeus the agent

[36] My interpretation predisposes me to accept the reading of Aristophanes at 13.158, so that Zeus continues with *mēde sphin oros amphikalupsai,* "but don't cover the city with a mountain" (the verse could also be interpolated from 13.152, although Aristophanes' reading proves its antiquity). Zeus thus mitigates a punishment which he finds excessive. The transformation of the Phaiakian ship to stone makes a bow to their Giant ancestry, as does Poseidon's proposal to encircle them with a mountain. Aristophanes' reading, which is accepted by Stanford and by Ameis and Hentze, but rejected by Allen and by van Thiel, has found a recent champion in Friedrich; for the contrary view, see Erbse (1972) 145–48; Peradotto, 78–80. In favor of *mēde* it should be observed that Homer mentions the departure of Poseidon from Scherie with the city still unharmed, although its enclosure by a mountain would surely require his presence. And are we to imagine the god taking pleasure in the expiatory hecatombs offered by the Phaiakes before he destroys them? Hera's maliciousness in the *Iliad* would pale by comparison. More important, Poseidon's essential aim has been achieved with his transformation of the ship: the Phaiakes cease to offer escort to mortals. What is more, he achieves his aim—thanks to Zeus—with a minimum of human suffering, thus returning us to the themes of the first divine assembly.

of punishment led to the selection of a god uninvolved in the issue of Odysseus' return to demand that punishment. Yet Homer paid a price for his choice of offended parties, since Poseidon is no longer overtly responsible for the continued sufferings of Odysseus. This would suggest that the theme of Helios' wrath was created to bring the destruction of the crew into harmony with that of the suitors. Poseidon's transformation of the Phaiakian ship to stone two hundred verses later does, however, present us with a scene in which the god punishes Odysseus' crew, albeit a different one.

Heubeck, Schadewaldt, and Fenik—to name but a few of the modern scholars to study this issue—have shown that parallelism is one of the most pervasive and important structural features of epic narrative.[37] It is first and foremost a tool of emphasis, one regularly employed to expose themes that might otherwise remain latent. The device is elegant and economical in that it provides tacit commentary on two or more events at once. There is, however, nothing intrinsic to structural parallelism which restricts its use to that of equating situations and characters; and in Homer, at least, it is often used to establish contrasts.[38] Whether the relationships so created are meant to equate, to contrast, or to do both must be determined from the context.

If the narrative architecture of the *Apologoi* points to an underlying similarity in the character of Poseidon and Zeus, then three interpretations seem possible: 1) Homer sought to emphasize the fact that the Zeus of the *Apologoi* and the Zeus of the divine assembly reflect widely divergent cosmologies; 2) our poet has appropriated these structures from an earlier version of the poem and has failed to neutralize or adapt them to his own thematic program; 3) Poseidon's actions are indeed consonant with those of the other Olympian gods.

As to the first alternative, what competent poet would select the most inappropriate story from his repertoire to illustrate his themes in the proem? Why should he then employ the resources at his disposal to draw attention to such discrepancies in the *Apologoi?* The second alternative seems hardly more plausible when one relates the passages under discussion to the larger context of the *Odyssey*. The prologue balances the fate of Odysseus, whose continued suffering elicits divine pity, with that of the crew, who die by their own reckless acts. The divine assembly is framed by the contrasting attitudes of Poseidon and the other

[37] Heubeck (1954); Schadewaldt (1966); Fenik (1968, 1974, 1986).

[38] In his most recent treatment of Iliadic battle scenes, Fenik (1986) chap. 1 to 3, himself concedes that parallels may also be used to contrast characters. See E. Cook (1990).

Olympian gods to Odysseus' suffering. Within the *Apologoi,* the positions of Thrinakie and the *Cyclopeia* in the sequence of adventures reproduce the contrast between Odysseus and the crew that informs the prologue. Both episodes conclude, moreover, with mention of Zeus and Poseidon. The organizing structures of the prologue and of the *Apologoi* are thus the work of the same poet, since the prologue relates the same characters as does the *Apologoi,* refers to the very scenes from the *Apologoi* in which they are related, and employs identical narrative devices to establish those relationships. If, as I have argued, the opposed attitudes of Poseidon and Zeus in the divine assembly point to a basic difference in their outlook, then these parallel scenes from the *Apologoi* echo, and thereby reinforce, that contrast.

Poseidon's behavior throughout the poem remains consistent with his portrayal in Book 1. Every time the god appears in the *Odyssey* he is angry and vengeful. When Poseidon's anger is aimed at Odysseus, his actions are motivated by ties of paternity. In his deliberations with Zeus in Book 13, Poseidon himself raises the issue of kinship, just as Polyphemos had done in the *Cyclopeia.* An ethical contrast between Poseidon and the other gods is rendered explicit at the end of the *Cyclopeia,* when Polyphemos prays to his father for vengeance and Poseidon hears his prayer. This follows closely upon Odysseus' own claim that Zeus and the other gods had punished the Cyclops for his outrages against *xenia.*[39] The Phaiakes, on the other hand, are made to pay dearly for offering hospitality to Odysseus. Thus, in avenging his son and in punishing the Phaiakes, Poseidon twice excludes himself from the institution of *xenia,* which is seen in the *Odyssey* to be a tag, even the tag, for the *themistes* authenticated by Olympian rule. Poseidon's twin acts of vengeance could not be more different from Zeus's punishment of the crew. The structure of the narrative calls attention to that difference.

Although Zeus acts to alleviate the sufferings of Odysseus in the first divine assembly, he destroys Odysseus' crew in the Thrinakian episode. His actions in Book 1 and in the *Apologoi* are then dissimilar, even opposed. In the assembly, however, the justice of the gods also includes their willingness to punish those who knowingly do wrong. If we are to see the destruction of the crew as punishment for a crime that they had been warned against committing, then Zeus's actions illustrate the complementary aspects of the theodicy that he himself announces in the divine assembly. The illustration is provided, moreover, by the con-

[39] It bears observing that the contrast holds regardless of the truth value of Odysseus' claim.

trasting fates of Odysseus and the crew, the same contrast that informs the proem.

The Thrinakian episode, then, maintains and further develops the themes of the Introduction. The actions and punishment of the crew affirm their portrayal in the proem and illustrate the theodicy of the first divine assembly. Thrinakie belongs to a family of Greek myths which may be called aetiological in that they describe the origin of sacrificial ritual. Such myths, though not intrinsically concerned with justice, regularly portray the first sacrifice as a criminal act. The poem constructs additional guilt for the crew by making them pervert the sacrificial ritual. Still more important, it reveals the full significance of the structural parallels that link Thrinakie to the *Cyclopeia* and *Mnesterophonia*. On the other hand, nothing suggests that structural parallelism equates the actions of Poseidon and Zeus at the end of the Thrinakian episode. The larger context of the *Apologoi* and of the *Odyssey* as a whole indicates instead that their actions are thereby contrasted. In the protracted sufferings of Odysseus we see the vengeance of Poseidon motivated by ties of family, while the destruction of the crew illustrates the justice of Zeus. The *Odyssey* is indeed driven coherently by theme, the theme of *mētis* versus *biē* in its ethical, religious, and cultural permutations. When, as often, we find ourselves at a loss to account for this or that feature of the text, it is better as a rule to explain that loss with our own ignorance of the world, mentality, and traditions that produced the *Odyssey* than with theories of compositional strata or the poet's incompetence. It is an irony of modern Homeric scholarship that the very passages which most clearly bear the stamp of the theodicy announced in the divine assembly are the ones most often singled out as belonging to more primitive strata of the *Apologoi*.

CHAPTER 5

Homer and Athens

"In no part of actual Greek religion was there any connexion between Pallas and Poseidon that points to an original affinity of character."[1] Farnell is unquestionably right: Athene never was, nor could she be, in any sense equated with Poseidon. Yet Poseidon is associated with Athene in Greek religious thought more often than with any other god. The literary and archaeological record finds them paired at Argos, Athens, Corinth, Olympia, Sparta, and Trozen.[2] On every occasion, Poseidon and Athene reify the Greek polarization of nature and culture, thus confirming our interpretation of their opposed outlooks in the *Odyssey*.[3] Athene reigns within the city gates, Poseidon without them; Poseidon embodies the power of nature, Athene the ingenuity which renders that power useful or protects us from it.

Each of the traditions surveyed is comparatively late; the earliest may be dated to the period that saw the rise of the Greek *polis,* the same period in which the *Odyssey* achieved its present form. On three occasions, Poseidon is the father and Athene the patroness of culture heroes who hailed from cities on or near the Saronic Gulf: Erechtheus, the au-

[1] *CGS* 1:270.

[2] For the spelling of Trozen, not Troizen, see Barrett (1966) at verse 12.

[3] Myths and cults not treated in this survey include the temples built by Kadmos to Athene and Poseidon at Thera (Theophrastos in the scholia to Pindar, *P.* 4.11; compare Diodorus Siculus 5.58), discussed by Wide, 36 ff. Livy 22.10.9 mentions a *lectisternium* of 217 B.C.E. at Rome in which Minerva and Neptune shared the same couch (see Weissenborn ad loc.). *CGS* 1:265–70 treats the cult of Athene Tritogeneia, in which the goddess was worshipped as daughter to Poseidon.

tochthonous king of Athens, Theseus, another Athenian king though born at Trozen, and the Corinthian Bellerophon, who figured in the myths of Athens and Trozen as well.[4]

Although the survey shows that the Odyssean roles of Athene and Poseidon are well precedented in Greek religious thought, my ultimate aim is somewhat more ambitious. It appears that the cult of Athene in the Erechtheum has exerted a formative influence on the *Odyssey*, in particular the Ithacan narrative. Our point of departure, then, will be the contest between Athene and Poseidon for the patronage of Attica. From there we shall turn to the legendary war between Erechtheus and Eumolpos, together with its ritual analogue, a festival known as the Skira. Correlation of the Attic material with the *Odyssey* will center on three areas: the relationship between Ithacan society and Attic year-end festivals, in particular the Skira, Bouphonia, and Panathenaia, the similar fates of Odysseus and Erechtheus, including their patronage by Athene and antagonism with Poseidon, and the presence of an olive tree and a lamp belonging to Athene in the homes of both rulers.[5]

Athene and Poseidon in Their Ritual Context

The Contest Myth

The contest between Athene and Poseidon for Attica is a multiform of a broadly attested myth in which Poseidon disputes the patronage of various territories with another god. These include reports of his defeat in a contest with Dionysos for Naxos, Zeus for Aigina, and Hera for Argos, and of compromises reached with Athene at Trozen and with Helios at Corinth.[6] The basic story pattern may be schematized as follows:

[4] Bellerophon's presence at Athens and Trozen is not insignificant, since his sphere of activity in myth is fairly restricted.

[5] I complete my survey of the myths and cults in which Poseidon and Athene are paired in Appendix 2.

[6] Athens: Herodotus 8.55; Apollodorus 3.14.1; Pausanias 1.24.5. Naxos: Plutarch 741a. Aiginia: Plutarch 7412; scholia to Pindar *I.* 8.92 (= Orphic *Fragment* 335 Kern, the authenticity of which is questioned by M. West [1983] 28, 268). Argos: Pausanias 2.15.5, 2.20.6, 2.22.4. Trozen: Pausanias 2.30.6. Corinth: Pausanias 2.1.6; Dio Chrysostomus 37.11; Lucian *Salt.* 42.293. Acrocorinth (ceded by Helios to Aphrodite): Pausanias 2.4.6.

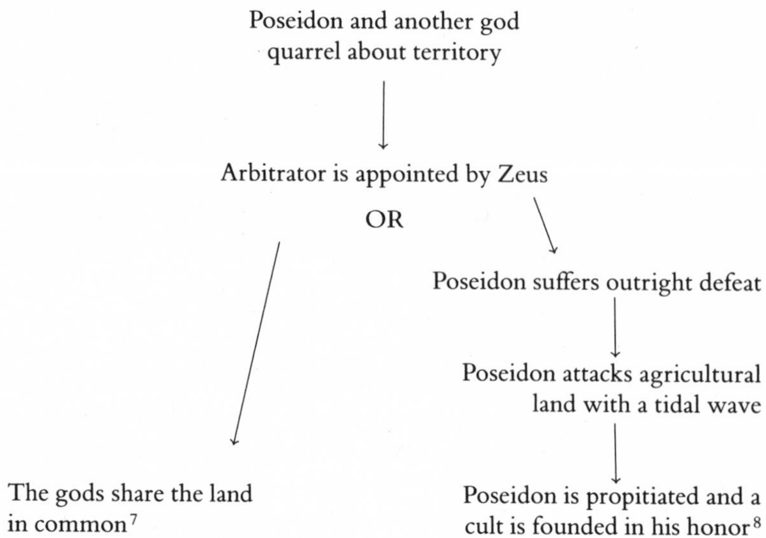

Of the disputes with Dionysos, Helios, and Zeus nothing further is known. The story of Poseidon's contest with Hera for Argos shares with the Athenian version the motifs of his defeat, revenge, and ultimate reconciliation, so that we may suppose the dependence of one account upon the other, or that both derive from a common source. Influence between the cults of Argos and Attica, however, seems to be anything but strong, and given the possibility that Hera and Athene developed out of an earlier divinity common to the indigenous cultures of Greece, the myth could predate their differentiation into separate deities.[9] In this case the basic pattern would be quite old indeed. On the other hand, a

[7] Briareos acts as judge at Corinth and Zeus at Trozen. Athenian accounts varied between Kekrops and all the gods: Apollodorus 3.14.1; Xenophon, *Mem.* 3.5.10; Callimachus, *fr.* 194.66–68, 260.25–26. Frazer at Apollodorus 3.14.1 discusses a later variant in which the Athenian citizens acted as jury, with which compare Aristides 1.41–42. Poseidon's exchange of Delphi for Tainaron with Apollo and of Delos for Kalaureia with Leto (Pausanias 10.24.4, 2.33.2; Strabo 8.6.14 [374]) may belong to this pattern.

[8] Cults to Poseidon were founded at Athens and Argos; in Argos he was said to have both flooded the land and caused a drought. Simonides, *fr.* 552 Page, reports that Hephaistos competed with Demeter for Sicily, and that Aetna was appointed judge of the dispute. Nothing is known of the outcome, but on analogy to the contests involving Poseidon, Hephaistos, who would seem to represent volcanic force, lost to Demeter. Be that as it may, an opposition between (agri)culture and destructive natural force is once more in evidence.

[9] See *MMR* 490–503. *GG* 179. Nilsson refers to an earlier Mycenaean palace goddess. He may well be right, although I distance myself from his conflation of the Minoan and Mycenaean material.

number of related accounts at Trozen—although they refract the contest into discrete elements—are clearly dependent on the Athenian version of the myth and should be so treated (see Appendix 2).

The Athenian contest is unique in that the gods base their claims to the land on *sēmata,* or 'tokens'. Each of our sources records that Poseidon made a "wave" of the sea appear atop the Acropolis, and that Athene created the first cultured olive. Both gifts could be found in the precinct of the Erechtheum, and the role of these tokens in the myth was recalled by a free-standing sculptural group on the Acropolis and by the west pediment of the Parthenon.[10]

The domestic olive is an obvious and frequently exploited symbol of culture. Most importantly, it is an agricultural product, and the Greeks of all periods held that civilized existence began with the development of the agricultural arts.[11] Olive oil provided fuel for torches and lamps, and was used as soap and in the preparation of food. As a ready source of calories olives were, together with bread, cheese, and wine, the most important item of the Greek diet. In fact, "without its oil the deficiency of fats would have kept the human population down to a fraction of the size it reached," so that the Athenian *polis* was in a direct sense predicated upon the cultivation of the olive.[12] Preserved olives and olive oil are practically imperishable, making them relatively easy to convey over large distances, and since Attic olives were known in antiquity as

[10] Athene as creator of the olive: Euripides, *Ion* 1433ff.; further references in *RE* 17:2.2015. The Attic origin of the olive: Herodotus 5.82. The location of the tree: Apollodorus 3.14.1; Philochorus, *FGrH* 328F67. Herodotus 8.55 likely refers to the precinct, although it must be remembered that the temple complex was rebuilt after the Persian wars. See the discussions in Paton, 125, 436, 448, 474–75; Jeppesen. For the statue group on the Acropolis, see Pausanias 1.24.3–7, who attests to salt waves at two other Poseidon temples (1.26.5, 8.10.2–4). The pedimental fragments are published in Brommer (1963); for interpretation of the central figures see *GG* 210–12; Binder. Harrison, 9, identifies U as a daughter of Erechtheus, U* as Praxithea, V as Eumolpos, and W as Chione, thus suggesting an association of the contest with the "Erechtheus myth" (on which see below).

[11] This theme is already a feature of Hesiod's *Works and Days* and the *Cyclopeia.* Classical authors include: Plato, *Mx.* 237–38, and Isocrates 4.28–29. Discussion in *GGR* 665–66. Pliny, *HN* 7.199, makes Eumolpos the inventor of arboriculture and viniculture, although Dionysos was elsewhere said to have taught Ikarios to cultivate the vine. Euripides, *Cyc.* 39, apparently alludes to a satyr play in which Dionysos gave wine to Oineus (see Seaford ad loc.). Plutarch, 402a, has the daughters of Anios divide the world of agriculture into cereal grain, wine, and olives.

[12] French, 5. Amouretti, 183, 195, estimates the average annual per capita consumption of olive oil for food at 20 liters, and the requirements of a middle-class family of four living in the city with three slaves at perhaps 200 liters per annum. Greek reliance on plant fat is correlated with climate by French, 1, 5. Herodotus 4.2 shows that the production and use of butter was a defining characteristic of "barbarians."

among the best of Greece, they came to play a role in the export economy of Athens.[13] Yet in order to realize any of these benefits, it was necessary to domesticate the olive. The cultured olive can thus stand for the technological achievements that make civilization possible. As Erika Simon remarks, it is typical of Greek religious thought to portray all such inventions as gifts of Athene.[14]

Athene's gift also served to guarantee the continued prosperity of the city. As such, it received the cult-title of *Morios,* or 'Tree of Fate'.[15] This is a role for which the olive is naturally suited: first, the tree is evergreen, a characteristic that receives frequent mention in classical authors.[16] It is also extremely long-lived: the *Morios* of Athens was said to be the first domestic olive in existence. In the fifth century B.C.E. it could thus pass for a tree created before the Trojan war. The shoot that sprouted from its stump after the *Morios* was burned during the Persian occupation survived into the second century C.E.[17] Finally, cultivation of trees requiring a generation to reach production assumes a state able to withstand external, and internal, threat. It is thus uniquely suited to represent peace and social concord. The archaic statue, or *xoanon,* of Athene Polias, another sacred object from the Erechtheum on which the welfare of Athens depended, was also made of olive wood. In the Erechtheum, olive oil fed Athene's lamp, which symbolized the continued well-being of the state.[18]

[13] Zimmern, 417; Jeffery, 85. French, 123, declares that the quality of Attic olives was not exceptional by Aegean standards, on what authority I do not know. Finley (1985) 133, rightly cautions that the significance of the olive in export trade should not be exaggerated, although he makes no allowance for variations in quality between growing regions or for colonies in places where the olive did not or could not grow.

[14] *GG* 180. In the Archaic period Athene is attested as patroness of agricultural technology; Hesiod, *Works and Days* 430. Cottage industry; *Od.* 7.109–11, 20.72; *h. Ven.* 14–15 (see also *Il.* 8.386, 14.178–79). Carpentry; *Il.* 15.410–12; *Od.* 8.492–93 with Kullmann (1960) 340. Inventor of the chariot; *h. Ven.* 12–13 (compare Cicero, *N.D.* 3.59; Pausanias 8.21.4; Callimachus, *Dian.* 234). Athene's cult-title Telchinia (Pausanias 9.19.1) is of some interest in this connection.

[15] See in particular Sophocles, *OC* 699, discussed below; compare the Herodotean account of the tree's regeneration after it was razed by the Persians (8.55). See also Hdt. 5. 82–88. A. Cook, 3:760–64, treats the cult-title. Pease, *RE* 17:2.2016, s.v. Ölbaum, observes that the word for 'olive' and 'lot/portion' in Phoenician and related languages is the same.

[16] See Detienne (1970) 7; *RE* 17:2.1998 with classical references.

[17] Pausanias 1.27.2, 8.23.5; Pliny, *HN* 16.240; Hyginus, *Fab.* 164. A parallel for the tree's miraculous regeneration is provided by the *ficus ruminalis* at Rome, for which see Tacitus, *Ann.* 13.58.

[18] For the lamp see Pausanias 1.26.6–7; Strabo 9.1.16 (396). For its location see Palagia. Apollodorus 3.14.6 states that the *xoanon* was set up by Erichthonios. The image was

Poseidon's gift to Athens was a natural element—his element. Upon suffering defeat, Poseidon threatened to use his gift to destroy its ungrateful recipients. In the oldest extant account of the contest, Poseidon inundated the Thriasian plain in the territory of Eleusis, one of the richest agricultural districts of Attica.[19] Nearby was Skiron, the site of a legendary war between Athens and Eleusis instigated by Poseidon after his loss in the contest. Skiron is characterized by local outcroppings of chalk rock, or *skirra gē,* said by Theophrastus to be the ideal soil in which to grow olives.[20] The ambivalent character of the god is reflected in the structure of the myth and in the nature of his gift.

Poseidon, as embodied natural *biē,* is by definition the original occupant of the lands from which he is displaced. Thus, Isocrates and Apollodorus report that Poseidon staked his claim to Attica first, but that Athene won the contest with the devices of *mētis,* specifically by bribing Kekrops, the first ruler of the territory.[21] Kekrops' choice is that of humankind to live together as a social unit. The contest myth dramatizes the evolutionary process that culminated in the *polis* as an instantaneous event and conscious choice. To become civilized implies Poseidon's defeat, though the Greeks felt that a reconciliation was ultimately necessary.

Olive trees, at once a product of nature and of technology, are well suited to represent that reconciliation. Theophrastus states, moreover, that the olive will not grow further than three hundred stades from the sea. This he attributes to the salubrious effect of salt on the tree. Elsewhere, he suggests that the olive oil of the Thebaid, though good, is less pleasant in smell than the Attic product, because of an insufficiency of salt in the soil.[22] The enclosure of the Erechtheum gives formal expression to the relationship that exists between the olive and salt: the *Morios* of Athens cannot thrive without the wave of the sea. Poseidon's very

---

said to be the Palladion taken by the Greeks from Troy, on which see Frazer at Pausanias 1.28.8; *GR* 140; Burkert (1970).

[19] Herodotus 8.55. See also Apollodorus 3.14.1; Augustine, *C.D.* 18.9; Hyginus, *Fab.* 164.

[20] Theophrastus, *CP* 2.4.4, 3.5.5. Connected to the cult of Athene Skira by Roscher, 1:683; Deubner, 46; Dietrich, 9. Compare Photius, *Lexicon* s.v. Σκίρος.

[21] Apollodorus 3.14.1; Isocrates 12.193. See also *RE* 17:2.2016. Scholars such as Farnell, *CGS* 1:270–73, have treated this as a historical record of the gradual displacement of Poseidon's cult by those of other gods.

[22] Theophrastus, *HP* 6.2.4, 4.2.9. See also Theophrastus, *HP* 4.4.1; Pliny, *HN* 15.1, 21.57; Columella, *de re rustica* 5.8. Elsewhere, at *CP* 2.5.3–4, Theophrastus states that salt sweetens bitter plants such as cabbages. Perhaps such thinking lies behind his assertion regarding the olive.

act of "revenge" ensured an abundant supply of sweet-smelling olive oil in Attica.

The opposition between Athene and Poseidon at Athens is complex: the rise of culture is a triumph over nature, and nature, jealous at any encroachment upon its domain, remains an ever-present threat. Yet civilization depends on nature for its well-being, indeed for its very survival. Myth represents this symbiotic relationship with a contest in which the instrument of victory symbolizes the well-being of the state and depends on the gift of the vanquished. On the level of cult, this symbiosis is achieved with the incorporation of Poseidon into the heart of the *polis*. It is embodied in the person of Poseidon-Erechtheus.

War with Eleusis as Sequel to the Contest

A number of related myths clustered around the Athenian contest, each of which restates the theme of Poseidon's defeat in his bid for the land of Attica. The most important of these is the legendary invasion of Attica by Eumolpos, which I shall call the Erechtheus myth after the Athenian king who defended the city.[23] Together, the stories of the contest and the war with Eleusis yield a continuous narrative culminating in the reconciliation of Poseidon with Athene and her *polis,* and in the creation of four Attic cults sanctified by the deaths of their founders: Erechtheus and his daughters, Eumolpos, and Skiros. At the same time, the Erechtheus myth does not simply continue, but reenacts the contest on the human level as a war in which the survival of the state is threatened by the progeny of Poseidon and defended by the protégé of Athene.

The *Erechtheus* of Euripides provides the earliest comprehensive treatment of the war in antiquity, and in its essential details appears to follow the *hieroi logoi* (sacred accounts) promulgated by the associated cults of

[23] For Erechtheus see Kron, 32–83; Mikalson. Herodotus 1.30 mentions a battle between Athens and Eleusis although he does not name the Eleusinian leader. Only Thucydides 2.15.1 and perhaps the scholia to Euripides, *Ph.* 854, make Eumolpos the leader of an Eleusinian army, although this is clearly the earliest version of the story. In later authors he became a Thracian so that the story could serve as a foil for the Persian invasion, just as Poseidon's earthquake at the end of Euripides' *Erechtheus* would have reminded the audience of the Persian destruction of the Acropolis. Eumolpos is a Thracian leader in Euripides, *Erechtheus Fragment* 50.48 (see also *Erech. Fr.* 57, 65). Oxyrhynchus Papyri 6.853, a scholia to Thucydides 2.15.1 (= *Erech. Fr.* 63), does not prove that Euripides mentioned Eleusinian forces, as is sometimes claimed. Eumolpos is also a Thracian in Lycurgus, *contra Leocratem* 98; Isocrates 12.193; Lucian, *Anach.* 34; Strabo 8.7.1 (383), who says that he was defeated by Ion; and possibly the scholia to Euripides, *Ph.* 854.

the Acropolis.[24] The play opens with war between Athens and Eleusis imminent: Eumolpos has arrived at Eleusis with an army of Thracians in order to avenge the defeat of his father, Poseidon, in the contest. Erechtheus, who had gone to consult the Delphic oracle concerning the war, returns to deliver a prologue describing the enemy general and the cause of the dispute.[25] He then repeats the oracular response to his wife, Praxithea, who arrives to greet him: victory will belong to Athens if they offer Chthonia, one of their three daughters, in sacrifice.[26] Surprisingly, Praxithea indicates her willingness to permit the sacrifice in an impassioned speech that continued to inspire patriotism in male audiences and readers throughout ancient times:[27]

ὦ πατρίς, εἴθε πάντες οἳ ναίουσί σε
οὕτω φιλοῖεν ὡς ἐγώ· καὶ ῥαιδίως
οἰκοῖμεν ἄν σε κοὐδὲν ἂν πάσχοις κακόν

(*Erechtheus Fragment* 50.53–55)

Dear land of our fathers, would that all who inhabit you
love you thus, as I do: we would dwell
within you free from care, and you would suffer no wrong.

Thus encouraged, Erechtheus overcomes his initial hesitation and permits the sacrifice of his daughter on behalf of Athens.

Ion, the adoptive son of Erechtheus, who is without male issue, now makes an appearance in order to rouse his father to battle.[28] The king re-

24 The fragments of Euripides' *Erechtheus* with select ancient testimonia and commentary are gathered in C. Austin (1967, 1968). For a reconstruction of the play see Looy. See also Carrara; Sissa and Detienne, 238–45.

25 *Erech. Fr.* 39, *Αἰθιοπίαν νιν ἐξέσωσ' ἐπὶ χθόνα* (I brought him safely to the land of Aithiopia), refers to a story known only from Apollodorus 3.15.4, whose account is used to reconstruct the prologue. Apollodorus and Lycurgus, *contra Leocratem* 98, who quotes the speech of Praxithea, report that Erechtheus consulted the oracle, and the *σέ* of *Erech.* 50.36 indicates that Praxithea's speech is directed to her husband. This version is followed by Plutarch, 310d, who adds that Praxithea learned of the oracle's contents from her husband. See also Demaratus, *FGrH* 42F4; Aristides, 1.87.

26 For the number of daughters, see *Erech. Fr.* 47, 50.36–37; scholia to Aratus 172. Looy, 120, suggests that before speaking to his wife Erechtheus encounters an ambassador from the Thracian forces who had come to announce the enemy's demands.

27 For this reason her speech was recorded in its entirety by Lycurgus; see also Plutarch, 604d. Her speech evokes the *epitaphios* formula of an *encomium* of Athens followed by a protreptic address to the survivors. Praxithea's daughter thus becomes the fallen soldier to whom she is directly compared in the speech. For the *epitaphios* formula in Athenian oratory see Loraux.

28 For Ion as adoptive son, see Wilamowitz (1926) 6; C. Austin (1968) 28. Owen, xv, followed by Webster, 130, and Van Looy, 122, argues that Xouthos is meant. For Erech-

sponds to the young man's appeals with approval and the offer of some paternal advice before departing for war. The scene between father and son is balanced by the appearance of Praxithea with the daughter to be sacrificed on behalf of Athens. Erechtheus departs in company with his wife to sacrifice their daughter, and from there he sets out to fight in a war in which he too will die in defense of the city.[29] His final words on stage contain an appeal to his wife and followers to pray to Athene for help.[30]

As the chorus of old men sings about their weariness of war, Erechtheus leads his forces to victory.[31] Erechtheus kills Eumolpos, but as he is erecting a trophy Poseidon slams him into the earth with his trident in revenge.[32] Meanwhile, Erechtheus' other daughters take their own lives at the Hyakinthian spring in accordance with a former pact. Praxithea returns from the sacrifice of Chthonia to learn of their suicide, whereupon a messenger arrives to announce that the Athenians have conquered, but that her husband has perished. She who willingly offered her own daughter on behalf of Athens discovers that the city's defense has claimed every member of her family. Praxithea and the chorus join in lamentation, but are interrupted by an earthquake that destroys the palace.

Athene answers the prayers offered by Erechtheus as he set out for battle. The goddess appears to Praxithea *ex machina:* a struggle that began as a contest between Athene and Poseidon returns to the divine sphere for its final resolution. At the sound of Athene's voice, the earth ceases to tremble, order is restored. Imperiously, she commands her uncle to desist:

---

theus without male issue, see *Erech. Fr.* 50.22–23 (also in the *Ion*). Hesiod, *fr.* 10a.20–23 M-W, makes Ion the son of Xouthos by Kreousa, daughter to Erechtheus. The Hesiodic genealogy is followed by Strabo, 8.7.1 (383); Pausanias, 1.31.3, 2.14.2, 7.1.5; Harpocratio Grammaticus, s.v. *Βοηδρόμια*. They state that Eumolpos was defeated by Ion, who was rewarded for his success with the throne. Herodotus 8.44 also makes Ion general.

[29] Erechtheus sacrifices the daughter himself in Lycurgus, Demaratus, Apollodorus, and Plutarch 310d. Although it is possible to take their statements in a causal sense, I find the analogy to Agamemnon's sacrifice of Iphigenia, with its implicit contrast in the attitudes of Clytemnestra and Praxithea, to be irresistible. This analogy suggests that the daughter is a willing victim, like Iphigenia in the *Iphigenia at Aulis*.

[30] *Erech. Fr.* 41 is so treated by Webster, 129. The appearance of the god *ex machina* following such appeals is precedented in Euripides.

[31] For the chorus of old men, see *Erech. Fr.* 60, 65.6–10. For the possibility of a second chorus of women, see Calder (1969) 153.

[32] For Erechtheus killing Eumolpos, see Apollodorus 3.15.4–5 (compare the scholia to Euripides, *Ph.* 854). For Poseidon killing Erechtheus, see *Erech. Fr.* 65.60; see also Euripides, *Ion* 281–82. Hyginus, *Fab.* 46, says that Zeus killed him with a thunderbolt at Poseidon's request.

αὐδῶ τρίαιναν τῆδ' ἀποστρέφειν χθονός,
πόντιε Πόσειδον, μηδὲ γῆν ἀναστατοῦν
πόλιν τ' ἐρείπειν τὴν ἐμὴν ἐπήρατον.

(*Erechtheus Fragment* 65.55–57)

Turn back your trident from this land,
Poseidon, god of the sea, nor convulse the earth
and cast down my lovely city.

Athene announces the creation of two cults to reward those who gave their lives: the daughters of Erechtheus shall be known henceforth as the Hyakinthides.[33] They are to be honored annually with "sober sacrifice" and dances of maidens in a sacred enclosure from which the enemies of Athens must be excluded lest they gain victory by sacrificing there.[34] Erechtheus shall be known as "holy Poseidon," although his citizens will continue to call him Erechtheus when they offer bulls in sacrifice.[35] The revenge of Poseidon for the death of Eumolpos is once again ambiguous: the god punishes Erechtheus by hiding him in the earth, yet the effect of his actions is to provide Athens with guardian divinities. In the play of Euripides, Eumolpos must content himself with a lesser honor: a descendant and namesake will found the cult to Demeter at Eleusis.[36]

[33] The Hyakinthides were daughters of Hyakinthos, who is associated with Demeter and identified with Apollo at Sparta. See Wide, 285–93; Mikalson, 144–47; Calame (1977b) 1:305–23. One of the Hyakinthides was named Orthaia, which makes an obvious reference to the chthonic cult of Artemis Orthia at Sparta; see Calame (1977b) 1:276–97. Another was named Lousia, a cognomen of Demeter at Thelpousa (Pausanias 8.25.6). Demaratus, *FGrH* 42F4, indicates that the eldest of the daughters was sacrificed to Persephone, but Apollodorus 3.15.4 says that it was the youngest. Hyginus, *Fab.* 46, states that Neptune himself demanded the daughter's sacrifice *upon the death of his son,* but elsewhere, *Fab.* 238, follows Euripides in saying she died on account of the oracle. He identifies the girl as Chthonia, the youngest of Erechtheus' daughters. Pausanias 2.35.5 relates that hyacinths were offered in the cult of Demeter Chthonia at Hermion.

[34] Sober sacrifices were called *nēphalia,* with libations of honey, rather than wine, poured into springs, rather than over fire. The cult is chthonic.

[35] These sacrifices presumably occurred during the Panathenaia. From *Il.* 2.550–51 (see also Herodotus 5.82), we learn that Erechtheus was "propitiated" yearly with bulls and lambs. Lorimer, 442–49, and Kron, 32–37, argue that the Iliadic passage dates at least to the sixth century. Thus, the idea of propitiation may have some significance for dating the cult of Poseidon-Erechteus, since it suggests apotropaic worship. Note also that bulls were the preferred sacrifice of Poseidon.

[36] *Erech. Fr.* 65.100: Εὔμολπος γὰρ Εὐμόλπου γεγὼ[ς. For Thracian Eumolpos as mystery founder, see Plutarch 607b; Lucian, *Demon.* 34; Photius, s.v. Εὐμολπίδαι; Pausanias 1.38.3; scholia to Sophocles, *OC* 1053; perhaps the scholia to Euripides, *Ph.* 854. For the mystery founder as a later descendent, see Istros, *FGrH* 334F22; Andron, *FGrH* 10F13. For further discussions see Jacoby. (1980) 73; Simms. The hierophant always came from the *genos* of the Eumolpidai, for which see Garland, 82–83, 96–104, 115–16.

Corresponding to the identification of Erechtheus as Poseidon is the close association of his wife Praxithea with Athene. Like the goddess herself in Aeschylus' *Eumenides,* Praxithea must choose between the competing demands of family and state. Like Athene she privileges those of the state. While Athene bases her decision on the fact that "no woman bore her," Praxithea denies her ties to family by offering her own daughter on behalf of Athens. Yet the demands of state are absolute. The death of Erechtheus and the sacrifice or suicide of her daughters leave Praxithea without the ability even to enter on such a choice: thus stripped of family, Praxithea comes to resemble Athene more closely still. In reward for allowing the sacrifice of her maiden daughter, Praxithea will serve as priestess to a virgin goddess, personification of the city over which her adoptive son, Ion, shall now rule. This arrangement mirrors Athene's own relationship with Erechtheus, whom the goddess received from the Earth and reared in the temple on the Acropolis as her foster son.[37]

In historical times the priesthood of Athene and of Poseidon-Erechtheus was supplied by the Eteoboutadai, who claimed descent from Boutes, or 'Neatherd,' the twin brother of Erechtheus and a co-inhabitant of the Erechtheum.[38] The reconciliation achieved between Athene and Poseidon is achieved with the physical union of their cults in the legendary home of the king, the cult of Poseidon-Erechtheus, and a priesthood descended from the brother of Erechtheus that served both gods. Corresponding to the mythological role of Erechtheus as the city's protector in a time of crisis, the Erechtheum housed cults and artifacts that guaranteed the security of the state: Poseidon-Erechtheus and the snake with which Erechtheus was identified; Athene Polias, her *xoanon,* lamp, and tree, and the cult of Pandrosos in whose precinct the tree was housed.

In the Erechtheus myth, the divine adversaries of the contest have been replaced by human counterparts, Eumolpos, the son of Poseidon, and Erechtheus, the foster son and protégé of Athene. The threat to civilization posed by the wave of Poseidon has been transformed into an army of invaders. Eumolpos suffers defeat in his bid for control of Athens as had his father before him, but it is with Erechtheus that Poseidon becomes identified in cult. Poseidon avenges the defeat of his son,

[37] *Il.* 2.547–48. The same was said of Erichthonios.

[38] Apollodorus 3.14.8–15.1 says that Boutes served as priest of both Athene and Poseidon-Erechtheus. For the *genos* of the Eteoboutadai see J. Davies 348–53, and on the priesthoods see Garland, 77–78, 106.

as he had his own loss in the contest myth, yet in both cases his vengeance ultimately benefits the city. The paradox of Erechtheus' personal defeat in triumph allows him to represent Poseidon as well. Erechtheus emerges from the earth to rule Athens; with a blow of his trident Poseidon hides him in a fissure of the earth. There he will continue to protect the city for all time. In like manner Poseidon staked his claim to Attica, yet the god's "burial" of Erechtheus reverses the act of calling forth a wave. Poseidon's revenge secures him a cult on the site of his earlier contest. His identity undergoes a corresponding reversal to that of city guardian.

Poseidon-Erechtheus embodies a polarity between destroyer and preserver common to all apotropaic cult. Myth has simply dissociated these aspects of the god into discrete personages in order to reunite them. Thus, Poseidon as Erechtheus also enjoyed the epithet Gaiaochos, or 'Earth-Mover'.[39] Yet Athenian cult has sharpened the beneficent aspect of the god into that of culture hero and king, something nowhere else attested in the worship of Poseidon.[40] The relationship between Athene and Poseidon in the cult of Poseidon-Erechtheus restates the outcome of the contest. The Athenians have attempted to neutralize the potential of the god for destruction through apotropaic cult, by identifying him with a culture-hero, and by twice subordinating him to Athene, first as defeated pretender for the possession of Attica, then as dependent king and foster son.[41]

[39] A. Cook, 3:11–12. Although it is a Homeric epithet, Gaiaochos is rare as a cult title.

[40] Trozen is a possible exception, for which see below, Appendix 2.

[41] Precedent for associating Athene's civic cult with the apotropaic cult of Poseidon comes from Sparta, where adjoining the *agora* was a temple to Zeus Agoraios and Ge, and another to Athene Agoraia and Poseidon Asphalios (Pausanias 3.11.9). The most prominent of the relief figures decorating the temple of Athene Poliouchos were those of Athene and Poseidon with Amphitrite (Pausanias 3.17.2–3; further references in Wide, 390). Inscriptional evidence from Amyklai (*IG* 5:1.559; see Wide, 368 ff., and *CGS* 1:399, note b) reveals that the cult of Poseidon Asphalios was the most important cult celebrated in the temple after that of Athene herself. The inscription is late, though the antiquity of the temple and the prominence of Poseidon on its reliefs suggest the presence of his cult, doubtless as Asphalios, from an early date. The Damonon inscription (*IG* 5:1.213; see A. Cook, 3.11, note 1, and Nilsson [1906] 90–91), found within the temple and dedicated to Athene, refers to a festival in honor of Poseidon Gaiaochos in which chariot races were featured. At Sparta as at Athens, Athene, *qua* civic goddess, is paired with Poseidon, whose cult is apotropaic, and both gods are served by the same priest in the temple of Athene, the chief temple of the city.

The Skira as Ritualized Myth

The ritual analogue to the war between Athens and Eleusis was the Skira, an Attic year-end festival.[42] Pausanias reports that as Eumolpos was preparing for war he was joined at Eleusis by a prophet named Skiros, who had founded a temple to Athene Skiras at Phaleron.[43] Like Eumolpos, Skiros was son to Poseidon (alternatively, his grandson), acted as coleader of the Eleusinian forces, and died in battle. In one rather late and suspect account, he is said to have been killed by Athene herself.[44] These accounts introduce a symmetry lacking in the Euripidean play: the Athenian king Erechtheus dies while defending the city and his cult is founded thereby on the Acropolis. The Eleusinian leader Skiros, who is also killed in battle, gives his name to the place where he fell and to the cult celebrated there. The cult of Poseidon-Erechtheus on the Acropolis is answered by that of Athene Skiras at Skiron.

The Skira began with a procession: the priestess of Athene Polias, the priest of Poseidon-Erechtheus, and in Hellenistic times at least the priest of Helios, withdrew from the Acropolis under a parasol carried by Eteoboutadai.[45] Their destination was the temple of Demeter at Skiron, where Demeter had once enriched the farmer Phytalos for his hospitality by creating the first fig tree.[46] At the temple sacrifices were

[42] *HN* 143–49; *GR* 230. See also Deubner, 40–50; Parke, 156–62; Calame (1990) 339–50.

[43] Skiros' activities point to the complementary relationship between the Skiraphoria and the Oschophoria with its processional led by transvestite Salaminian youths to the temple of Athene Skiras at Phaleron. Skiros was also said to have married Salamina, who bore Poseidon a son Kychreus after he carried her off to the island, where the cult of Athene Skiras was also celebrated. Like Megara, Salamis boasted an outcropping of chalk rock, and local tradition had it that the island used to be known as Skiras. See the discussions with references in *HN* 146, note 44; Calame (1990) 339–41. The Salaminian tradition suggests a cult explanation for the statement in Euripides, *Tr.* 799–808, that the olive first appeared on Salamis.

[44] For Skiros as son, see Apollodorus, *Epitome* 1.2; Aulus Gellius, *noctes atticae* 15.21 (Skiron as opponent of Theseus); Hesychius, Σκ[ε]ιρὰς Ἀθηνᾶ. For alternative traditions see *RE* 3:A 540–41; Brommer (1982) 14. For Skiros killed by Athene, see the scholia to Clemens Alexandrinus, *Protr.* 2.17.1 (Dindorf, 420); citation in Roscher, 4:1014.

[45] The priest of Helios has sometimes been seen as a late addition to the procession, although see Simon (1983) 23.

[46] It seems unlikely that there was a temple to Athene Skiras at Skiron. The scholia to Aristophanes, *Ec.* 18, could be taken as evidence that her cult was celebrated in the temple of Demeter which was known to exist there. The problem revolves around the possibility of a confusion with the attested temple of Athene Skiras at Phaleron and the fact that Pausanias in his discussion of the place makes no reference to a temple of Athene there. See Frazer at Pausanias 1.36.4; *CGS* 1:291, n.d. But see also Appendix 2. In *HN* 144–45, Burkert was of the opinion that there were temples to both Demeter and Athene Skiras at Skiron, a position which he has since changed in *GR* 230. Pausanias 1.37.2

offered. It is an attractive theory that women also threw piglets into underground chambers to be recovered during the Thesmophoria. The latter rite is connected with the rape of Persephone, whose disappearance from the earth resulted in the angry withdrawal of Demeter from Olympos and drought on earth.[47] Two days later, on the last full moon of the year, Eleusinian priests who traced their line to Kekrops or to Eumolpos occupied the deserted Acropolis, where they performed the Bouphonia at the altar to Zeus Polieus.[48] Priests of Demeter thus reenact an ancient crime in which a bull ceases to be an agricultural laborer as his own body becomes a source of nourishment.

The destinations of these processions correspond to the theaters of the war where the opposing generals had fallen: the tomb of Skiros was to be found adjacent to the temple to Demeter in Skiron, and that of Eumolpos—appropriately enough—at salt-water inlets somewhat nearer to the bay.[49] The grave of Eumolpos' son Ismaros/Immarados, who in some accounts led the Thracian army in place of his father, was located at the base of the north west face of the Acropolis, in a precinct dedicated to Demeter and known as the Eleusinion.[50] Nearby, Erechtheus was said to have been "hidden in the earth" by Poseidon.[51]

The Erechtheus myth describes a political crisis which takes the form of an external threat, an invasion that would displace an autochthonous Greek people with an army of usurpers.[52] The Skira reenacts this crisis at year-end, the seasonal correlate to the historical date of a war fought at the dawn of civilization. The destination of the procession is the ancient border between Athens and Eleusis. The religious analogue to foundation myth is the erection of temples on the border to the city.[53] Thus

---

mentions another temple to Demeter and Kore near the tomb of Themistokles in which Athene and Poseidon were worshipped.

47 Deubner 40. See Dietrich; Parke 158–59; Calame (1990) 342–43.

48 For the priesthood see Garland, 97–100.

49 Pausanias 1.36.4, 1.38. Note in this context that Praxithea was daughter to Cephissus.

50 Clemens Alexandrinus, *Protr.* 3.45.1. Pausanius 1.27.4 (see also 1.5.2, 1.38.3) insists that those familiar with antiquities knew that Immarados, not Eumolpos, was the leader of the war, although he also indicates that most people believed it to have been Eumolpos.

51 Euripides, *Ion* 281–83, with Owen's notes to verses 13 and 17; Grégoire and Parmentier, 160–61. The absence of a tomb implies Erechtheus' apotheosis. A. Cook, 2:794, argues that the hypaethral opening in the floor of the Erechtheum was the place at which Erechtheus sank, while Burkert, *HN* 148, argues from the Skira that his death occurred at Skiron.

52 The usurpers are barbarian in the play of Euripides and in some other authors, elsewhere Eleusinian.

53 See de Polignac, reviewed by Snodgrass (1986). See also Morgan, 6–16.

the cult of Athene is celebrated in a temple to Demeter at Skiron. The synchronic, diachronic, and topographic settings of the myth and ritual mark the location at which the city and its laws cease to exist. It is here that the crisis "takes place," and it is here that the *polis* reaffirms its prerogatives. As in the contest myth, and as on Ithaca, the Skira unites an agricultural and a political crisis at the cusp of change and renewal.

During the Skira, the crisis is not simply external. The absence of the king and goddess marks an interregnum in the political and religious life of the *polis,* during which the domestic order is also dissolved: when the king disappears together with his divine patroness, hostile neighbors occupy the palace.[54] As the male citizens engage in games of dice and licentious behavior, the women leave their quarters and set up an anti-*polis* complete with elected officials and sacrifice.[55] The departure from the Acropolis of the forces regulating Athenian political life is thus mirrored in the desertion of the home by the female. An external threat to civilization, represented in the contest myth by a divine assault on agricultural land and in the war by an invasive force, becomes in ritual a threat from within. Stated from the perspective of the cult's participants, the story of the war with Eumolpos places this yearly drama of dissolution in the context of a myth-historical crisis in which the survival of the state had been threatened.

Burkert has shown that the Skira belong to a larger cycle of religious festivals celebrated at year-end, in which the fabric of society is temporarily dissolved and reconstituted.[56] To this same period belong the ritual extinction of Athene's lamp, presumably during the Kallynteria, and the Plynteria, in which the clothing of Athene's olive-wood *xoanon* was removed for washing. During the Plynteria, the temples to the city were closed and most other business was postponed, for the day was felt to be inauspicious. Shortly thereafter the Athenians celebrated the

[54] *HN* 158.

[55] *HN* 145. The suitors first appear in the *Odyssey* playing board games at 1.106–8. MacDowell, 21, offers a general definition of hubris as "having energy or power and misusing it self-indulgently." He argues that the javelin-throwing of the suitors at *Od.* 4.625–27 reveals their hubris, in that they are "'larking about', as opposed to doing something seriously; expending surplus energy in a useless manner" (18). These remarks are also applicable to their gaming in Book 1. The objections of Fisher to this interpretation are undermined by Michelini's demonstration that plants were thought to be hubristic when through excess of food they expend their energy on producing foliage rather than fruit.

[56] *HN* 136–161; *GR* 227–36.

Kronia, during which slaves were allowed to feast with their masters and to revel through the streets of the city.[57]

Periods of ritual dissolution, during which the hierarchies that govern political and domestic life are effaced or inverted create an environment in which change in the social organism can occur. Such changes in society are, moreover, predicated on changes among its members, and the pattern of normalcy, its inversion, and its—frequently violent—restoration is common to other rituals of transition, such as adolescent rites of passage. The polis is reconstituted, but it includes new citizens; the initiate is reintegrated into society, but as an adult.[58] Thus, the Arrephoria, which belongs to the cycle of year-end festivals at Athens, can be seen as a maiden initiation ritual. Not only are the patterns of year-end festival and initiation cognate, but the processes imply one another. The interregnum is a time of crisis, yet the crisis preserves the state by renewing it. Ritual offers the assurance that the forces of disorder will be contained, even as it acknowledges their necessity with annual reenactments of the formative violence that gave the state birth.

The Panathenaia celebrates and reaffirms the political order in the coming year.[59] During this festival, the chief magistrates of the city, including the king, polemarch, and eponymous archon, entered office. Myth records that king Erichthonios introduced the festival in honor of Athene's victory in the war against the Giants, and that he set up the *xoanon* of Athene Polias. The Panathenaia celebrates the restoration of order with the arrival of Erichthonios and his patroness Athene after the departure of Erechtheus and the goddess during the Skira. Yet even in antiquity Erichthonios was seen as a doublet of Erechtheus, and his name may well be a Hellenized version of Erechtheus' own.[60] The new king is thus in a sense the old king returned, just as Odysseus returns at new year to restore order on Ithaca.

The festival began with a Pannychis, in which young men and women joined in an all-night celebration of singing and dancing on

[57] For the Plynteria, see Deubner, 17–22; Burkert (1970). For the Kallynteria, see below. For the Kronia see Deubner, 152–55; *GR* 231–32.

[58] The classic work on initiation remains that of Gennep; more recent literature on the subject is vast. Of particular significance are the studies of Jeanmaire; Brelich; Calame (1977b).

[59] Burkert, *HN* 154–58, *GR* 232–34, lays particular stress on the Panathenaia as a reaffirmation of the civic order. For the festival see also Deubner, 22–35; Davison (1958); H. Thompson; Mikalson; Simon (1983) 55–72; Robertson; Connor; Kyle, chap. 1 and 2; Morgan, 207–12.

[60] *HN* 156 with note 95; Mikalson, 141 with note 1.

the Acropolis. New fire was also conveyed by a torch race from the Academy to the Acropolis where it was used to light the sacrificial altar. The Panathenaic procession followed at dawn. Already in the sixth century it seems that the focal point of the procession was the presentation of Athene's *peplos,* a robe embroidered with the Gigantomachy and conveyed to the Acropolis by a ceremonial ship-wagon.[61] At the head of the procession girls from the leading families of Athens carried baskets holding sacrificial grain. Cows and sheep followed, to be offered to Athene and to Pandrosos, in whose precinct the olive tree was housed. Representatives of all ages and classes joined in the larger procession: metics followed the sacrificial animals, the men carrying trays of offerings, cakes, and honeycombs, the women pitchers of water. Pipers and lyre players followed them, to offer musical accompanyment to the sacrifice. Specially chosen old men carried olive branches in honor of the goddess from the Dipylon gate to the Acropolis. Freed slaves and "other barbarians" carried oak branches through the market place. The procession was accompanied by a military escort in which hoplites marched under arms and rode in chariots, while the ephebes paraded on horseback. The entire community took part in the Panathenaic procession to the Acropolis and above all in the sacrifice that followed, for it was by these very acts that the body politic reconstituted and articulated itself.

The role of the cavalry and charioteers in the procession looked forward to the Panathenaic games that followed. Athletic events offered a forum in which those of military age could demonstrate the physical prowess necessary to defend the *polis.*[62] At early festivals athletes competed in the *stadion,* a foot race of about 200 meters, the *pentathlon,* including the long jump, discus, javelin, foot race, and wrestling, separate events for wrestling and boxing, and in the *pankration,* an especially violent event combining both boxing and wrestling. But the most important and distinctive events at the Panathenaia were equestrian. Such events, though popular elsewhere, acquire special meaning in an Athenian context, since Poseidon was the traditional sire of horses, while Athene as the inventer of the chariot and bridle made the *biē* of horses available to humans.[63] One of these events, the *apobates,* in which a soldier in hoplite uniform leapt from a moving chariot, involved tactics

[61] For the date, see Deubner, 33–34. Andromache's presentation of a robe to Athene at *Il.* 6.271–311 has been taken to suggest a Homeric date for that part of the ceremony.

[62] I say this while acknowledging that explicitly military events reflecting contemporary practice were a later development.

[63] See Appendix 2.

that would have been outmoded in the sixth century and may well belong to the Mycenaean period.[64] As founder of the games, Erichthonios was also said to have invented the chariot and to have instituted and won the first *apobates* event.[65] The arrival of order in the polis is thus celebrated as a military act, an act of seizure: "In this way the warrior and king took possession of the land at his advent."[66] Victors were awarded amphoras containing olive oil from the *Moriai,* a grove of trees propagated off the *Morios,* together with a crown of olive leaves. In this setting, rhapsodes gave competitive recitations of the *Iliad* and *Odyssey.* Tradition had it that Troy fell during the Skira.[67]

Ithaca at Midnight

Similarities between the fates of Erechtheus and Odysseus invite speculation that one story has to some degree modeled itself on the other, yet at no point can we determine the direction of influence, and indeed there is no reason to assume that such influence was entirely unidirectional. So far as can be determined, however, the manifestation of Athene's *numen* in the home of a Mycenaean king, particularly in the form of a sacred lamp and olive tree, finds an Odyssean echo that is unique in literature and cult. My conclusion, based chiefly on the strength of the cult evidence, is that the *Odyssey* acquired the form in which we have it today at Athens.

Comparison of the *Odyssey* to Athenian year-end festival will consist of three parts, devoted to Ithaca and the Skira, Erechtheus and Odysseus, and the significance of the olive tree and lamp in the homes of the kings. In the first part of this comparison, I shall seek to establish that the *Revenge* reflects the typical elements of a ritual pattern common to year-end festivals *such as we find at Athens.* I shall not argue on the basis of this evidence for the dependence of the *Odyssey* on Athenian cult per se.[68] It cannot be overemphasized that the ritual pattern in which the social order is dissolved and restored at year-end is attested for regions other

[64] H. Thompson; *HN* 156; *GR* 232–33; Kyle, 188–89.

[65] The invention of the chariot was elsewhere ascribed to Athene.

[66] *HN* 156.

[67] For ancient references to Homeric recitations at the Panathenaia see Allen (1924) 226–27; further bibliography may be found in Nagy (1990b) 21–22. For the Skira and the fall of Troy, see *HN* 158.

[68] Auffarth, who also places the *Odyssey* in a ritual context, singles out the Anthesteria and identifies the reunion of Odysseus and Penelope as a *hieros gamos* (564–65 and 571–72).

than Attica. Indeed, were our evidence as complete for all of Greece as it is for Athens, the basic pattern would doubtless emerge as ubiquitous. As such, a narrative recreation of this pattern would be accessible to a Panhellenic audience even if it had been influenced at various points by the cults of one or more cities.

There is, moreover, an important discrepancy between the *Odyssey* and Athenian cult: the Athenian new year was set at the summer solstice, but Odysseus kills the suitors during a festival on the winter solstice. There is no difficulty, however, in seeing both the ritual cycle at Athens and the *Mnesterophonia* as taking place at year-end, since some regions of Greece celebrated the new year at the winter solstice and some at the summer—for example, on the first new moon after the winter solstice at Delos, and apparently after the summer solstice at Delphi and Elis, as at Athens.[69] The seasonal setting of the *Mnesterophonia* may be explained by observing its effect. Odysseus reaches Ithaca after the onset of the winter storm season, whose victim he very nearly became. His herds on Ithaca number approximately six thousand, yet the suitors consume them at a rate of four thousand three hundred per year.[70] Had Odysseus waited until spring, Penelope and quite possibly his son would have married: there would have been no home to which he could have returned.[71]

Revenge *in Its Narrative Context*

Social conditions during Athenian year-end festivals overlap conceptually with mythological representations of Paradise, in which cultural categories and hierarchies are effaced. The enchanted realm, bordered by the world of Troy and by Scherie, site of athletic competition and Homeric performance, is a geographic analogue to year end in the festival cycle. Consequently, the Ithacan sections of the *Odyssey* can be—and in fact are—thematized by the system of relations established in the *Apologoi*. The suitors have created an anti-Paradise in the heart of the Ithacan *polis,* within the very home of its king. Cultural institutions are irrelevant in Paradise. Thus the suitors are never shown sacrificing or participating in the festivals of the gods, whose warnings they repeat-

[69] Samuel, 64, 73–74, 95–97, 99. The Athenian calendar may date to the first half of the seventh century, for which see Garland, 80–81. The dates assigned to various other Greek cities by Bishoff, *RE* 10:2.1569, are somewhat optimistic.

[70] Erbse (1972) 122, who concludes that the suitors have only recently occupied the palace.

[71] N. Austin (1975) 242–43; Nagy (1985) 64–68.

edly dismiss.[72] The pattern of behavior observed among the Cyclopes returns: luxuriance leads to excess (*koros*) and a hubris manifested in unrestrained *biē* that violates *themis,* in particular the laws of *xenia.* Thus, the name of the ringleader Eurymachos, or 'Widespread-Battler', specializes the *biē* of the suitors into organized fighting. He alone dies a heroic death. Antinoos, either 'Anti-Mind' or 'Anti-Return', is in terms of Odyssean thematic categories synonymous with *biē.* Of all the suitors he is the most conspicuous for his unrestrained behavior.[73]

On the afternoon before the *Mnesterophonia* Odysseus delivers a warning to Amphinomos that recapitulates the themes of the divine assembly. In so doing he also echoes his earlier description of the Cyclopes:[74]

καὶ γὰρ ἐγώ ποτ' ἔμελλον ἐν ἀνδράσιν ὄλβιος εἶναι,
πολλὰ δ' ἀτάσθαλ' ἔρεξα βίῃ καὶ κάρτει εἴκων,
πατρί τ' ἐμῷ πίσυνος καὶ ἐμοῖσι κασιγνήτοισι.
τῶ μή τίς ποτε πάμπαν ἀνὴρ ἀθεμίστιος εἴη,
ἀλλ' ὅ γε σιγῇ δῶρα θεῶν ἔχοι, ὅττι διδοῖεν.
οἶ' ὁρόω μνηστῆρας ἀτάσθαλα μηχανόωντας,
κτήματα κείροντας καὶ ἀτιμάζοντας ἄκοιτιν
ἀνδρός, ὃν οὐκέτι φημὶ φίλων καὶ πατρίδος αἴης
δηρὸν ἀπέσσεσθαι . . .

(18.138–46)

For once I too was supposed to be a prosperous man,
but I did many reckless deeds (*atasthala*) yielding to my *biē*
since I trusted in my father and my brothers.
Therefore let no man ever be lawless (*athemistios*),
but let him receive the gifts of the gods in silence, whatever they give.
What reckless deeds (*atasthala*) I see the suitors devising,
devouring the possessions and dishonoring the wife
of a man whom I think will not be far from his friends and paternal land
much longer.

The impulse to punish criminal acts and to show compassion for human suffering are embodied in the same characters and satisfied by the same condition: the return of Odysseus. Thus, Athene's desire for the return

[72] Pucci (1987) 196–97. See also Vermeule (1974) 95.

[73] See Felson-Rubin, 115–20. Mühlestein, 76, connects Antinoos' name to *nostos.* Frame has demonstrated that interpretations based on *noos* and on *nostos* need not be treated as exclusive.

[74] Segal (1994) 160, 222, offers further parallels between Polyphemos and the suitors. Also note the nautical imagery that links both scenes of punishment. For the *Cyclopeia* see above Chapter 3, and for the Revenge see 21.390–91, 22.384–88, 465, 23.233–38.

of Odysseus is practically undifferentiated from her desire to punish the suitors.

On the morning of the *Mnesterophonia,* the prophet Theoklymenos serves the earlier function of Teiresias in providing a divinely inspired warning to the suitors (20.347–57). His vision evokes the sacrifice of the crew on Thrinakie. The eerieness of the scene in the palace is matched only by the creeping hides of Helios' cattle and their meat lowing on the spits; the severity of the suitors' crime is once again registered by the extinction of the sun.[75] The *Mnesterophonia* begins with a horrific confirmation of this prophecy. As Antinoos raises a goblet of wine to his mouth Odysseus strikes him on the throat with an arrow. Blood spurts forth from his nostrils, defiling the food that he drags to the floor as he falls (22.9–21). Odysseus traps the other suitors in the *megaron* just as Polyphemos had once trapped him in the cave. Yet in their improper feasting and crimes against *xenia,* it is the suitors who resemble Polyphemos.

When Odysseus kills the suitors, their parents attempt to retaliate, as had Poseidon after Odysseus blinded the Cyclops. On this occasion, in which Odysseus acts within his own domain and the would-be avengers are human, Zeus imposes an arbitrary end to the conflict by imposing a truce (24.539–48). The *Odyssey* concludes with the opposition between a patriarchal code of reciprocal violence and the theodicy authorized by Zeus that informs the Introduction and the narrative architecture of the *Apologoi.*

Archaeology offers an important clue as to why the behavior of the suitors is so harshly condemned. Excavations at Greek Iron Age sites suggest that the dwelling of the ruler had cult functions, among the most important being that of a ritual meal offered at the hearth.[76] These meals would have served to identify the local rulers as such, and to place them under obligation to the king. It may be possible to catch a glimpse of just such a meal in Book 7 of the *Odyssey,* in which Odysseus arrives at the home of king Alkinoos as the "leaders and counselors" of Scherie are pouring libations to Hermes before retiring for the evening (7.136–38). The suitors are guilty of perverting the ritual meal offered in the home of the archaic king, just as the crew pervert the sacrificial ritual on Thrinakie. Their feasting constitutes an assault not only on the laws governing *xenia,* but on a ritual verification of the social order.

[75] Whitman, 122; Reinhardt (1960) 90; Erbse (1972) 52–54; Nagler (1990) 340.

[76] Discussion and further bibliography in Mazarakis (1987) 20–21; Mazarakis (1988); Morgan, 132. For the improper feasting of the suitors, see above, Chapter 1.

Odysseus triumphs over the suitors with the devices of *mētis*. As we have seen, the enchanted world repeatedly threatens to deny Odysseus a return to civilization with attacks on consciousness and cultural identity. In so doing, it also poses a threat to *kleos*. Political life, on the other hand, requires the subordination of personal identity to that of the group. Thus, in the civilized world as in the enchanted realm the greatest resource at Odysseus' disposal remains his ability to conceal his identity.[77] The warfare of *mētis* is likewise anonymous: the tactic that Odysseus employs against the suitors is the *lokhos*, or ambush, and his weapon is the bow.[78]

It has long been noted that the *Iliad* never refers to Odysseus as an archer and that a passage from the *Phaiakis* carefully prepares for his weapon in the *Mnesterophonia* (8.215–25; see also 1.260–62).[79] Scholars have concluded from these observations that the *Iliad* and *Odyssey* cannot be the work of the same poet, although the name Telemachos, or 'far-fighter', is known to Iliadic tradition and can be taken to reflect an awareness of *kleos* acquired by Odysseus through archery.[80] Nor is it hard to find a motivation for an Iliadic suppression of Odysseus' bowmanship. In that poem, *kleos* is won by defeating a worthy opponent in battle; the mutual identification of combatants is thus necessary in order to assess the risks involved and the stature of one's intended victim.[81] In such an environment, anonymous warfare such as archery and ambushes are objects of reproach. Reference to the fact that Odysseus is a "far-fighter" in the *Iliad* would have undermined his status *as defined by the tradition in which he is operating*. Odysseus did well to leave his bow at home.

Archery is a natural attribute of a hero of *mētis*, and hence an honor-

[77] Odysseus is very much a "team player" in the *Iliad*. In his comparison of Iliadic speeches by Odysseus and Nestor, Martin, 122, observes that "nowhere does Odysseus assert an individual role, unlike Nestor in his reminiscences."

[78] For the *Mnesterophonia* as a *lokhos* see A. Edwards (1985) 35–38. Burkert (1973), followed by Auffarth, 516–23, explains the bow as a ritual legitimation of Odysseus as ruler.

[79] Kirk (1962) 290. The parallel between the passages is noted by Lang, 166.

[80] The Iliadic passage in which Odysseus calls himself the father of "Far-Fighter" could be read as a sort of metatextual bragging by the Odysseus character about his Odyssean tradition. For the tendency of the names of offspring to function as virtual epithets of their fathers, see most recently Peradotto, 106, 134–39, 164–65. Scholars are divided as to whether "Far-Fighter" refers to Odysseus as an archer or as a hero who fought in faraway Troy. The latter epithet could be applied to every hero who fought in the war; yet there is no reason to treat these meanings as mutually exclusive. Any term which characterizes Odysseus can be expected to be ambivalent.

[81] Beidelman, 230–33.

ific attribute in a poem that privileges *mētis* over *biē*. Just as the *Odyssey* offers the promise of return with *kleos,* it celebrates the paradox from an Iliadic perspective of a *kleos* won by archery. Thus, in the Ithacan sections of the poem, an opposition between *mētis* and *biē* returns us to a rivalry with the Iliadic tradition detected in the poem's Introduction. I can now take my earlier analysis of that rivalry somewhat further. In concealing his identity so as to insinuate himself into the palace, Odysseus employs the stratagem by which he conquered Troy and recovered Helen, another object of improper courtship.[82] The *Odyssey* calls attention to the analogy in Book 4 with the story of Odysseus' disguised entry into Troy as a beggar, which is followed by the complementary account of the Trojan horse.[83] As Odysseus uses a bow to punish the suitors, he becomes aligned with the ritual antagonist of Achilleus, who died by an arrow from Paris or Apollo himself.[84] Odysseus kills the suitors during a festival to Apollo; he strings the bow effortlessly, as a poet would a lyre (21.406–9).[85] The instrument of punishment becomes the musical instrument that will accompany future mimetic recreations of his exploit in song, the lyre in the hands of Homer. The *Odyssey* insists that the deed and the poetry which celebrates the deed are one; a bow of horn verifies the fact that Penelope's dream came from the gates of horn. The bow is, moreover, Apollo's weapon, and the lyre his musical instrument. Theoklymenos, in many ways a doublet of Odysseus himself, represents Apollo's third function of prophecy, which is likewise brought to bear against the suitors.[86]

The antagonisms between Apollo and Achilleus and between Poseidon and Odysseus are inversely related in that Apollo, a natural repre-

[82] The pattern thus relates Penelope to Helen, on which relation see Katz; Fredricksmeyer.

[83] The relation of both episodes to the *Mnesterophonia* is discussed by Erbse (1972) 96–97; Andersen (1977); Goldhill (1989) 19–22; Katz, 46–47, 78–79.

[84] Already prepared for by *Od.* 17.494.

[85] My interpretation provides a thematic motivation for the festival, which has been assigned by Analytic scholars such as Fernándes-Galiano, *CHO* 3.132-33, to the *Bearbeiter.* It should be observed that axes are formidable weapons. Either the contest took place in the courtyard so that Odysseus could trap the suitors in the *megaron* (then was anyone watching?) or the axes lacked handles.

[86] On the antithetical pairing of the bow and lyre in art to represent the punitive and beneficent aspects of the god see *h. Ap.* 3.131; Callimachus, *Ap.* 19, with F. Williams' note to the verse. On the association of horn with oracular and poetic truth note that Apollo's altar on Delos was made of horn, and it may have been tradition that Homer sang the *Homeric Hymn to Apollo* there, for which see Callimachus, *Ap.* 61, with F. Williams' note. For Theoklymenos and Odysseus, see Page (1955) 86–87; Fenik (1974) 233–44; Katz, 74–75.

sentative of *mētis* and civilized values, protects the Trojan *polis* from the *biē* of Achilleus.[87] Odyssean tradition asserts its superiority to the Iliadic by identifying Odysseus with Achilleus' antagonist in a reenactment of his former conquest of Troy, the conquest denied the hero of *biē*. The competition between these poetic traditions is signified by a basic incompatibility in the tactics and weapons of its heroes. At the same time, the *Odyssey* and *Iliad* are thematically consistent in their identification of unrestrained *biē* as a threat to civilization. Indeed, it is this very consistency that permits the alignment of Odysseus with Apollo. The *Odyssey* inverts the Iliadic relationship between Greek and non-Greek, however, for in the *Iliad* Troy is the higher culture but the Greeks are the better fighters. The *Odyssey,* by contrast, represents the enchanted realm as a partial or complete negation of Greek culture and aligns it with *biē,* while Greece itself belongs to *mētis*.

Biē is also a defining characteristic of the heroic persona. By instituting the contest of the bow, Penelope allows Odysseus to establish himself as a model of the successful hero, since not only is archery a symbol of *mētis,* but the bow of Odysseus can only be strung by someone of heroic strength. The bow provides a tangible symbol of the subordination of *biē* to *mētis* in those capable of wielding it. Yet the very act of portraying Odysseus as a conquering warrior also threatens to assimilate him to the character of Achilleus. This problematizes the ethical themes of the *Odyssey,* as becomes explicit in the case of Leiodes, "the only suitor for whom *atasthaliai* were hateful" (21.146–47; compare 22.314). When Leiodes pleads for his life on the grounds that he is a soothsayer and attempted to prevent the suitors from committing *atasthaliai,* Odysseus kills him with the sarcastic remark that "you doubtless prayed for my death so that you could marry my wife and have children by her" (22.322–24). The issues here are complex: Leiodes does not deny that he actively courted Penelope, and his father's name, *Oinops,* or 'Wine-Face', together with his position among the suitors by the mixing bowl, points to his gluttony.[88]

Once again, Odysseus is denied the omniscient perspective on Leiodes that might have mitigated his response. More importantly, however, Odysseus acts in passion, for which his momentary loss of self-restraint at the close of the *Cyclopeia* provides an exact parallel. In the

[87] See Whitman, 229, 236–37.

[88] The mind of the other "good suitor," Amphinomos, also turns quickly to food (22.245–46). K. Usener, 135–36, argues that the scene with Leiodes is modeled on Achilleus' encounter with Lykaon during his *aristeia*.

fury of his revenge, Odysseus becomes, as it were, an Achilleus. Comparison with the *Iliad* yields similar results. The *Mnesterophonia* is organized as an *aristeia,* and its position in the larger narrative is analogous to that of Achilleus' own *aristeia* in the *Iliad*. Like its Iliadic counterpart, the *Mnesterophonia* is also the hero's greatest exploit, the climax of the poem, and an act of vengeance marked by unrestrained behavior.[89] The alignment of Odysseus with Apollo at the beginning of the *Mnesterophonia* gives way to his realignment with Achilleus, the ritual antagonist of the god and his own archrival in epic. The *Odyssey* affirms that the very qualities which make heroism possible inherently threaten the social order, even as they are used to punish the suitors for their crimes against it. In Book 24 Zeus himself must prevent Odysseus from continuing his attack on the parents of the suitors after they had turned in flight. The poem thus closes with Zeus endorsing the need for restraint in the form of mitigated punishment. The *Odyssey* does not shrink from dramatizing the paradox of cultural foundation: as Odysseus restores order he becomes assimilated to the forces of disorder. By describing the punishment of the suitors as an *aristeia* Homer creates a dramatic equivalent to the cult of Poseidon-Erechtheus at Athens.

Revenge *in its Ritual Context*

The suitors, like the Cyclopes, disregard or oppose the laws and institutions of society in the belief that they are more powerful than their opponents. Yet the savage existence of the Cyclopes is described as a negation of culture, while an internal political crisis on Ithaca is accompanied by an inversion of the ethical norms that characterize Greek society.[90] Thus, the *biē* of the suitors derives from their capacity for organized activity. As an inversion rather than a simple negation of culture, conditions on Ithaca correspond to the year-end festival pattern at Athens.[91] In either case, this inversion is accompanied by the absence of the king and his patron deity, Athene. Odysseus' journey from civilization into the enchanted realm and back again mirrors, even as it is ultimately responsible for, the dissolution and reestablishment of social order on Ithaca.

The scene from *Odyssey* 13 in which Athene greets Odysseus on the shores of Ithaca foreshadows the situation that awaits him in the

[89] Schröter, 121 ff.; Müller, 136–45; Krischer, 13–14, 58–59.
[90] Compare the remarks of Vidal-Naquet, 25.
[91] For Ithaca and year-end festival, see Foley, 60–61; Auffarth, chap. 6.

palace (13.221–439). Each of the three principal narrative sequences of the poem, the *Telemachy, Phaiakis,* and Revenge, include a sea voyage followed by the hero's welcome on the beach upon arriving at his destination. In the first two sequences, he is met by a royal youth in a social setting emblematic at once of the place and of his mission: Telemachos is greeted by Peisistratos during a sacrifice to Poseidon, Odysseus by Nausikaa and her maidservants. On Ithaca, however, Athene appears to Odysseus alone in the guise of a royal shepherd. The contrasting scenes from Books 3 and 6 underscore the fact that a social context for the welcome of the hero has become impossible on Ithaca.

Athene's choice of disguise is appropriate to the island, since as Athene and Telemachos remark, Ithaca is unsuited to extensive farming or raising horses (13.242–47, 4.601–8; see also 9.25–27). More to the point, circumstances will presently require that Odysseus adopt a false identity himself. The goddess thus engineers a scene of greeting in which Odysseus' first action on Ithaca is to adopt the strategy of concealment and deception that ensures his success against the suitors. By disguising Odysseus as a beggar, Athene also reverses his natural position within the social hierarchy. Athene, whose natural seat as goddess of civilization is the heart of the *polis* and the home of the king, undergoes a corresponding reversal by identifying herself with a socially marginal occupation.[92] In so doing she takes on the professional identity of Odysseus' most deadly adversary, Polyphemos.

Thus, although we may detect a certain irony in Athene's masquerade, her disguise perfectly represents Ithacan society and contains an implicit warning: the forces normally consigned to the margins are in control; the outside has become the inside. The youth of Ithaca have occupied the home of the king, and with them dines the goatherd Melanthios, the worst of Odysseus' servants. Our first image of the suitors finds them, like the male celebrants of the Skira, engaged in board games emblematic of their idleness and licentious behavior (1.106–8). To gain entry into the palace, Odysseus assumes the identity of one who can have no formal relationship with it; he becomes ostensibly what the suitors in fact are, a "mere belly." The king of Ithaca "makes the threshold his regular seat," while in her appearances to the suitors Penelope remains at the door to the *megaron,* and takes her seat at the hearth only in their absence.[93]

The inside has also become the outside. With the prolonged absence

[92] On goatherding, see above, Chapter 3.
[93] *CHO* 3:3; see also Segal (1994) 80–81.

of Odysseus and the death of Antikleia, Laertes withdraws to a secluded part of the island, effectively renouncing any claim to control the household and in particular the status of Penelope within it. Yet Laertes remains faithful to the memory of his son by tending an orchard, that is, by acculturating nature, while the returned Odysseus proves his identity to Laertes with his knowledge of the grove and its contents (24.327–46). Thus, in demonstrating his legitimacy Odysseus also reaffirms his ties to the land. The reunion of father and son takes place in an agricultural space created and filled by Laertes but possessed by Odysseus.

On the previous afternoon, Penelope tricked Odysseus into relating how he had built their marriage bed on the stump of an olive tree (23.174–204). Penelope thus confirms the identity of her husband in a way that demonstrates her own fidelity to him through continued protection of a tree within the bedroom. In so doing, she compels Odysseus to prove his legitimacy with a story in which he acculturates nature. Odysseus goes beyond the ministrations of his father when he incorporates the tree into the home and separates it from the cycles of nature by transforming it into a cultural artifact.[94] The tree's annual production of fruit is displaced onto the larger cycle of human procreation by making it the locus of conception, birth, and even death. Odysseus effected his return to civilization by performing similar tasks within the enchanted realm, although the ship which he built on Ogygie and the objects to which the olive-wood staff of Polyphemos are compared relate him to economic and political, rather than domestic, activities (see Chapter 3). The image of Odysseus as a *homo faber* predicates the social and domestic orders on the subordination of nature to *mētis*. He owes his return to his carpentry, just as he proves his identity as husband and ruler with the knowledge that in the heart of the *oikos* a piece of nature serves as the unmovable foundation of his marriage bed. Odysseus' manipulation of an olive tree transforms it into a symbol of the domestic order; Polyphemos, by contrast, uproots a tree to make a shepherd's staff, symbol of wandering and social isolation. At the moment of reunion, the bed becomes the setting for a tale of wanderings in the enchanted realm.

On the outside Odysseus meets his faithful servant, Eumaios, in whose hut he is made to witness firsthand the ongoing depletion of his herds by the suitors. Eumaios supplies a personal dimension to the effect of Odysseus' prolonged absence: the reciprocal relationship between master and servant has been broken so that the loyal servant merely benefits, but is not benefited by, the *oikos* which he serves. In particu-

[94] Katz, 178–82. See also Pitt-Rivers 95–125.

lar, there is no one to provide Eumaios with a wife (14.61–66). He thus faces a predicament similar to that of Penelope and Telemachos. The absence of Odysseus from Ithaca results in a loss of fertility within his *oikos* analogous to the depletion of his herds. The serving girls within the palace provide a converse example of disloyal servants characterized by flagrant promiscuity (18.325, 20.6–8).

Corresponding to this topographic inversion is one of social hierarchy. Odysseus' assumed identity as a beggar reverses his social standing relative to that of his own servants, whose behavior toward him accurately reflects their loyalty to his memory. Odysseus is, moreover, apparently unable to reciprocate his potential benefactors on Ithaca, thus rendering the institution of *xenia* irrelevant. *Xenia* is twice irrelevant in the case of servants, since like the Cyclopes they do not travel. Eumaios, who receives the beggar into his home, explains his hospitality with appeal to the fact that "all guests and beggars are under the protection of Zeus" (14.57–58).[95] The sole obligation to receive the beggar or to treat him well, and thus the criterion by which the behavior of Odysseus' intended hosts will be judged, is religious.

Odysseus does have one possession that enables him to establish *xenia* with Penelope, knowledge by which he is able to reawaken memories of her long absent husband (19.220–50). Marylin Katz has called attention to an Odyssean homology between the institutions of marriage and *xenia,* both of which incorporate an outsider into the *oikos* in an inferior position.[96] In terms of this homology, Odysseus seeks and obtains an identity that reverses his relationship with Penelope as her husband. This reversal is not simply hierarchical, but sexual as well. In the very scene in which Odysseus establishes *xenia* with his wife, he compares the *kleos* of Penelope to that of a king whose people flourish under his just and pious rule (19.108–14).[97] The restoration of order on Ithaca entails a further reversal that restores Odysseus to his position as head of the household. The complementary relationships that Odysseus establishes with Penelope, first as *xeinos* and then as husband, parallel the inversion of social norms on Ithaca and the restitution of those norms. The change in their relationship is achieved with a story pertaining to the arrival of Penelope in the *oikos,* where Odysseus incorporates another "outsider," the olive tree, into his bedroom.

[95] Note the triple repetition of *xeinos* at the beginning of verses 56–58, which creates an emphasis analogous to that achieved by Odysseus at 9.267–71, as he counsels Polyphemos to respect the laws of hospitality.

[96] Katz, 134–37.

[97] For the simile see Foley; Felson-Rubin, 44, 56–57.

Athene urges Odysseus to collect loaves of bread from the suitors, "so that he might learn who were just and who were unlawful (*athemistoi*); but not even so was anyone destined to escape destruction" (17.363–64). It is significant for our analysis that guilt is a function of collective rather than individual identity, as is brought out most forcibly in the case of the "good" suitor Amphinomos. Yet the antisociety created by the suitors does have its leaders, Antinoos and Eurymachos, who are especially hostile to the beggar. Odysseus couches his request to Antinoos for food in a pointed lesson on the dangers of yielding to *biē* (17.415–44). When Antinoos rejects this request, Odysseus reminds him that the food which he is withholding is not even his, whereupon Antinoos strikes him with his footstool. Later that same evening, Eurymachos throws a second footstool at Odysseus, who avoids being hit by assuming a suppliant posture at the feet of Amphinomos (18.394–96). Eurymachos' attempt to be a poor host makes it impossible for the suitors to be improper guests; he strikes the wine steward on the arm, thus disrupting the feast (18.401–4). Telemachos sees in this the hand of a god:

> δαιμόνιοι, μαίνεσθε καὶ οὐκέτι κεύθετε θυμῷ
> βρωτὺν οὐδὲ ποτῆτα· θεῶν νύ τις ὔμμ' ὀροθύνει.
>
> (18.406–7)

> Madmen! you rage like men possessed, and in your spirit
> no longer conceal your food and drink, for some god incites you.

Mistreatment of a *xeinos* who is a beggar identifies Antinoos and Eurymachos as *athemistoi;* Polyphemos had been marked in the same way for eating *xeinoi* who were suppliants. Thus, despite his disguise or because of it, Odysseus becomes a shifting value, creating a hierarchy of relationships with Penelope, Eumaios, the other servants, and the suitors. This new hierarchy corresponds to Odysseus' natural affinities, as head of the household, toward these same individuals. The gradually intensifying influence of Odysseus and Athene on Ithaca is accompanied by a deterioration in the antisociety of the suitors.

Order is restored during a new-moon festival to Apollo at the beginning of the new year, in which an athletic contest devolves into open military conflict.[98] The festival was celebrated at Athens; during it the citizens "assembled on the Acropolis in order to pray for one's

[98] Wilamowitz (1884) 54; Wilamowitz (1927) 43–44; H. Thompson, 57, note 41; N. Austin (1975) chap. 5; *CHO* at 19.306–7; Auffarth, 388–410.

own well-being and that of the state."[99] Yet the affinities between the *Odyssey* and Athenian civic festivals extend well beyond this one cult. In its conflation of athletic competition and warfare, the *Odyssey* has a direct parallel in games such as those at the Panathenaia. The "new king" of Ithaca, whose arrival signals the restoration of order, is the old king returned, just as Erichthonios was seen as a doublet of Erechtheus. Erichthonios founded the Panathenaic games, in which he competed and won, to celebrate the victory of Athene over forces of disorder. In the *Odyssey,* Penelope institutes an archery contest in which Odysseus competes and wins. He then uses the instrument of victory to punish the suitors for their crimes. The suitors die to a man, while the Panathenaia celebrates the incorporation of the ephebes into adult society, yet myth and ritual alike describe such transitions as the death of the old self, and Telemachos furnishes a paradigm of the successful initiand. In Odysseus' struggles with the suitors, represent the polarity between culture and disorder, as happens in the Erechtheus myth. At the same time, the suitors are chiefly Ithacans or citizens of regions within the Ithacan political ambit, so that the forces of disorder come from within the society, as in the Skira.

Erechtheus and Odysseus

In order to establish a connection between the *Odyssey* and Athenian cult, we must look beyond these shared structural patterns to actual characters and artifacts. One such point of contact lies in the central roles played by Athene and Poseidon and in their contrasting attitudes towards Odysseus and Erechtheus. In supplying the hero with a divine patron and adversary, however, the *Odyssey* can be seen as drawing on a generic feature of hero cult, or even on a specific cult to Odysseus that is no longer attested. In this case, the coincidence of gods in the *Odyssey* and in the Erechtheus cult remains simply that, a coincidence. It is also true that Athene and Poseidon are frequently paired in Greek religious thought, where they represent a polarity between culture and the forces of nature. The contrasting relationship between these gods both in the *Odyssey* and in the Erechtheum belongs to Panhellenic tradition. Thus the analogous function of these gods in Homer and in Athenian cult could be seen as an accident of a religious system that Homeric epic at once reflected and helped codify. Yet nowhere else in extant myth or cult

[99] Deubner, 203.

do we find this polarity expressed as the gods' support and persecution of a king, nor is Poseidon elsewhere identified with a culture-hero.

At first glance, parallels in the fate of Erechtheus and Odysseus would permit us to go somewhat further: both heroes are Mycenaean kings under the patronage of Athene, and both kings are punished by Poseidon for harming one of his sons in self-defense. Erechtheus defends Athens against an invasion led by Eumolpos. Erechtheus triumphs in the war, killing Eumolpos, but is himself killed by Poseidon in revenge. Like Erechtheus, Odysseus departs for war, disappears, and is presumed dead. In the course of his return, Odysseus defends himself and a group of soldiers under his command against Polyphemos, and suffers continued persecution from Poseidon for blinding the Cyclops. Poseidon is responsible for the disappearance of the Ithacan king, although in deference to Zeus he merely delays Odysseus' homecoming rather than kill him as he had Erechtheus. Yet as a result of this delay, Poseidon is directly responsible for the disarray in which Ithacan society finds itself as the poem begins. When the king departs for war, Athene deserts the city with him. The ensuing interregnum is marked by a corresponding dissolution of the social order linked to an agricultural crisis.

Odysseus reestablishes order on Ithaca with an act of war during an athletic contest held at a religious festival on the winter solstice. Erechtheus defends Athens from an external threat in a war remembered in a ritual celebrated at year-end in which the social order is dissolved. Order is restored with the reappearance of the king during a new-year festival dedicated to Athene and featuring athletic competition. While Athenian cultural tradition differentiates between an external crisis remembered in myth and an internal crisis institutionalized in cult, Odyssean poetic tradition distributes these crises among complementary narratives, the *Cyclopeia* and the Revenge. A final reconciliation is achieved by identifying the king with his ritual antagonist: Odysseus becomes priest of a cult to Poseidon which he himself founds, while the death of Erechtheus leads to the creation of a cult to the god with whom he is equated. Thus at Athens, rhapsodes sang an epic that dramatizes a radical exclusion of disorder during a festival that reaffirms the social order. By calling for a severe condemnation of the suitors, the *Odyssey* promotes a corresponding exclusion of disorder within the individual members of the audience—a disorder with which they had identified throughout the preceding festivals.[100]

[100] In this context see the remarks of Felson-Rubin, 109.

The priority of a hero-cult to Erechtheus over the text of our *Odyssey* seems assured, although due to a general lack of material evidence from the Archaic period it must be inferred. This much can be said: a *terminus ante quem* for Athene's patronage of Erechtheus is provided by the *Odyssey* itself, in which Athene makes her landfall *en route* from Scherie to Olympos in the "tightly constructed home of Erechtheus" (7.81).[101] On the other hand, Solon included the Skira, the Bouphonia, and the Panathenaia in his religious calendar, and the festivals are doubtless much older.[102] There is no difficulty in supposing that Odyssean tradition drew on an Athenian ritual pattern in which the departure of the king from the city signals a time of crisis resolved with his return during a new-year festival. The temporal and geographic liminality of the cult and the social disruptions that attend upon it strongly suggest that the king was venerated for protecting Athenian society from the time that his cult was founded on the Acropolis.

The *terminus* for the role of Poseidon as the antagonist of Erechtheus remains problematic. Our first evidence for their identification is provided by an inscription from the fifth century B.C.E., although it should be noted that this is our first archaeological evidence for the cult of Poseidon of any kind on the Acropolis at Athens.[103] Herodotus' account of the destruction of Athene's tree by the Persians suggests the presence of a cult to Poseidon at an earlier date. How much earlier is, however, impossible to determine. Versions of the contest myth are attested for a number of cities throughout Greece. In surviving tradition, Poseidon is opposed by Athene only at Athens and at Trozen, which may have appropriated the legend from Athens (see Appendix 2). Athenian cult is also unique in that the gods base their claim to the land on tokens, of which the olive tree had an independent role in cult as the *Morios* of the city. These facts are most easily explained with the assumption that the olive tree was already an object of veneration before the contest myth arrived at Athens.[104] Given the importance of olive oil to the Bronze Age

[101] For the Iliadic reference to Erechtheus, 2.550–51, see my discussion above.

[102] See the references in *HN* 144, 157.

[103] *IG*² 580 (= Raubitschek Inscription 384) to which Raubitschek assigns the date supplied above based on letter forms. The date must therefore be regarded as tentative. See the bibliography in Raubitschek. The statue group of Erechtheus and Eumolpos on the Acropolis, if it is in fact the work of Myron, would date to the same period. Further references to Poseidon-Erechtheus, most of them late, may be found in A. Cook, 3:12; *HN* 149. According to Pausanias 1.26.5 the Athenians believed that Poseidon was worshipped as Erechtheus in obedience to a prophecy, and Pausanias himself gives priority to the cult of Poseidon.

[104] Simon, *GG* 180–81, treats Athene's tree cult in the Classical period as a Bronze Age survival. Elsewhere, *GG* 61–65, she discusses the pillar cult to the Argive Hera and

palatial economy, it seems highly plausible that the olive tree was also the *Morios* of the royal household. This would explain its association with Athene in the home of a Mycenaean king, and even the apparent age of the tree in 479 B.C.E. It bears observing in this context that an olive tree hundreds of years old in the Homeric period could well have survived until the time of the Persian wars. The salt-water spring of Poseidon does not permit us to make a similar assumption regarding the antiquity of his worship on the Acropolis, since it apparently did not enjoy an independent cult function. It is of course possible that the story of Poseidon's retaliation upon losing the contest with Athene was taken from a local version of the flood myth. This is, however, impossible to verify, nor does it even prove that the flood or its *sēma* is earlier than the contest.

Thus far, our discussion of Athenian cult and the *Odyssey* supports the following conclusions. Ithacan society reflects a period of social inversion institutionalized in year-end civic festivals at Athens and elsewhere. The events surrounding Odysseus' return to Ithaca have a social meaning equivalent to those surrounding Erechtheus, and the two heroes experience similar fates. Odysseus and Erechtheus have the same divine patroness and adversary, Athene and Poseidon, whose pairing in both the *Odyssey* and in Athenian cult represents a fundamental tension between nature and Greek culture. The internal evidence of the *Odyssey* indicates that the cult of Athene was already celebrated in the Erechtheum during the Archaic period. Recognized as the protégé of Athene, Erechtheus received worship in hero-cult as a defender of the city in a time of crisis; an ancient olive tree, worshipped as *Morios* and associated with the goddess, was located in his temple precinct and former home. Yet the apparent antiquity of Athene's tree-cult does not entitle us to assign a similar date to the role of Poseidon as the ritual antagonist of Erechtheus. We may only say that the casual manner in which Herodotus alludes to the contest fails to betray any awareness that in the fifth century the cult of Poseidon on the Acropolis was of comparatively recent introduction.

Although each of these points of contact can be dismissed individually as generic attributes of year-end festivals and hero-cult, or as simple coincidence, their sheer extent may lead us to suspect otherwise. Yet the normative influence exerted by the Panhellenic audience of Homeric

Theban Dionysos. The *Odyssey* twice mentions sacred trees: Apollo's date palm at the oracular site of Delos is a locus of divine birth (6.163–64), and the oak tree of Zeus at Dodona had the gift of prophecy (14.327–28). An oak tree near the Scaean gate at Troy also belongs to Zeus (*Il.* 5.693, 7.60).

poetry would have tended to remove specific references to local cult from the poem, thus leaving us precisely with generic parallels such as these. Conversely, the composition of the Homeric audience also requires that the interpretation of such features as may remain not depend on knowledge of a strictly local cult. Our interpretation should, however, be reinforced or even deepened by knowledge of the poem's interaction with a specific ritual or ritual cycle. Two artifacts from the home of Odysseus can be said to meet these criteria: Athene's lamp in Book 19 and the olive tree in Book 23.

Cult Artifacts in the Home of a Mycenaean King

Tree-cult is relatively uncommon in Classical Greece, and the association of Athene with olive trees is less common still, being virtually restricted to Athens and its satellites.[105] In the *Odyssey,* however, the olive tree is repeatedly associated with Odysseus, particularly in the context of Athene's protection or assistance (see above, Chapter 3). By far the most prominent olive tree in the poem serves as the post of Odysseus' own marriage bed. Odysseus demonstrates his legitimacy as ruler with the story that he had once built the walls of his bedroom around this tree, which was growing within the *herkos* (23.190). What precisely the *herkos* designates is open to debate, but it is clear that the tree once grew in an enclosure of some sort attached to the house. Thus, the former location of the tree corresponds to the Pandroseion, which housed the *Morios* at Athens and abutted directly onto the Erechtheum in the Classical period. Although we have no way of determining whether this arrangement faithfully preserves the association of the tree with the pre-Classical structure, it is clear that they stood in close physical proximity to one another. If we are right to see the cult of the *Morios* as a survival from the Bronze Age, then the tree was always associated in some fashion with the home of the king, whose fate, or *moira,* it embodied.

The thematic significance of the olive tree in the bedroom of Odysseus corresponds perfectly to its function in Athenian cult. When Penelope tests the identity of her husband by suggesting that the bed could be moved, Odysseus' impassioned reply reveals that her words contain a latent threat: if the bed has been displaced by another, then he returned in vain (23.173–204). The suitors' courtship of Penelope thus becomes a figurative assault upon the tree, an attempt to uproot it as

105 For the restriction of the cult, see *CGS* 1:293, but note that Near Eastern parallels are easily supplied. The Bronze Age material is discussed in *GGR* 278, 84; *MMR* Chap. 7; *GR* 39–40; Rutkowski; *GG* 180–81, 61–65.

Polyphemos had done to fashion his shepherd-staff. The scene of recognition is formulated in such a way that an olive tree comes to represent the *moira* of the house of Odysseus, just as the olive tree in the Pandroseion is the *Morios* of Athens. The position of the tree at the epicenter of Odysseus' house corresponds to its axial function in cult.

Like the cult object at Athens, the marriage bed—and Penelope herself as the faithful wife—represent a symbiotic relationship in which culture both subordinates nature and depends upon it.[106] From the perspective offered by Athenian cult, we may add that by constructing his bed upon an olive tree, Odysseus places his marriage under the protection of Athene, even as Penelope in her protection of the tree effectively becomes a priestess in the cult to the goddess. Thus, Penelope defends the tree and her own chastity by weaving, an activity under the patronage of Athene Ergane in which agricultural products are transformed into cultural artifacts. As a cunning stratagem used to deceive the suitors, Penelope's weaving relates her to Athene for a second time and to her own *polumetis* husband, Odysseus. Yet weaving is also a common symbol of fate, and through her weaving Penelope controls the destinies of the suitors, Odysseus, and the entire household. As a protector of the household, she thus assumes a function analogous to that of the *Morios* at Athens. Odysseus' own transformation of an olive tree into a bedpost makes the marriage bed a symbol of the immutable and immobile wife on whom the fate of the *oikos* depends, just as the security of Athens was assured so long as the olive wood *xoanon* of the virgin Athene remained undisturbed in the Erechtheum.[107] For this as for so much else, the house of Atreus provides a negative foil: Helen is the paradigm of the mobile wife.

Finally, Penelope is associated not only with an olive tree in the bedroom, but with pillars as well.[108] On four occasions Penelope, holding a veil before her face and flanked heraldically by two attendants, stands beside a pillar upholding the roof (*para stathmon tegeos*) as she appears to the suitors in the *megaron*.[109] The internal evidence of the poems indi-

[106] Nagler (1977) 82–85, treats the bed as an axial symbol; for more on the symbolism of the tree see Katz, 178, who elsewhere describes it as the center of the house (182).

[107] For the relationship between the *xoanon* and the Palladion at Troy, on which the fate of the city likewise depended, see above.

[108] Rutkowski offers a recent discussion of the relationship between tree and pillar cult. I have also benefited from the written comments of N. Yalouris and N. Marinatos on an abstract of this part of the discussion, and hasten to acknowledge Dr. Marinatos' objections to understanding the Odyssean passages in terms of cult.

[109] *Od.* 1.333–35, 16.415–16, 18.209–11, 21.64–66; the passages are connected to the marriage bed by Nagler (1977) 82. Penelope likewise spins wool as she sits *para stathmon*

cates that the veil and attendants are symbols of chastity, and the scene in Book 1 announces her continued fidelity to her husband with her first appearance in the poem.[110]

Nausikaa is also related to pillars and to a tree venerated in historical cult. When Odysseus first supplicates Nausikaa on the shores of Scherie, he compares her to Artemis and then to the date palm at Delos at whose base the goddess was born (6.150–52, 160–69). The second comparison may not be explained by the supposed beauty of a palm sapling (*phoinikos neon ernos*), which is a squat and spiky growth;[111] the tree's religious significance as an object of cult veneration would seem to be primary. Nausikaa later bids farewell to Odysseus as she stands beside a pillar upholding the roof—the verse is otherwise restricted to Penelope—whereupon Odysseus promises that on his return to Ithaca he shall "pray to her as a goddess every day" (8.464–68). The association of Penelope with pillars and the parallel afforded by Nausikaa offer striking support for interpreting the olive tree in the bedroom of Odysseus in terms of Athene's tree-cult.

The golden lamp of Athene provides a further point of contact between the homes of Erechtheus and Odysseus. On the night before the *Mnesterophonia,* Athene guides Odysseus and Telemachos by the light of her lamp as they bury the weapons lining the walls of the *megaron* (19.34). These verses have long been the object of Analytic attack:[112] in Book 16, Odysseus instructs Telemachos to hide the weapons at his signal, with the exception of two swords, spears, and shields for themselves (16.281–98). In Book 19, however, Odysseus abandons his advice on a number of points, for he and his son hide all the armor in secret (19.1–46). As a consequence, Telemachos must fetch armor from the

---

megaroio when she interviews Telemachos and Theoklymenos (17.96–97). Several otner characters are related to *kiones:* Arete and Alkinoos lean their thrones against a *kiōn* (in the feminine) and create a heraldic flanking of the pillar itself (6.307–8). Odysseus sits *pros kiona makrēn* as Penelope tests his identity as master of the house (23.90). A poet, Demodokos, who sits *pros kiona makron* (8.66, 473; his lyre apparently hangs from the same place, 8.67–69), is the only good character associated with a pillar who does not belong to the royal household. Conversely, there is not a single instance in which any of the poem's bad characters is related to a *stathmos* or *kiōn* at any location *except in the context of his or her punishment* (22.181, a *stathmos* in the sense of doorpost; 22.176, 22.193, 22.465, all *kiones* in the feminine), while the instruments of the suitors' punishment are associated with the pillars of the *megaron* (1.127–29 with 99–101, *pros kiona makrēn;* 22.120, *stathmos*).

110 Nagler (1974) 45 and chap. 4.

111 Harder discusses the difficulties involved in the comparison and proposes a solution.

112 Kirchhoff, 590; Woodhouse, 158–93; Page (1955) 92–98; *CHO* at 16.281–98, 19.1–50.

storeroom as the *Mnesterophonia* begins, so that Melanthios, who apparently sees him emerge from the storeroom, is able to supply the suitors with armor as well (22.101–41). Analysts have seized on the overt discrepancy between the plan announced in Book 16 and its execution in Book 19 to argue that the latter passage was an interpolation.[113] The difficulties encountered by Odysseus during the *Mnesterophonia,* which the plan in Book 16 was designed to prevent, were taken as a further sign of clumsy adaptation by the *Bearbeiter.*

The *Mnesterophonia* in Book 22 is organized as an *aristeia.* If we are to see the episode as a heroic exploit, rather than a simple act of retribution, the suitors must be able to arm themselves, since otherwise Odysseus would have enjoyed an unfair advantage despite their superior numbers. Homer thus decorated the walls of the *megaron* with weapons *in order to arm the suitors.* Odysseus would have shown an intolerable lack of foresight had he failed to dispose of these weapons in advance, yet something must go wrong with whatever plan he concocts. This is precisely what happens: the oversight that sends Telemachos to the storeroom permits the scene to be read as an *aristeia,* since from it Melanthios discovers the location of the weapons.[114] Moreover, this temporary setback corresponds to a standard element of the *aristeia,* in which the hero suffers a minor wound after achieving some noteworthy initial success in battle.

Analysts have focused their attention on the latter passages in large part because of the golden lamp of Athene in Book 19. This is the only example of a lamp, or *lukhnos,* in Homeric epic, in which the torch (*dais, daos,* and *detē*) or the brazier (*lamptēr*) are the usual sources of illumination.[115] The ancient scholiasts offered a historical explanation for its absence by asserting that "the *lukhnos* is not an ancient invention." [116] The archaeological record both confirms and refutes that claim: lamps were common during the Bronze Age, but apparently went out of use with the decline of Mycenaean culture, only to reappear at the beginning of the seventh century B.C.E. We may surmise from references to a lamp belonging to Athene at *Batrachomyomachia* 180 and at Pausanias 1.26.6–

113 Kirchhoff, 573 ff., Bethe, 80. Focke, 292, on the other hand, argued that Book 19 was the original. For a Unitarian defense, see Erbse (1972) 5–7.

114 Odysseus could not, however, have anticipated the fact that Eumaios and Philoitios would assist him during the *Mnesterophonia,* so that the scene in which Telemachos retrieves armor from the storeroom, together with its consequences, is motivated for a second time by their fortuitous appearance at the beginning of the episode.

115 Jantzen and Tölle.

116 Athenaeus 15.700e. See Nilsson (1950) 98; Pfeiffer (1960) 2–3; Jantzen and Tölle, 87.

7 that it was shortly thereafter incorporated into the cult of the goddess in the Erechtheum.[117]

Our seventh century *terminus post quem* for the Homeric reference to Athene's lamp is provided by the finds at Athens, which has thus far furnished the earliest examples of lamps on the Greek mainland.[118] These lamps must be dated by their position in stratified deposits, a notoriously difficult enterprise. However, we are greatly aided by the fact that "over 1200 closed deposits, consisting of wells, cisterns, shafts, graves, building fills and other strata . . . have now been analyzed and dated. . . . A large number of deposits contain lamps or lamp fragments which acquire the over-all dates assigned to the deposits."[119] Our dates are thus more secure than they might be. By 650, at any event, lamps had become considerably more numerous, and within a generation afterwards they are to be found throughout Greece. The distribution pattern thus suggests a technology that had been lost and reintroduced at what turns out to be the height of the Orientalizing period, when a number of other artifacts arrived from the Near East.[120] At the center of this cultural exchange were Athens, Aigina, Corinth, and Euboea.

For scholars such as Hilda Lorimer and Rudolf Pfeiffer, the seventh century seemed an intolerably late *terminus post quem* for a Homeric artifact. As a result, Lorimer concluded that the lamp was an Athenian interpolation. Pfeiffer saw it as a reminiscence of a lamp belonging to the cult of the Mycenaean palace-goddess who was later worshipped as Athene.[121] More recently, Ulf Jantzen and Renate Tölle have argued that the lamp did not entirely pass out of existence during the Dark Ages, but that its use was severely restricted due to a supposed scarcity of olive oil.[122]

In Book 19, the light issuing from Athene's lamp provokes wonder, whether because lamps were a relative scarcity or because it belonged to the goddess. Yet Homer felt no need to gloss his word for lamp with a description, and if his audience knew what lamps were they could have made one. The theory that lamps continued to be used from the Bronze Age into historical times has received little support from the quarter-century of excavations conducted since the theory was first proposed.

117 Deubner, 20; Pfeiffer (1960) 6.

118 It is worth remarking in this context that burn marks left on a stone or ceramic surface by an oil-fed wick are virtually indelible, thus rendering the consistent misidentification of primitive lamp forms which had seen actual use somewhat unlikely.

119 Howland, 2.

120 Burkert (1984) 19–29.

121 Lorrimer, 509–11; Pfeiffer (1960) 7. See also Nilsson (1950) 98.

122 Jantzen and Tölle, 96–97; accepted by Powell (1991) 201–2.

Moreover, the pollen samples taken by the Minnesota Messenia Expedition suggest that in the western Peloponnesos, at least, the cultivation of olives actually increased during the Dark Ages.[123] This is explained by John Chadwick in a letter to the surveyors with the fact that olives are a subsistence crop suited to the diminished circumstances of the period. On the other hand, those who conclude from the archaeological evidence that the lamp went out of use and explain the Odyssean lamp as a reminiscence of Bronze Age cult must argue that the palace-goddess possessed such a lamp, although there is no evidence for this, that the Athenians preserved the memory of such an artifact over four centuries in which lamps were no longer in use, although armed with this memory they could have made lamps at will, and that the lamp was reintroduced into the cult of the city-goddess upon its arrival in Greece.[124] It is worth observing in this context that Athene's lamp in the *Odyssey* was designed to be carried. This corresponds to seventh century designs, but apparently not to the Mycenaean.

Of the theories developed to account for the Odyssean lamp, that of Lorimer remains the most plausible; yet not only Athene's lamp but the larger narrative context in which the lamp occurs has a direct analogy in Athenian year-end festival.[125] Sacred flames are attached to the cults of several gods, where they commonly symbolize the well-being of the state. In this, the significance of Athene's lamp corresponds to that of

123 Wright, 195–99. See also Lukermann and Moody, 94; Snodgrass (1980) 35–36. Dickinson, 83, however, considers a late Bronze Age date more likely.

124 For the issue of Mycenaean survivals in Homer, see Micknat, 341, who refutes Pfeiffer's explanation of the *lukhnos*. Micknat's argument that there are no Mycenaean reminiscences in Homer is supported by the recent discovery of the remains of a sub-Minoan boar's tusk helmet from Crete, for which see Catling, 53. A Bronze Age plaque depicting a warrior in a boar's tusk helmet could still be seen at Delos in the eighth century B.C.E. See Coldstream (1977) 215.

125 The connection between the Odyssean lamp and Athenian cult is made by Auffarth, 290–91, 407–9, 582. On what evidence, however, Auffarth bases his claim that the lamp was rekindled during the Panathenaia I do not know. Of the authors whom he cites, Deubner, 20, follows Hock's suggestion that the lamp was cleaned during the Kallynteria, while Burkert, *HN* 151–52 and *GR* 229, argues that the implements used to clean the lamp were placed in the *kistē* used in the Arrephoria. Either interpretation would require that the lamp remain extinguished for upwards to two months before the Panathenaia. Therefore, I cannot follow Auffarth in holding that the rekindling of Athene's lamp symbolizes the restoration of order in Athens. Note that Euphorion, *fr.* 11 Groningen (although the tradition may have been known to Nonnus 27.112–7, 319–23) provides a version of the *aition* to the Arrephoria in which Athene leads the way with her lamp as the *kistē* is removed, thus offering a parallel for the disposal of the weapons. Even if the cult *aition* were drawing on the *Odyssey,* this would suggest that an association between the *Odyssey* and Athene's lamp-cult was recognized in antiquity and supports Burkert's theory that the contents of the *kistē* were associated with the lamp.

her tree, although flames have a property which makes them uniquely suited to play a role in the festivals of year-end: they can be extinguished. In the cult of Hephaistos on Lemnos, the ritual extinction of fire on the island ushers in a disruption of the social order remembered in myth as the murder of the men of Lemnos by their wives. Order is restored with the return of fire to the island.[126] Thus, at Athens Kallimachos apparently redesigned Athene's lamp so that it could burn for an entire year without refueling in order to bring its ritual extinction and cleansing into coincidence with the year-end festival cycle.[127]

Athene's golden lamp in the *Odyssey* serves a function analogous to that of the cult object in the Erechtheum:[128] it represents Athene's assurance that the house of Odysseus will continue to stand through her support. The light of her lamp, which magically appears on the night before the restoration of social order on Ithaca, guides Odysseus as he sets in motion his plan to restore that order. When Telemachos sees its light bathe the walls of the *megaron,* he exclaims:

ὦ πάτερ, ἦ μέγα θαῦμα τόδ᾽ ὀφθαλμοῖσιν ὁρῶμαι·
ἔμπης μοι τοῖχοι μεγάρων καλαί τε μεσόδμαι
εἰλάτιναί τε δοκοὶ καὶ κίονες ὑψόσ᾽ ἔχοντες
φαίνοντ᾽ ὀφθαλμοῖς ὡς εἰ πυρὸς αἰθομένοιο.
ἦ μάλα τις θεὸς ἔνδον, οἳ οὐρανὸν εὐρὺν ἔχουσι.

(19.36–40)

Father, this is truly a great wonder that I see.
The walls of the great hall, the finely wrought tie-beams,
the roof-beams of fir, and the columns that hold them aloft,
appear to my eyes as if lit by blazing fire.
Truly one of the gods is within, who dwell on Olympos.

Although Telemachos correctly surmises the presence of a god, his wonder could well reflect the novelty of the lamp throughout the first half

[126] See the discussion in *HN* 190–96. Nilsson (1950) 111, mentions that lamps, decorated with Victoria and Fortuna, were a common gift during new-year festivals at Rome.

[127] I conclude that the lamp was extinguished for the purpose of cleaning and refueling, although this is not strictly necessary. The Skira took place just after the summer grain harvest, although olives would most likely not have been harvested for oil until November or even later. See Dickinson, 91; Morgan, 41. Burkert, *HN* 151–52, *GR* 229, argues that the sacred *kistē* carried during the Arrephoria held the implements used to clean the lamp, which would presumably be relit immediately before the procession.

[128] For the symbolism of light in Homer see Whitman, 121–22; *CHO* at 19.36–40. See also Nagy (1990b) 124–25.

of the seventh century. The reaction of his father, however, sounds specifically like an injunction from cult observance:

> *σίγα καὶ κατὰ σὸν νόον ἴσχανε μηδ᾽ ἐρέεινε·*
> *αὕτη τοι δίκη ἐστὶ θεῶν, οἳ Ὄλυμπον ἔχουσιν.*
>
> (19.42–43)

> Silence, restrain your thoughts, and do not question;
> for this is the way (*dikē*) of the gods who dwell on Olympos.

These words connote a relationship between Odysseus and Athene quite at odds with their familiar tone in Book 13. They are every bit as striking as the lamp itself. It is the significance of Athene's lamp in cult that explains its unique occurrence in Homer. The ancient scholiasts, who had lost the cult reference, complained that Athene performed the service of a maid by holding the lamp for Odysseus and his son.

For Athenian audiences of Homeric performance, the *Odyssey* was a mimesis of the year-end festival cycle at Athens; the home of Odysseus brings to life the ritual realia of Athene's cult in the Erechtheum. Moreover, Athene's sacred olive tree is virtually restricted to her cult at Athens, while it is repeatedly associated with the goddess and her protégé in the *Odyssey*. Just as the only lamp to occur in Homer belongs to Athene, the Erechtheum provides the sole extant example from cult in which the goddess is associated with a sacred lamp.[129] The validity of isolated parallels for the tree or lamp from other cults may be insisted upon, or new evidence may be uncovered, but the combination of Athene, lamp, and olive tree in the home of a Mycenaean king provides at least four independent points of contact between the *Odyssey* and Athenian cult. Finally, not only is this combination unique to the *Odyssey* and Athens, but the lamp and olive tree have analogous narrative and religious functions. Our *Odyssey* acquired its present form in the region of the Saronic Gulf during the seventh and sixth centuries B.C.E.[130]

If we assume that the final crystallization of the text which has come down to us occurred at Athens, then perhaps we can date that text more

[129] Nilsson (1950) 99–100, mentions lamp deposits in the Phoenician temple of Anat-Athene in Idalion and a possible deposit on the Acropolis of Lindos.

[130] West (1988, 1992) and Powell (1991) assign a Euboean provenience to the *Odyssey*. The themes of the *Apologoi* well accord with Euboean interests in Italy during the seventh century, and its leading cities lay on the coast facing Attica, with which the Euboeans

closely. Archaeologists have noted a period of decline at Athens during the first half of the seventh century, particularly evident in the quality of the ceramic artifacts.[131] Our *Odyssey* belongs to the period of gradually increasing prosperity, and social and cultural ferment that began in the latter half of the seventh century and culminated in the tyranny and the achievements of Peisistratos. The trajectory from the divine assembly to fifth century Athenian democracy is direct; fallible kings can be found somewhere along the path laid down by human responsibility.

At about the time that lamps first reappear on the Greek mainland, the inhabitants of Sounion may have begun offering sacrifices to Phrontis, whose death is mentioned at *Odyssey* 3.278–83.[132] Yet the Odyssean passage also describes Sounion as *akron Athēneōn,* the 'headland of Athens'. The description is inconceivable before the end of the seventh century, as it not only presupposes the unification of Attica under Athenian political control, but implies a territorial definition of the polis. After 700 B.C.E. regular Greek contact with Egypt had resumed, reaching an early zenith under Psamtik I whose accession in 664 brought an end to the Ethiopian Dynasty.[133] The *Odyssey* reflects the fascination which this newly rediscovered, exotic, and ancient culture held for Homer and his audience. From the poet's reference to the wealth of Egyptian Thebes at 4.126–27, Burkert arrives at a *terminus post quem* for the *Odyssey* of approximately 660.[134] During this time a Greek noble might well accumulate fabulous wealth in Egypt, become part of the Egyptian court, be called Aigyptios, or have a Nubian slave.[135] Within a decade of this date, a wealthy Athenian commissioned a burial amphora for his ten-year-old son illustrated with the blinding of Polyphemos and the pursuit of Perseus by the Gorgons.[136] The vase painter, or his

---

were in regular contact. It is thus easy to account for how these references to Athenian cult could be found in a Euboean poem; less clear is why.

131 On Athens in the seventh century see Dunbabin (1936–7) 88–91; Dunbabin (1950) 200–202; Coldstream (1968) 360–62; Camp, 401; Snodgrass (1980) 93, 111; Snodgrass (1983); S. Morris, 104–7; I. Morris (1987) chap. 9 to 10; Osborne.

132 Morris (1988) 753.

133 Carpenter, 3–16; Levin. In this context see *CHO* 1:33–34 and 192; Boardman. Corinthian involvement in the Egyptian wars is suggested by the name of Periander's nephew and successor, Psammetichos, on whom see Nagy (1990b) 157, note 51. The name Psamatichos may appear on a mid-seventh century cup at Athens (see J. Cook, 823).

134 Burkert (1976); see also West (1966) 46–47.

135 *Od.* 2.15, 3.300–302, 4.84–91, 126–32, 228–32, 14.278–86, 19.244–48.

136 Simon (1967) 42, dates the vase to 670–660 B.C.E.; Arias and Hirmer, 26–27, date it to 670–650. Photographs may be found in Simon (1981), pl. 4; Arias and Hirmer, pl.

patron, apparently knew a version of the Cyclops story in which Odysseus subdues his adversary with cultural artifacts. In his right hand, Polyphemos is shown holding a goblet of Maron's wine.

13. S. Morris, 37–51, 115–16, assigns an Aiginetan provenience to the Eleusis amphora although she assumes that the Polyphemus Painter trained in Athens. Gorgons, which begin to appear in Greek art after 700, are mentioned once in the *Odyssey* (11.633–35), and thrice more in the *Iliad* (5.741–42, 8.348–49, 11.36–37). These mentions are used to support a seventh century *terminus post quem* for the Homeric epics by West (1966) 46, note 2; Burkert (1976) 19; Burkert (1983) 82.

APPENDIX I

Homer and the Analysts

Previous attempts to explain the reference to Thrinakie in the Odyssean proem have met with limited success. Samuel Bassett, Bernhard van Groningen, and Klaus Rüter concluded from their separate inquiries into epic introductions that it would be anachronistic to expect a table of contents from the proem.[1] Thus it would also be wrong to demand that mention of the hero's wanderings or the demise of the crew represent the events of the entire *Odyssey,* or even the *Apologoi.* Yet as Stephanie West remarks, this brings us no closer to understanding why these references were made, or why they are formulated as they are.

Bassett explains the reference to Thrinakie with Aristotle's assertion that the poet "must define his theme at the outset, and must give a 'sample' (δεῖγμα) to illustrate his treatment of this theme, 'that the listener's mind may not be kept in suspense, for vagueness causes the mind to stray.'"[2] D. M. Jones responds with the claim that Aristotle is merely describing the Odyssean prologue, although Jones ignores the fact that Aristotle had at his disposal a number of Greek epics now lost to us. At the same time, neither Bassett nor Aristotle indicate how Thrinakie illustrates an Odyssean theme, or what that theme might be.

[1] Bassett (1923) 347; Bassett (1934) 106–7, 109; Groningen, 282ff.; Rüter, 44. See also *CHO* 1:68–69; Ford, 20.

[2] Bassett (1934) 105. See also Bassett (1934) 106; Bassett (1923) 342; A. Lenz, 12–13. Bassett's further explanation, that the poet focuses our attention on Odysseus by stripping the hero of his companions, does not account for the emphasis awarded the crew.

Groningen suggests that Homer composed by free-association and that the issue of the crew's destruction derailed his train of thought.[3] This is of course tantamount to admitting the poet's incompetence at the most elementary level of composition.

Focke notes that the *Odyssey* begins with Odysseus alone on a desert island. From this he argues that the proem must prepare the audience for the initial situation with mention of the fate of the crew *and the assurance that Odysseus attempted to save them* (1.5–6).[4] This leads to the further assurance that the crew—and not Odysseus—were responsible for their demise (1.7–9). Verses 7–9 are then necessary elaborations of verses 5–6. Like verses 5–6, those which follow are meant to exonerate Odysseus *rather than* to blame the crew.

The events on Thrinakie are the immediate cause of Odysseus' plight on Ogygie, so that it would be natural to explain the initial situation of the poem with reference to the episode. Yet Homer could have dispensed with this explanation in a single verse by remarking that Odysseus lost his crew when they ate the cattle of Helios. More important, even though it may have been "natural" to defend Odysseus with the statement that he attempted to save his men, such a defense was by no means necessary. Why then did the poet go on to declare that the crew were to blame for their destruction? Why raise the issue of guilt and responsibility at all? Were Focke's explanation correct, four lines of a ten line proem would be simple accidents of psychology, that is, of Homer's partiality for his hero. Moreover, these verses would solve a problem which they themselves introduced. Focke offers a partial defense of verses 4–5, but not of verses 6–9.[5]

Analytic scholars, most notably Jaeger, have long maintained that the first divine assembly presents an "enlightened" concept of justice alien to Homeric thought. Jaeger accordingly dismissed the scene as the

[3] Groningen, 286; objected to by Jones, 20, and Clay (1983) 35.

[4] Focke, 26, and 248–251. Desperation alone accounts for the fact that Heubeck (1954) 86, note 121, followed by Jones, 13, and Clay (1983) 36–38, 218, resorts to Focke's further claim that verses 6–9 emphasize Odysseus' innocence. Focke himself dismisses verses 28–47 as an interpolation (78), so that he is able to avoid the consequences of the repetition of *atasthaliēsin* at verse 7. Those who follow him do not: Heubeck (see also Rüter, 50) claims that the verse is "formulaic" so that the repetition is insignificant, while Jones resorts to vituperation. Eisenberger, 2–4, accepts Focke's reading of verses 6–9, although he argues that Homer contrasts Odysseus with men who die by *atasthaliai*.

[5] Some reference to the crew's demise would still be necessary. A statement to the effect that they perished in the harbor of the Laistrygones and at Thrinakie would satisfy the objections of S. West. No progress over the positions of Focke and Groningen is made by Rüter, 43–45; Eisenberger, 1.

interpolation of a *dichtender Problematiker.*[6] Analytic reconstructions of Homeric thought fed into theories of Greek intellectual history proposed by scholars such as Fränkel.[7] As noted in Chapter 1, Fränkel employed a teleological approach to intellectual history, in which the *Iliad* with its archaic world-view represented the point of departure and mature Attic tragedy the goal. Revolutionary developments in Ionic philosophy during the Archaic period supplied a motive for the formulation of the divine assembly to advocate a new code of justice.[8]

A theoretical basis for this teleological approach was provided by Hegel. Fränkel is by no means the first to apply Hegelian theory to the study of ancient literature, although his attempt remains among the most ambitious and influential. In addition to Fränkel, belief that clear signs of intellectual progress distinguish certain passages of the *Odyssey* from the *Iliad* is fundamental to the hermeneutics of Jaeger, Jacoby, Snell, von der Mühll, Pfeiffer, Lesky, Schadewaldt, Heubeck, Jones, Rüter, and Fenik, among others.[9] The attraction of Fränkel's approach for scholars of Analytic inclination is obvious—it allows them to find the textual strata on which two centuries of Homeric scholarship have been based.

Analysts and Unitarians have found themselves generally agreed that Poseidon belongs to a more primitive stage of the *Odyssey* and Greek thought than that which we find reflected in the divine assembly.[10] The Analysts, moreover, can provide an elegant explanation for Poseidon's limited role in the events of the poem despite his prominence in the Introduction. They begin with the observation that the curse of Polyphemos is fulfilled in each of its points—late return, on the ship of another, in evil plight, companions lost, and troubles at home—yet Poseidon's actual interference is restricted to a pair of scenes from Books 5 and 13. Therefore, in an earlier—and apparently much shorter—version of the *Odyssey,* it was Odysseus who caused the death of the crew by revealing his name to the Cyclops. When Polyphemos cursed Odys-

[6]Jaeger, 74.

[7]See especially Fränkel, 94. Also the approach of Jacoby (1933), especially 178, 187–89.

[8]On the other hand, others find nothing new in Zeus's speech: Wilamowitz (1931–32) 2:118–19; Jones, 18; *GGR* 363; *CHO* at 1.32ff. Lloyd-Jones (1971) 28, sees in Zeus's speech "a belief radically different from that found in the *Iliad,*" but does not find it necessary to account for this with theories of cultural evolution.

[9]See Lesky (1967) 118–19. Important early exceptions are the work of Reinhardt (1948 = 1960); Segal (1962 = 1994, chap. 2 and 3).

[10]For Poseidon see Woodhouse, 39–40; Jacoby (1933) 189–90; Focke, 156–61; Heubeck (1954) 84–85; *CHO* at 9.526–35; Jones, 11–12; Reinhardt (1960) 69–76; Fenik (1974) 208–30; Rüter, 44–45, 89–90; Clay (1983) 229–30; Dawe at *Od.* 1.20, 1.71–75.

seus to his father, Poseidon destroyed the flotilla immediately on its departure.[11]

According to this reconstruction, the changes worked on the text by a later moralizing poet left Poseidon without a meaningful role in the poem. The god's primitive outlook is the residue of an earlier conception of the gods. For whatever reason, Homer could not or did not wish to dispose of or even alter that outlook so as to harmonize it with his own very different cosmology. The characterization of Poseidon in the Introduction thus becomes a simple accident of his "fixed" role in the story of Odysseus' wanderings.

The relationship of the divine assembly to the Thrinakian episode is somewhat more complicated: the proem insists on the guilt of the crew and even links their demise to that of Aigisthos with close repetition of *atasthaliēsin,* or 'by their reckless acts'. The fate of the crew thus illustrates the code of justice announced in the assembly. We have the theme required by Aristotle—or so it would seem. Yet Homeric scholars since Focke have regularly argued that the episode itself represents the "older" outlook of the *Iliad* (see Chapter 4). As a result, these same scholars have censured the reference to Thrinakie in the proem. Jones, for example, declares that "if the poet had wished deliberately to conceal and confuse the moral issue of the retribution that overtook Aegisthus and the suitors, he could not have done so more effectively than by comparing it to the vengeance of the Sun-god." He concludes that "as evidence for the poetic meaning or intention of the Odyssey, the prologue is valueless."[12]

Fenik, who argues that the Thrinakian episode "remains in disharmony with Zeus' lecture *and* with the poet's own editorial comment," sees the prologue as colored by its local narrative environment:

> Here is a case where I . . . am inclined to see a hasty attempt to harmonize the Helios story with the ethical norms set forth by Zeus in his first speech, an attempt that is simply abandoned within the wrath-tale [Thrinakie] itself. No significant internal changes were made within the story to adapt it to Zeus' speech, and given its distance from the prologue, the discrepancy can easily pass unnoticed.[13]

Yet Fenik's explanation cannot be applied to the wrath of Poseidon, which figures prominently in the first divine assembly and is manifestly

[11] Pfeiffer (1928) 2361–62; Jones, 13.
[12] Jones, 14, 21.
[13] Fenik (1974) 216, 225–26.

at odds with its central themes.[14] Moreover, does the Introduction seem a likely place to find signs of haste or carelessness?

Those who argue that the Thrinakian episode reflects an "older" cosmology are unable to account for the portrayal of the crew in verses 7–9 as responsible for their own demise. As a result, reference to the episode in the prologue is regularly excised by Analysts and disparaged by Unitarians. As in the case of factual discrepancies, such criticism of the prologue has been determined by a prior interpretation of the *Apologoi*. Schadewaldt avoids this difficulty by arguing that Thrinakie was modified to represent the new cosmology; but he does so at the cost of transporting these same inconsistencies into the episode itself, which in his view belongs to the earlier system of belief (see Chapter 4).

Nor have scholars been entirely unsuccessful at finding traces of an earlier, more "primitive," cosmology in the Revenge narrative. Perhaps the most famous such attempt was made by Schadewaldt, who argued that such moral concerns were lacking from the *Urtext,* and that the *Bearbeiter* sought to provide a moral justification for the suitors' death by burdening them with crimes of varying severity.[15] With Schadewaldt's analysis compare the interpretation offered by Whitman, whose monumental *Homer and the Heroic Tradition* has been called "the acme of New Criticism":

> . . . the moral design of the poem, the somewhat schematized view of poetic justice announced by Zeus in the exordium, is far more an assertion of the validity of forms and quasi-ritual observances than a real exploration of the issues involved. The evil of the suitors is a house of cards, carefully piled up to be knocked down, with the appearance of justice at the appointed time. In the case of Amphinomus and Leiodes, the poet seems to struggle with the story a little. . . . Here one feels that a primitive story . . . has resisted the efforts of the poet to moralize and universalize it.[16]

Harry Levy, who approves Whitman's analysis, goes so far as to reconstruct from the Revenge an unattested folk-tale tradition "in which the generous host is beset by guests who abuse his hospitality to such an extent that they threaten his livelihood. . . . The gods intervene, and

[14] Rüter's interpretation runs aground on this same point (for which see above, Chapter 1).

[15] Schadewaldt (1958, 1960); Erbse (1972) 131–32.

[16] Whitman, 305–6. For the assessment of his work see Martin, 3. Fenik (1974) 222, also assigns Amphinomos to a primitive stratum of the poem. Compare the interpretations in *CHO* 1:56–57; Nagler (1990).

punish this symbolic homicide with death." Despite the poet's efforts to adapt the story to an epic context, "the emotion-laden denouement which . . . was appropriate to the early form of the tale was too deeply embedded . . . to be discarded. Conflated with the theme of a returning hero's identification by a test of strength, it resulted in the story of the massacre as we have it."[17]

The critic who protests against the treatment of Amphinomos and Leiodes is merely responding to tensions that these characters were designed to introduce. It is characteristic of Analytic method to identify such tensions as imperfections and to explain them with the *Bearbeiter* or the tradition. Yet censure is not the only critical response available to us. It is often more fruitful to proceed from the assumption that the text is sound, the poet competent, and ask instead to what are such tensions meant to direct our attention. In the present case, note that Athene herself "binds" Amphinomos so that he will die at the hands of Telemachos (18.155–56). As Rüter remarks: "This is not a case of entrapment by the gods. The suitors have long since ensnared themselves in their crimes; Athene merely sees to it that these crimes are a matter of public record and that no one escapes the punishment they have earned."[18] The suitors are for some reason so offensive to Athene that even the best among them deserves his fate.

What is it, then, about the suitors that provokes Athene's implacable hatred? In Chapter 5 I argued that her hatred is based not merely on what they have done or hope to do, but on who they are and what they represent. Although Homer goes to great lengths to construct guilt for the suitors, as he does for the crew, this is but the moral dimension of a larger complex of oppositions which sets the suitors against civilized values and hence the divine embodiment of those values, the civic goddess Athene.[19] The fate of Amphinomos does not subvert these oppositions so much as it affirms them, by privileging group over individual identity while insisting on the criminality of merely being a suitor.

[17] Levy, 150, 147.

[18] Rüter, 78.

[19] The events of Book 16 (see especially verses 364–92) reveal the suitors to be cold-blooded assassins willing to murder the lawful heir to the Ithacan kingdom simply so that they may go on ravaging his estate. In desperation, Penelope reminds Antinoos, the leader of the attempted ambush, that his father owed his life to Odysseus. Eurymachos' hypocritical assurance that, owing to gratitude for Odysseus' past acts of kindness, Telemachos was dearest to him of all men, depicts precisely what should have been the case but was not (*Od.* 16.445–47). See Nagler (1990) 345. Yet, as I have argued, this is but one aspect—albeit an important one—of their portrayal. For more on the suitors' behavior, see Felson-Rubin, chap. 6; Saïd.

Unitarian scholars must also explain why such widely divergent views on justice should coexist in the text. Those who accept the evolutionary model of Fränkel have a ready explanation—the cosmology that produced the divine assembly was not yet fully integrated in Greek thought:

> The new outlook that appears in the *Odyssey* could not permeate and reformulate the tradition in an even manner, especially since these new ideas first attain their complete expression in lyric poetry and philosophy rather than epic. In the *Odyssey,* old and new ways of thought are often juxtaposed; the old remains unemphasized because it is self-understood, while the new is occasionally thrown into high-relief.[20]

Fenik supplies Homer with a positive motive for leaving unaltered episodes that belong to the older outlook:

> There is, in fact, good reason to believe that one poet could incorporate discordant ideas into a single poem. He was, after all, working within a tradition that preserved masses of older material—indeed, in a tradition that looked upon such preservation as one of its chief functions. A god's wrath directed against a hapless mortal *is* something relatively primitive, and doubtless older than the concept of the gods as arbiters and overseers of justice on earth. . . . It is hardly outrageous to suppose that he [the poet] would incorporate these older elements into a poem whose basic theodicy was in contradiction to them *if* they were useful from a narrative point of view or simply interesting in themselves.[21]

Thus, Homer was willing to sacrifice the coherence of his poem for the sake of incorporating all that the tradition had handed down. The Homeric poems become a pastiche, a witness to many periods and outlooks, representative of none.

A generation earlier, Pfeiffer employed similar arguments to explain discrepancies between the plan that Odysseus announces in Book 16 to hide the weapons in the *megaron* and the execution of his plan three books later:

> There are an entire series of analogous difficulties in the latter half of the *Odyssey.* This can be explained with the fact that the poet of *our Odyssey* had at his disposal a richer fund of earlier epic poems than he did

[20] Rüter, 73 (see also 82). Similar views may be found in Jacoby (1933) 135, 188, 190–91; Whitman, 308; Andersen (1973) 21; Fenik (1974) 221.

[21] Fenik (1974) 218–19; see also 221.

> in the case of Odysseus' earlier fate and adventures. In his characteristic desire for comprehensiveness, he appropriated all sorts of material from such poetry in order to shape his own epic, although such material was not entirely harmonious, both in terms of motif and in other respects as well.[22]

This theory flatly contradicts Aristotle's own pronouncement that the *Odyssey* does not incorporate conflicting traditions into the narrative.[23]

It is worth rehearsing some of the premises on which the above arguments are based. First, divergence equals contradiction—it is, in short, a question of logical error. Second, if a contradiction can be found, the explanation for it is genetic/historical—this is a preconditioned response of the Analytic tradition from which the arguments themselves are derived.[24] The Odyssean prologue was thus composed for an earlier version of the poem. In a prior version of the Thrinakian episode the crew were depicted as guiltless and the gods as malevolent, while the Revenge is based on "a primitive story . . . [that] has resisted the efforts of the poet to moralize and universalize it." Such an approach requires a text of the prologue and of the Thrinakian episode no less stable and carrying no less authority than the *Urtext* of nineteenth century Analysis. Homer followed these earlier "texts" for whatever reason down to their minute details, and was either willing to tolerate or simply unaware of significant discrepancies in the moral universe of his poem. It would be difficult for anyone who subscribed to this approach to believe that the Odyssean plot is shaped by the theodicy announced in the first divine assembly. Why then is the assembly awarded its programmatic position as the first scene of the poem?

Detailed analysis of the Introduction shows that the explanations proposed by Rüter and Fenik for how incompatible world-views could coexist in the text are deficient on several important points (see Chapter 1). First, whatever may be said about Thrinakie, divergence in the ethical values of Poseidon and the other Olympians are not separated by nine or more books, so that it may "pass unnoticed." Instead, the divergence frames the very scene in which Zeus articulates the principles of his rule. Nor can it be claimed that "old" and "new" ways of thought simply "stand side-by-side." Rather, they are brought into the sharpest

[22] Pfeiffer (1960) 1 (with which compare Whitman, 306).

[23] Aristotle, *Po.* 1451a. For interpretation of the passage, see Gantar, followed by Dimock, 3–4.

[24] See Clay (1983) 3–7; Goldhill (1989).

possible contrast. But even if we were to assume that these discrepancies only become evident some nine or more books later, what, short of simple capriciousness, could explain the fact that Homer singled out those stories from the *Apologoi* most at odds with his own outlook for mention in the passage where that outlook is first announced; indeed, not content with this, he chose one of them, the Thrinakian episode, to illustrate his own very different conception of divine justice? This is truly not the work of a poet who has advanced very far in his craft.

Clay, who recognizes the difficulties inherent in traditional approaches to the problem of justice in Homer, attempts a novel way out of the impasse. Clay accepts the Analytic premise that Odyssean theology is not uniform, but rejects a historical interpretation of the phenomenon.[25] She observes that on numerous occasions the poem's human characters depict the gods both as overseers of justice and as dispensers of evil. From this she concludes that the *Odyssey* is informed by a "double theodicy." In other words, Clay equates the world-view of the *Odyssey* with that of its characters.

Now there can be no doubt that Greeks at all periods could entertain ambivalent attitudes towards the gods. Yet Clay does not explain why "the [Odyssean] poet unlike the poet of the *Iliad,* never in his own person blames the gods."[26] Her *exempla,* moreover, conform to Jørgensen's law: whereas the authorial voice and the gods themselves always name the divine agents responsible for an event, the poem's human actors employ the generic terms *daimōn, theos,* or "Zeus," unless they are acting on specific knowledge.[27] The fact that Zeus is the only god regularly named by humans explains another recurrent phenomenon in the *Odyssey:* humans regularly blame Zeus for their troubles even when they know that another god is in fact responsible.[28]

25 Clay (1983) 3–7, 218.

26 Lloyd-Jones (1971) 29.

27 Although Jørgensen's interpretation requires some refinement ("Zeus," for example, has a special affinity for fate and the weather), the observation is correct that virtually all uses of *theos/theoi* and *daimōn* occur in direct discourse and exceptions usually admit of a ready explanation. When, for example, Odysseus says at 5.304 that Zeus began the storm that wrecked his craft off Scherie, the text preserves a theology far older than Homer. Here to be sure are strata belonging to different stages of intellectual development, but of a kind tolerated throughout the history of Greek religion—they do not indicate an incomplete transition from one mode of thought to another. Clay's oversight, if indeed it is one, is curious since she is among the few scholars to recognize the full significance of Jørgensen's findings (which can incidentally be extended to cover other contexts such as the speech of Amphimedon in Book 24).

28 See, for example, *Od.* 1.326–27, with 1.346–49, 3.131–36, 145 (with which compare 4.173), 23.352.

Clay offers a different interpretation for Athene's absence from the enchanted realm: the goddess was angry at Odysseus these last ten years rather than merely indifferent to his sufferings. For this reason Clay makes no reference to the theme of Athene's wrath in her discussion of the double theodicy. As we saw in chapter 2, however, not only the Olympians but their values are conspicuously absent from the world of the adventures. This can be explained neither with divine wrath nor with a double theodicy. I conclude that while the poem's human actors entertain ambivalent views of the gods, the authorial perspective is consistently that of Zeus and Athene as guarantors of justice. Athene fails to assist her protégé during his years of wandering because he finds himself in a world over which she has no jurisdiction, a world in apposition to the Greek cultural sphere.

APPENDIX 2

Poseidon and Athene in Myth and Cult

The Contest Myth at Trozen and Argos

In the Athenian contest myth, Poseidon avenges his loss to Athene by destroying agricultural land with a tidal wave. Other versions of the contest myth told at Trozen and Argos suggest that the theme of agricultural crisis is an integral feature of the contest. The correlative material also suggests that the association of Eleusis with the god's revenge at Athens is an accident of neither geography nor history. The possible implications of this association are great, since an agricultural crisis also leads to the foundation of the Eleusinian cult of Demeter. Moreover, the arrival of Demeter at Eleusis, the drought that precedes it, and the cult that results from it, were assigned by tradition to the reign of Erechtheus.[1]

In the Argolic contest, Poseidon flooded the Argive plain in revenge for his loss to Hera and then "made the water disappear."[2] Hera no less than Athene represents the natural order of the *polis,* so that the Argive myth reproduces the opposition that informs its Attic counterpart.[3] Flooding is a simple inversion of drought, and like drought an excess of salt water can render the land barren. In the satyr play that concluded the Suppliant trilogy of Aeschylus, Amymone brought the water back to

[1] *Marmor Parium* 23–9; Diodorus Siculus 1.29.1–3; Scholia to Aristides 3.55. Apollodorus 3.14.7, however, assigns the creation of Demeter's cult to the reign of Erechtheus' father, Pandion.

[2] See above, Chapter 5, and Plutarch, *Symposiacs* 9.6.

[3] *GR* 164–65.

Argos by sleeping with Poseidon, who presented her with the springs of Lerna in exchange.[4] We should recall that according to Herodotus the Danaids introduced the cult of Demeter in Argos, and Aeschylus may have concluded the Suppliant trilogy with the foundation of the Thesmophoria.[5] In Arcadia to the north Poseidon was said to have raped Demeter at a spring, and she bore him Kore and the horse Areion.[6] Perhaps the version of the Athenian contest in which Poseidon produced a horse to support his claim reflects an earlier association of the contest myth with Kore's birth and disappearance.[7]

Although Poseidon was said to have lost the contest at Athens and to have reached a compromise at Trozen, the final outcome of either story is the same in that Athene and Poseidon received joint worship as patrons of the city. The title of Poseidon Basileus, or 'Poseidon King', which is unique to his cult at Trozen, draws the analogy still closer.[8] Pausanias, our source for the Trozenian contest myth, follows it with mention of a cult to Poseidon Phytalmios, whose temple was adjacent to that of Demeter Thesmophoros: for some unspecified reason, Posei-

[4] Seaford (1984) 24. The springs produced the Lernaean Hydra, a monster that threatened agricultural land. In Hesiod, *fr.* 128 M-W, the Danaids or Danaos taught the Argives to dig wells.

[5] For the Danaids, see Herodotus 2.171. For the trilogy, see Garvie, 227, note 6; Seaford (1984) 24.

[6] The story is told in connection with both the cult of Demeter at Thelpousa (Pausanias 8.25.5–7) and her related cult at Phigalia (Pausanias 8.37.1–9, 8.42.1–3). Statius, *Theb.* 6.301–3, calls Poseidon the master of Areion. Poseidon is said to have sired Areion at the spring of Tilphousa in Boeotia by Erinys (Scholia to *Il.* 23.346–47). The Thelpousan union also took place by a spring (*GGR* 448).

[7] Poseidon was also worshipped as Pater in a joint temple to Artemis Propylaia at the entrance to the temple complex of Demeter at Eleusis (Pausanias 1.38.6). In Arcadia, where Poseidon and Artemis were worshipped in the temple complex of Demeter, Artemis was said to be the daughter of Demeter (Pausanias 8.37.6). The myths surrounding the family of Kerkyon, most notably the myth of Hippothoon, are also suggestive of the cult of Poseidon as Hippios (*CGS* 4.37–38). Admittedly, there is no reference in any author to the worship of Poseidon as father of Kore at Eleusis, and the title of Pater is usually explained with the fact that he was father to Eumolpos, but are these points of contact mere coincidence?

[8] Pausanias 2.30.6. For the temple, see Welter, 43 ff., who dates the cult to the beginning of the eighth century. Cult connections between the two cities were strong: Athene Polias was worshipped on the acropolis of both cities (Pausanias 2.30.6, 2.32.5), and the cult of Poseidon Kalaureatos was celebrated at Athens (*IG*[3] 369.74). The most important correlation between the cults of these two cities must be inferred, however. Although Poseidon is said to be one of the two principal deities of Trozen, Pausanias makes no mention of a temple belonging to him there. It seems plausible that Poseidon Basileus shared the temple of Athene on the Acropolis of Trozen, the same arrangement that Poseidon-Erechtheus enjoyed at Athens. This would not be the only place where Pausanias requires his readers to make such inferences; see, for example, 1.24.3 with Frazer's remarks ad loc.

don became angry with the inhabitants and sent "salt water upon the seeds and roots of the plants," until, mollified by prayer and sacrifice, he relented. The Trozenian account thus resembles the Athenian version of Poseidon's revenge in which he attacked the agricultural land by flooding the Thriasian plain.[9]

Pausanias goes on to say that Althepos, a son to Poseidon by Leis, established the cult of Demeter Thesmophoros at Trozen, just as his son Eumolpos introduced the mysteries at Eleusis.[10] In Attica, moreover, a certain Phytalos was said to have housed Demeter in her search for Kore, and was rewarded for this service with the fig tree.[11] Phytalos lived at Skiron, and on the site of his house was built the temple to Demeter in which Poseidon and Athene received worship during the Skira. The clan of the Phytalidai purified Theseus upon his arrival at Athens from his birthplace at Trozen.[12]

The Cult of Athene-Apatouria at Trozen and Athens

Pausanias relates that near Trozen was an island, Sphairia, separated from the mainland by water shallow enough to be forded.[13] Legend had it that Bellerophon came to Trozen to ask Pittheus the king for his daughter Aithra in marriage. Athene, however, appeared to Aithra in a dream and instructed her to offer sacrifice to Sphairos, the eponymous hero of the island. When Aithra crossed over to the island with libations, she was raped by Bellerophon's father, Poseidon. After the rape, Aithra founded the cult of Athene Apatouria, a cognomen held by the Trozenians to mean 'deceit', and renamed the island Hiera. She also established the custom that maidens dedicate their girdles to the goddess before

[9] Note that this version of the myth presupposes the annexation of Eleusis, which the invasion by Eumolpos was designed to explain.

[10] Pausanias 2.32.8. The descendants of the Trozenian Anthes, another son of Poseidon, maintained the god's cult at Halicarnassus, a Trozenian colony, for over five centuries (*PR*[3] 480; A. Cook, 1:74).

[11] Pausanias 1.37.2 (a fig also marked the location of Kore's descent into the underworld).

[12] *CGS* 4.53. Pausanias 2.31.1–2 also relates that Trozen, like Eleusis, boasted an entrance to Hades located within a temple complex to Artemis. In the Eleusinian temple, Poseidon was worshipped as Pater, and the temple at Trozen was said to have been built by his son Theseus. Pausanias 2.35.10 also indicates that Hermion, near Trozen, also had an entrance to Hades and a temple to Demeter with which it was associated.

[13] Pausanias 2.31.9, 2.32.1, 2.33.1, 10.10.8. For the dedication of a lock of hair to Hippolytos see also Euripides, *Hipp.* 1423–27. Aithra is said to be the daughter of Pittheus at *Il.* 3.144. Note the similarity to the story of Bellerophon's own birth.

marriage. Bellerophon meanwhile was driven out of Corinth, whereupon Aithra married Phalanthos. The child of her union with Poseidon was Theseus.[14] At the temple of Theseus' son, Hippolytos, it was also custom for maidens to dedicate a lock of their hair before marriage.

Trozenian myth represents Aithra's rite of passage as a journey across salt water, in which Athene's permanent maidenhood and Poseidon's sexuality furnish the starting point and destination. Athene sends the girl to a liminal zone where the crime of change can take place, and she returns a woman. Hippolytos, whose initiation into adult sexuality is represented in more drastic form as the death of the virgin, provides a male counterpart to his grandmother.

Although Pausanias himself fails to mention the fact, Athene's title relates this myth to the Ionian festival of the Apatouria, which celebrated the incorporation of infants, wives, and ephebes into the phratry.[15] At Athens, the festival took place over the course of three days, and on the third, entitled *koureōtis,* three kinds of sacrifice were offered: the *meion,* which was apparently performed when infants were entered in the register of the phratry, the *koureion,* when young men became ephebes, and the *gamēlia,* which was offered by a newly married husband on behalf of his wife upon her inclusion in his phratry.

The Apatouria places the story of Aithra in a civic context, and it can only be this which explains Athene's involvement in the transition from maidenhood to motherhood. Aithra journeys from the *polis* in which Athene is seen to be active, to a place controlled and embodied by Poseidon. There she conceives the king who would unite Athens and Trozen politically. Aithra's journey is analogous to that of a newly wed

[14]Hyginus (*Fab.* 37; see also Apollodorus 3.15.7 with Frazer's note) offers another version of the story, in which Aigeus and Poseidon raped Aithra on the same night in the temple of Athene, so that Theseus is the son of both his human and divine parents (H. Usener, 332, has shown that the combination of human and divine parents is a pervasive element of heroic myth). Athene's temple serves as the functional equivalent of the dream in the Apatourian myth, in that it represents her authorization of the rape. Bellerophon's relationship with Poseidon extends beyond the fact that he is his son and the master of Pegasos. In an account known from Plutarch, *Mul. Virt.* 248, Bellerophon, like his father in the contest myth, attempted to punish the Athenian king Iobates by drawing a wave upon the land. The Athenian women, however, exposed their genitals, thereby forcing him to desist (scurrilous behavior was noted feature of the Demeter cult, where it had, as here, an apotropaic function). Bellerophon may have been explicitly identified with the god in a late Corinthian crater now in Bari; Dunbabin, (1953) 1172, however, assumes that Poseidon and Areion are meant.

[15]Frazer on Pausanias 2.33.1; *CGS* 4.53–54; *MO* 167–68; Deubner, 232–34; Parke, 88–92.

bride from the home of her parents to that of her husband, and with it incorporation into his phratry.[16] Once again myth represents the *polis* as controlling the forces on which it depends—forces associated with the cycle of birth and destruction in man and nature, forces associated with Poseidon, at once excluded from and incorporated into the very heart of the *polis*. Athene remains sterile, like the political order that she embodies.

Athene and Poseidon Hippioi

Throughout the Greek world Poseidon was celebrated as the father of the first horse and on at least two occasions Athene was seen as responsible for the horse's taming.[17] In our first example, a variant of the contest myth at Athens, Poseidon was said to have struck a rock and brought forth a horse, whereupon Athene bridled and rode it.[18] We may elucidate the story with reference to the cult of Poseidon Hippios at Colonus, where the god shared his temple with Athene: there it was said that Poseidon spilled his semen on the cliff and so sired the horse Skyphios.[19] A passage from the *Oedipus at Colonus* suggests that in his cult at

16 Calame (1990) offers a recent and thorough study of the Theseus myth. See also Calame (1986) chap. 8. Trozen was the birthplace of Theseus, and archaeological evidence for a city on the site begins in the Geometric period (see Welter). The Theseus saga, as is generally recognized, is a comparatively young tradition (*MO* 163; Brommer [1982]) and it has even been argued that Poseidon's paternity dates from after Salamis (Binder, 22). Nilsson, *MO* 165, argues that the story of Theseus' journey to Athens belongs to the early historical period, and on somewhat slender evidence assigns a post-Iliadic date to the association of Aithra with Trozen (167). In all likelihood, Theseus was associated with Trozen virtually from the city's foundation, and the myth of Aithra and Athene likewise dates to this period. Be that as it may, the pairing of Poseidon and Athene in myth belongs once more to a tradition whose origins could scarcely antedate the historical period.

17 In addition to the cults discussed below, Wide (see above, Chapter 5) argues that both gods were worshipped as Hippioi in Cyrene and Pheneos. One is tempted to make a similar case for their joint temple at Asia in the vicinity of Pheneos, which was located at the source of the Alpheus and Eurotas.

18 Sources may be found in Frazer at Apollodorus 3.14.1; see also Detienne and Vernant (1974) 198, note 92. Although this "hippic" contest is only found in later authors, Athene was regularly associated with Pegasos in the fifth century at Athens. On the Acropolis the winged horse was to be found on the helmet of the Athene Parthenos, a statue of Bellerophon astride Pegasos may have crowned the apex of the pediment of the temple of Athene Nike (Yalouris, 51; Hiller, 84). Yalouris 48–55 also notes that the image of the winged horse occurs with great frequency on the Panathenaic prize amphoras and on Attic coins.

19 Nagy (1990) 232–33.

Colonus Poseidon was also said to have introduced the art of horseback riding.[20] This is an achievement assigned to Athene at Corinth, where the goddess was honored as the inventor of the bridle, the instrument by which she secured her victory over Poseidon at Athens. The tokens on which the gods base their claims provide an even more explicit affirmation of the subordination of nature to technological *mētis* than did the wave and olive tree. The "hippic" version of the contest between Athene and Poseidon would thus seem to draw on traditions known from the cults of Colonus and Corinth so as to restate the themes of the orthodox account.

The tradition that Athene had invented the chariot gave rise to yet another incarnation of the contest myth: in an account found in Nonnus, Erechtheus defeated Skelmis, another of Poseidon's sons, in the first chariot race.[21] The literary model for the passage is the chariot race at the funeral games of Patroklos in Book 23 of the *Iliad:* Skelmis assumes the role of Menelaos, and Erechtheus of Antilochos.[22] The ritual model for the passage is the chariot races at the Panathenaic games, and the mythological model for the games is the victory of Athene in the war against the Giants. Nonnus thus draws on two independent sources in which *mētis* triumphs in competition with *biē*.[23]

Pegasos and Bellerophon at Corinth

The Bellerophon Saga was of particular importance at Corinth, where Athene received cult worship as Chalinitis, or 'The Bridler'.[24]

20 Sophocles, *OC* 714–15, who also refers to the contest myth. The word *akestēra* at verse 714 suggests that Sophocles was thinking of the violent metaphors *philtron* and *pharmakon* in Pindar, *O.* 13.68, 85, which relate the Corinthian bridle to Medea's magic.

21 Nonnus, 37.103 ff., who draws the comparison to the contest himself at 37.320–23. Some said that Erichthonios himself was the inventor of the four-horse chariot which he drove in the first Panathenaic games. See *Marmor Parium,* 18; Yalouris, 58–59; Frazer on Apollodorus 3.14.6; *HN* 156.

22 Detienne and Vernant (1974) 197–98.

23 Athene's role in the *Iliad* might lead one to expect her hippic cult to have military attributes, but I am aware of only one other case where this occurs. At the Hippodrome in Olympia there were altars to Poseidon and Hera Hippioi at the starting point, and nearby, at the entrance to the "wedge," there was another pair of altars to Athene and Ares Hippioi (Pausanias 5.15.5–6). The grouping suggests a contrast between the wartime and peacetime *agōnes* of charioteering.

24 I accept Yalouris' argument that effective equitation began in Greece during the Orientalizing Period. There is definite evidence for horseback riding as early as the Late Bronze Age (Hood), and evidence for the use of bits may be even earlier (Crouwel, 101–8). But Yalouris has certainly established that improved riding and the introduction

The account of Bellerophon's life in Book 6 of the *Iliad* indicates that it was sufficiently well known to be understood by a Panhellenic audience in highly condensed form.[25] Hesiod relates that Poseidon sired Bellerophon on Eurynome in the house of Glaukos and presented his son with Pegasos.[26] Bellerophon is ostensibly the son of Glaukos in Homer, who betrays an awareness of Poseidon's paternity by alluding to Bellerophon's divine birth.[27] Thus, when Pindar and Hyginus make Bellerophon the son of Poseidon, while Eumelos and Pausanias indicate that he is the son of Glaukos, the distinction is one of perspective.[28] Historians would naturally represent Bellerophon as the son of Glaukos, while those who traffic in myth, although they could still acknowledge that Bellerophon numbered among the Aiolidai, made Poseidon the father. In like manner, Pindar could include the bridle in a list of Corinthian inventions at Olympian 13.20, and forty-five verses later in the same poem ascribe its creation to Athene.

The paternity of Glaukos and of Poseidon coexist in the tradition and are not mutually exclusive.[29] As the human master of Pegasos, Bellerophon acts as the mortal counterpart to Poseidon, the only Olympian god regularly depicted on horseback. The affinity between them is ex-

---

of a new form of bit from the East are more or less contemporary. Note that Hood's "cavalryman,"—unarmed, though being headless he may have worn a helmet—rides on a "donkey seat," from which it would have been virtually impossible to fight, since it was insecure and the horse would have been difficult to control. Sitting on a horse is not the same thing as effective riding. Vase paintings indicate that Bellerophon and Pegasos were known at Corinth before the mid-seventh century (Yalouris, 21–26; Dunbabin [1953] 1164–65), and the numismatic evidence suggests a cult association of Athene with the bridling of Pegasos at least by the final quarter of the sixth (the earliest coins depicting Pegasos and Athene are dated by Kraay, 340, to approximately 515 B.C.E.; see also Kroll and Waggoner, 333–35).

25 *Il.* 6.119 ff. See Will, 146–47; Peppermüller. *Il.* 6.206 gives Bellerophon an otherwise unattested son, Hippolochos. The name may suggest that the story of Pegasos, and with him horseback riding, was known to Iliadic tradition but suppressed as an obvious anachronism. For the tendency of the names of sons to reflect important attributes of their fathers, see above, Chapter 5.

26 Hesiod, *fr.* 43a M–W. The same genealogy may be found in the scholia to Pindar, *O.* 13.99, and fourth-century Asclepiades Tragilensis, *FGrH* 12F13, who adds that Poseidon provided Bellerophon with Pegasos.

27 Peppermüller, 6, note 7, assumes that *gonos* at *Il.* 6.191 refers to Zeus's paternity of Aiolos. But Iobates only recognized that Bellerophon, his own son-in-law, was the *gonos* of a god after he had killed the Chimaira, Solymoi, and Amazons, and had survived an ambush of the king's men. That Aiolos was the son of Zeus had, of course, always been known to him.

28 For Bellerophon as son of Glaukos, see Eumelus, *Corinthiaca* fr. 6; Pausanias 2.4.1, in a discussion of the sanctuary of Athene Chalinitis. For Bellerophon as son of Poseidon, see Pindar, *O.* 13.69; Hyginus, *Fab.* 157. See also Aristides 46.29.

29 *GG* 82; Malten, 155.

pressed in genealogical terms by making the god father to the mortal. The quasi-divine Glaukos is, moreover, a virtual hypostasis of Poseidon, so that conceptually the distinction between Bellerophon's divine and mortal fathers is minimal.[30]

Opposed to the role of Poseidon as father to Bellerophon is that of Athene as creator of the bridle by which Bellerophon could tame and ride Pegasos. This account was promulgated by the cult of Athene Chalinitis at Corinth, where it served to validate Corinthian claims to have invented the bridle.[31] Athene's role as technology goddess—specifically the technological aspect of the equestrian arts—was always fundamental to her cult: this is confirmed by renderings of Pegasos on Corinthian pottery and coins that consistently depict the horse as bridled, by the *xoanon* of Athene which apparently showed the goddess holding the bridle in her right hand and a spear in her left, and by the cult-title Chalinitis.[32] The role of Athene as inventor is, however, well precedented in Greek religious thought and her worship as Chalinitis is doubly appropriate since Athene was also a hippic deity. Horses were the most powerful force that humans could control and render useful:[33] in the cult of Athene Chalinitis, Pegasos as the archetypal horse represents the *biē* of an untamed nature, and the bridle is the technology by which that power could be exploited. As we have seen, this is also the message of the hippic version of the contest myth at Athens.

The "Corinthian bridle" seems to have arrived from Assyria in the seventh century B.C.E. At this time, Bellerophon, a local Herakles-type who perhaps already numbered among Athene's protégés, was set on the back of a winged horse in order to represent the possibilities of effective equitation.[34] Accounts of the horse's actual taming varied, although

30 Will, 188–91, treats the relevant classical references.

31 For the site of the sacred precinct see C. Williams, 102–4.

32 See Frazer on Pausanias 2.4.1, and Yalouris, 24, both citing a study of Corinthian coins from the reign of Hadrian by Imhoof-Blumer.

33 *GR* 139.

34 On Herakles and Bellerophon, Dunbabin (1953) 1180–82, remarks the affinity between the Chimaira and the Lernaian Hydra. Hesiod, *Th.* 313–25, indicates that the Chimaira and Hydra were sisters; there are also several artistic representations of Herakles battling the Chimaira. Both heroes were also said to have fought the Amazons, and Herakles was in some accounts the original owner of the winged horse Areion (Hesiod, *Aspis* 120; Pausanias 8.25.7–10; see also Dunbabin [1953] 1172–73). Bellerophon's association with Tiryns deserves mention in this context. An aryballos (Boston 397) depicts a hero in Corinthian hoplite armor attacking a lion with a human head projecting from its back in the place later occupied by the goat. If the hero is indeed Bellerophon (see Dunbabin [1953] 1165–67), then we have direct evidence for a Bellerophon Saga at Corinth which

each has a Corinthian origin: whereas Pindar, our earliest source, indicates that Bellerophon broke the horse himself, Pausanias, who most likely reports the version urged by the cult of Athene Chalinitis, indicates that Athene bridled Pegasos and gave him to Bellerophon already tamed.[35] In still another version which Strabo says is the story told at Corinth, Bellerophon tames Pegasos apparently unassisted by Athene or Poseidon.[36]

The story of the horse's taming is attested first in connection with the cult of Athene Chalinitis, where it is motivated by the worship of Athene as inventor of the bridle. Strabo, then, provides a secularized version of the accounts in which Athene gave the horse to Bellerophon or assisted him in its taming. In a similar vein, Pliny includes Bellerophon as the original horseback rider in a list of human firsts that assigns the invention of the four-horse chariot to Erichthonios and of the first ship to Danaos. The latter two inventions are elsewhere said to have been gifts of Athene to these same individuals.[37]

The Thirteenth Olympian Ode of Pindar

Pindar offers the most complete story of the taming of Pegasos in an Olympian ode celebrating the victories of the Corinthian Xenophon.[38] After a number of unsuccessful attempts to bridle the horse, Bellerophon went to the seer Polyidos, who advised him to sleep on the altar of Athene.[39] As he slept, the goddess appeared to Bellerophon, presented him with a Corinthian bridle, and instructed him to show the gift to

by my chronology predates the introduction of the bridle and the hero's association with Pegasos.

[35] Pausanias 2.4.1, who reports the genealogy supplied in Homer. For Pausanias as a witness to cult belief see Hubbard (1986) 28–29. The *Etymologicum Magnum* explains Athene's title of Hellotis with the Pindaric version that the goddess actively assisted in the capture. The Scholia to Pindar, *O.* 13.56, explain the term with the version found in Pausanias, saying that Athene captured Pegasos herself by bridling him. On the cult of Athene Hellotis at Corinth see Will, 129–43.

[36] Strabo 8.6.21 (379); see Yalouris, 22.

[37] Pliny, *HN* 7.202. For ships and chariots see above, Chapter 3 and 5.

[38] Pindar, *O.* 13.63–92. See the discussions in Detienne and Vernant (1974) 176–200; Hubbard (1986).

[39] For a Corinthian seer named Polyidos, see *Il.* 13.663–68. For a Cretan Polyidos, who resurrected Glaukos, the son of Minos, see *RE* 21:2.1653–55, s.v. Polyidos (5); for the character Panteidyia, who helped the Corinthian Glaukos in his search for horses in Lakonia, see Eumelus, *Corinthiaca fr.* 6.

his 'tamer-father', *Damaios Patēr,* and to offer the god a white bull in sacrifice. When Bellerophon related his experience to Polyidos, the seer urged him to do as the goddess had commanded and, additionally, to dedicate an altar to Athene Hippia.

Pindar apparently departs from the traditions attached to the cult of Athene Chalinitis in having Bellerophon rather than Athene bridle Pegasos.[40] If, however, we are dealing with a genuine departure from her cult, then it is reasonable to ask whether Bellerophon's sacrifice to Poseidon, his consultation with Polyidos, and even his incubation on the altar of Athene are not likewise Pindaric innovations. Indeed, nothing suggests that Athene's cult celebrated a detailed orthodox account of the taming of Pegasos. In all likelihood, the claim that Athene invented the bridle and with it tamed the first horse to be ridden were the only invariable features of the cult-version of the myth.[41]

There is no apparent basis in Corinthian cult for making Poseidon the father of Bellerophon, or even for the association of Poseidon with the story of the horse's bridling. It is also unlikely that the epithet *Damaios,* or 'tamer', at *O.* 13.69 implies an actual cult to the god. Pausanias makes no mention of such a cult, although one would have certainly been invited by the discussion of Pegasos and the hippic cult of Athene; nor, this one passage excepted, is there archaeological or literary evidence of any kind which suggests that a hippic cult to Poseidon existed at Corinth or that the god was ever worshipped under this title. Finally, nothing in our extant sources indicates that Poseidon was worshipped in conjunction with the cults of Athene Chalinitis or Bellerophon. The role of Poseidon in the Pindaric ode need not—and in all likelihood should not—be explained with reference to a particular cult to the god, at Corinth or elsewhere.[42] Bellerophon's sacrifice to his father was suggested by Poseidon's role as the patron of horseback riding throughout Greece.[43]

[40] Hubbard (1986) 32, argues that Pindar's version of the myth was meant to reconcile competing claims from the cults of Athene, Poseidon, and Bellerophon. This is certainly possible in the case of Bellerophon, whose cult was celebrated at Corinth (Pausanias 2.2.4). I do not, however, believe that a cult to Poseidon Damaios existed at Corinth, for the reasons given below.

[41] The Scholia to Pindar, *O.* 13.27, imply a general conception of Pegasos as the first horse to be ridden, a view supported by Pliny.

[42] Farnell (1932) at *O.* 13.69: Δαμαῖος, 'the tamer of horses', a title perhaps invented by Pindar, in place of the more usual Poseidon-Ἵππιος, as he wished to use this latter to designate Athena."

[43] *GR* 138–39. See the comprehensive survey of the subject in Schachermeyr. Pausanias mentions three temples and seven cults to Poseidon-Hippios, the most important being

Precedent for the association of Athene and Poseidon in Corinthian cult may, however, be suggested by the legends surrounding the Argo, the first ship. Pindar in fact mentions the Argo in his catalogue of Corinthian inventions at the beginning of Olympian 13. The Argo was said to have been built at Corinth, and was there to be found in historical times dedicated to Poseidon, but its builder and thus the creator of naval technology was Athene.[44] To Poseidon one dedicated the instruments by which his powers were harnessed, and these were the gifts of Athene. This is incidentally the only evidence we possess for a cult to Poseidon within the city of Corinth, and his cult is maritime.[45]

The Pindaric account of Bellerophon, with the constellation of Athene, Bellerophon, and Poseidon in an integrated narrative, is best seen as the poet's own reformulation of material gleaned from more than one source. The invention of the bridle by Athene is the only aspect of the story to which we can assign a Corinthian provenience with anything approaching confidence. Its selection to serve as the mythic *exemplum* is explained with the importance of her cult in Xenophon's native city and with its appropriateness to the larger themes of the poem. More surprising is the poet's decision to portray Bellerophon as the son of Poseidon rather than of Glaukos, as might have been expected in a poem honoring a Corinthian athlete and his city. Here, I suggest, the poet wished to exploit the latent contrast between Athene and Poseidon as hippic divinities.[46]

That contrast is developed with the Pindaric collocation *Damaios Patēr:* the epithet *Damaios* refers to Poseidon in his capacity as the tamer of horses, while the bridle is the means by which Bellerophon is able to tame the horse and thus assume a role assigned to his father in cult. The relation between the god and the bridle is underscored with the

---

in Athens (Pausanias 1.30.4). Only one of these cults seems not to have been associated with another divinity.

[44] Built at Corinth: Aristides 46.29 (this was not the only version, however; see *RE* 2.722). Dedicated to Poseidon: Dio Chrysostomus 37.15; Apollodorus 1.9.27; Diodorus Siculus 4.53.2.

[45] The only other evidence of which I am aware that can be taken to indicate an association of Athene and Poseidon in Corinthian cult are two clay dedications, one of which bears the names Athene and Poseidon (*IG* 4.166), and another with Poseidon, Amphitrite, and Athene (*IG* 4.265). A number of other dedications pair Poseidon with Amphitrite: *IG* 4.219, 224, 246, 294, 297. Athene-Poseidon-Amphitrite is the same combination one finds at the temple of Athene Chalkioikos at Sparta (for which, see above, Chapter 5) and may relate to the tradition that Athene was daughter to Poseidon by Amphitrite.

[46] Detienne and Vernant (1974) 176.

verbal echo between Athene's command that Bellerophon "show it [the bridle] to your tamer-father" in verse 69 and the narrative statement that Bellerophon "showed Polyidos . . . how . . . she provided him with the spirit-taming gold [the bridle]" six verses later.

Reference to Poseidon as *Damaios Patēr* casts Bellerophon in the role of his father, just as Xenophon had continued a tradition of athletic excellence in his own family by winning victories at Olympia. At the same time, the poem celebrates Athene and Corinth as the creators of important technology, so that a harmony between tradition and innovation—itself a powerful metaphor of the poet's own craft—emerges from Pindar's description of the city and from his juxtaposition of the hippic deities Athene and Poseidon.

Yet *Damaios* is an ambivalent epithet, since Poseidon is father to both the horse and its master. It is the Poseidon within the hero that helps him tame manifestations of Poseidon in the external environment. Corresponding to the role of Poseidon as father is that of Athene as the creative intelligence that allows heroic man to transgress his physical limitations. Her gift of a technological device enables Bellerophon to assume the role of his *Damaios Patēr.* The plastic image of the bridled Pegasos, by contrast, refracts the subordination of *biē* to *mētis* into its constituent elements. Bellerophon's subsequent exploit in which he destroys the Chimaira, the monstrous progeny of the sea god Phorkys, represents a more extreme act of subordination. Thus, a combination of *mētis* and *biē* allows Bellerophon to appropriate additional *biē* from nature in the form of a marvelous horse: with his native *biē* thus enhanced, Bellerophon can destroy the wholly destructive force represented by the Chimaira.

The story of the taming of Pegasos is linked thematically to the catalogue of Corinthian civic virtues that precedes it. We have already remarked that the invention of the bridle, attributed to Athene in the mythic *exemplum,* is listed among the Corinthian inventions with which the poem begins. Bellerophon's ancestry includes two characters from the catalogue of illustrious Corinthians that follows: Sisyphos, his grandfather, and Glaukos, his grandson, whose role at Troy effects the transition to the mythic *exemplum.* Bellerophon is, moreover, called "Aiolida" within the *exemplum* itself, and since Aiolos was father to Sisyphos the choice of patronym further emphasizes the relationship between all three characters. On the other hand, the metaphors 'hippic charm', *philtron . . . hippeion,* and 'drug', *pharmakon,* applied to Athene's bridle at verses 68 and 85, evoke the magic of Medea, another famous inhabitant of Corinth who figures in the catalogue. Medea and Sisyphos both owe their fame to "cunning intelligence," which as we have seen is central to the story of Bellerophon and Pegasos.

Still more important for our purposes, Pindar indicates that Corinth owes its continued well-being to the self-restraint exercised by its citizens. *Eunomiē, Dikē,* and *Eirenē,* daughters of *Themis,* provide a check on the innate human disposition towards *hubris* in the face of egregious prosperity, just as the bridle controls the daimonic forces of nature. The bridle is an effective metaphor for *themis/nomos* in that it both restrains and directs behavior: this is evoked by the very term *metra*—literally 'measure', 'due measure', or even 'poetic meter'—with which the bridle is introduced at verse 20. The analogy is further emphasized by the phrase "spirit-taming gold," applied to the bridle at verse 78.[47] Just as Corinth embodies the potential of a city disciplined by *nomos,* Bellerophon and Xenophon realize these same possibilities on the level of the individual.

The theme of restraint reveals the significance of Bellerophon's sacrifices to Poseidon and Athene: they constitute necessary acts of propitiation, since heroic accomplishment infringes on the prerogatives of the god or gods who are the embodied perfection of that activity. Bellerophon shows himself able to master his own spirit, just as the creative intelligence of Athene manifests itself in a technological invention used to control a marvelous horse. Self-control is thus seen to be a precondition to achieving mastery over the *biē* of nature, whether that mastery be an individual or corporate accomplishment. In keeping with a well-known feature of Pindaric thought, Bellerophon's later fate reveals the dangers of unrestrained behavior just as the Chimaira provides a negative counterpart to Pegasos in nature. Pindar thus offers a tacit commentary on the sacrifice that Xenophon will presently offer Zeus in thanks for his victories at Olympos (24–31).

The themes of Olympian 13 provide a close analogy to those of the Homeric *Cyclopeia* (see Chapter 3): the motifs of intelligence, restraint, society, *themis/nomos,* piety, and technology are common to and similarly associated in both accounts. Significantly, Homer and Pindar both couch a celebration of technology in a broader discussion of *themis* and *eunomiē.* The same pair of gods appear and assume analogous roles. The means by which Odysseus triumphs over Polyphemos is related to technological innovation, just as Bellerophon tames Pegasos with the newly invented Corinthian bridle. Bellerophon, like Odysseus, offers

[47] Note that *metra* continues the musical imagery of the preceding passage and that its overt meaning of restraint is reinforced by verses 47–48.

a positive and a negative example of the theme "success through self-restraint." Moreover, Pindar's *nomos,* like Homer's *themis,* signifies an external as well as internal form of restraint, and the *eunomiē* of Corinth is verified in its numerous technological achievements. Thus, the *mētis* of the civic goddess Athene manifests itself in the creation of the bridle, a technological artifact that provides an external form of restraint.

In the *Cyclopeia,* as in Pindar's ode, self-restraint is a defining aspect of *mētis.* Yet Pindar, who is here engaged in praising a contemporary *polis,* celebrates the advantages that fall to a state blessed with *eunomiē,* technological products among them. Homer, by contrast, describes a precivilized race of Cyclopes. His perspective is accordingly that *themis* and technology first become possible with society. While *nomos* provides a curb on *hubris* in Pindar, the *hubris* of the Homeric Cyclopes is wed to the fact that they are *athemistoi.* For all the similarities between them, the themes of Olympian 13 do not constitute an intellectual inheritance from Homer; rather both narratives reflect the common intellectual categories of archaic and even classical Greek culture.[48]

[48] In this context, see Hubbard (1985) 5–7, 107–24; Hubbard (1986) 34.

Bibliography

Multivolume works are cited by volume and page number: *CHO* 1:27 = *A Commentary on Homer's "Odyssey"*, vol. 1, page 27 (note, however, that *CHO* at 1.27 = the commentator's note to Book 1, verse 27 of the *Odyssey*). Citations of the *Odyssey* are based on the edition of H. van Thiel (Hildesheim, 1991), those of the *Iliad* on the edition of D. Monroe and T. W. Allen (Oxford, 1920). Works with commentaries are listed by commentator.

Abbreviations

CGS Farnell, L. 1896–1909. *The Cults of the Greek States*. 5 vols. Oxford.

CHO Heubeck, A., et al., eds. 1988–1992. *A Commentary on Homer's "Odyssey"*. 3 vols. Oxford.

FGrH Jacoby, F. 1923–58. *Die Fragmente der griechischen Historiker*. Berlin.

FHG Müller, C. 1841–70. *Fragmenta Historicorum Graecorum*. 5 vols. Paris.

GG Simon, E. 1980. *Die Götter der Griechen*. 2d ed. Munich.

GGR Nilsson, M. 1955. *Geschichte der griechischen Religion*. 2d ed. Munich.

GR Burkert, W. 1985. *Greek Religion*. Trans. J. Raffan. Cambridge, Mass.

HN Burkert, W. 1983. *Homo Necans*. Trans. P. Bing. Berkeley.

IC Kirk, G., et al., eds. 1985–1993. *The "Iliad": A Commentary*. 6 vols. Cambridge, Eng.

IG *Inscriptiones Graecae* (For publication history and contents of individual volumes, see H. Liddell, R. Scott, and H. Jones. 1940. *A Greek-English Lexicon*. 9th ed. Oxford. xxxix.)

Leaf, W. 1900–1902. *The Iliad*. 2d ed. London.

MMR Nilsson, M. 1950. *The Minoan-Mycenaean Religion and Its Survival in Greek Religion*. 2d ed. Lund.

MO Nilsson, M. 1932. *The Mycenaean Origin of Greek Mythology*. Berkeley.

PR Preller, R. 1894–1926. *Griechische Mythologie*. 4th revised ed. in 3 vols. by C. Robert. Berlin.

RE Wissowa, G., et al., eds. 1893–present. *Paulys Realencyclopädie der classischen Altertumswissenschaft*. Stuttgart.

SH Burkert, W. 1979. *Structure and History in Greek Mythology and Ritual*. Berkeley.

Adkins, A. 1960. *Merit and Responsibility*. Oxford.

——. 1971. "Homeric Values and Homeric Society." *JHS* 91:1–14.

——. 1972. "Homeric Gods and the Values of Homeric Society." *JHS* 92:1–19.

——. 1987. "Gagarin and the 'Morality' of Homer." *CP* 82:311–22.

Allen, T. 1924. *Homer: The Origins and the Transmission*. Oxford.

—— et al. 1963. *The Homeric Hymns*. 2d ed. Oxford.

Ameis, K., and C. Hentze, eds. 1920–40. *Homers "Odyssee"*. Revised ed. in 4 vols. by P. Cauer. Leipzig.

Amouretti, M.-C. 1986. *Le pain et l'huile dans la Grèce antique*. Paris.

Andersen, Ø. 1973. "Der Untergang der Gefährten in der *Odyssee*. " *SO* 49:7–27.

——. 1977. "Odysseus and the Wooden Horse." *SO* 52:5–18.

Arend, W. 1933. *Die typischen Szenen bei Homer*. Problemata 7.

Arias, P., and M. Hirmer. 1960. *Tausend Jahre griechische Vasenkunst*. Munich.

Arthur, M. (see also M. Katz)

——. 1981. "The Divided World of *Iliad* VI." In *Reflections of Women in Antiquity*. Ed. H. Foley. New York. 19–44.

——. 1982. "Cultural Strategies in Hesiod's *Theogony:* Law, Family, Society." *Arethusa* 15:63–82.

——. 1983. "The Dream of a World without Women: Poetics and the Circles of Order in the *Theogony* Prooemium." *Arethusa* 16:97–116.

Auffarth, C. 1991. *Der drohende Untergang. "Schöpfung" in Mythos und Ritual im alten Orient und in Griechenland am Beispiel der "Odyssee" und des Ezechielbuches*. Religionsgeschichtliche Versuche und Vorarbeiten 39.

Austin, C. 1967. "De nouveaux fragments de l'*Erechthée* d'Euripide." *Recherches de papyrologie* 4:11–67.

——. 1968. *Nova Fragmenta Euripidea*. Kleine Texte 187:22–40.

Austin, N. 1975. *Archery at the Dark of the Moon: Poetic Problems in Homer's "Odyssey"*. Berkeley.

——. 1983. "Odysseus and the Cyclops: Who Is Who." In *Approaches to Homer*. Ed. C. Rubino and C. Shelmerdine. Austin. 1–37.

Ballabriga, A. 1990. "La question homérique. Pour une réouverture du débat." *REG* 103:16–29.

Barrett, W. 1966. *Euripides. Hippolytos*. Oxford.

Bassett, S. 1923. "The Proems of the *Iliad* and *Odyssey*." *AJP* 44:339–48.

——. 1934. "The Introductions of the *Iliad*, the *Odyssey* and the *Aeneid*." *CW* 27:105–10 and 113–8.

——. 1938. *The Poetry of Homer*. Berkeley.

Beidelman, T. 1989. "Agonistic Exchange: Homeric Reciprocity and the Heritage of Simmel and Mauss." *Cultural Anthropology* 4:227–59.

Benveniste, E., and L. Renou. 1934. *Vṛtra et Vṛθragna*. Paris.
Bergren, A. 1983. "Odyssean Temporality: Many (Re)Turns." In *Approaches to Homer*. Ed. C. Rubino and C. Shelmerdine. Austin. 38–73.
Bergquist, B. 1967. *The Archaic Greek Temenos: A Study of Structure and Function*. Lund.
Bethe, E. 1929. *Homer. Dichtung und Sage*. 2d ed. 2 vols. Leipzig.
Binder, J. 1984. "The West Pediment of the Parthenon: Poseidon." In *Studies Presented to Sterling Dow on his Eightieth Birthday*. GRBS Monogr. 10:15–22.
Boardman, J. 1980. *The Greeks Overseas*. 2d ed. London.
Bona, G. 1966. *Studi sull' Odissea*. Turin.
Brelich, A. 1969. *Paides et Parthenoi*. Incunabula Graeca 36.
Bremmer, J. 1983. *The Early Greek Concept of the Soul*. Princeton.
——. 1986. "A Homeric Goat Island (*OD*. 9.116–41)." *CQ* 36:256–57.
Brommer, F. 1963. *Die Skulpturen der Parthenon-Giebel*. 2 vols. Mainz.
——. 1982. *Theseus: Die Taten des griechischen Helden in der antiken Kunst und Literatur*. Darmstadt.
Brown, N. 1947. *Hermes the Thief: The Evolution of a Myth*. Madison.
Burkert, W. 1970. "Buzyge und Palladion." *ZRGG* 22:356–68.
——. 1973. "Von Amenophis II. zur Bogenprobe des Odysseus." *Grazer Beitr.* 1:69–78.
——. 1976. "Das hunderttorige Theben und die Datierung der *Ilias*." *WSt* 89:5–21.
——. 1977. "Le myth de Geryon." In *Il mito Greco*. Ed. B. Gentili and G. Paioni. Rome. 273–83.
——. 1983. General discussion following a paper by J. Schäfer. In *The Greek Renaissance of the Eighth Century B.C.: Tradition and Innovation*. Proceedings of the Second International Symposium at the Swedish Institute in Athens, 1–5 June, 1981. Ed. R. Hägg. Stockholm. 82–83.
——. 1984. *Die orientalisierende Epoche in der griechischen Religion und Literatur*. Heidelberg.
——. 1987. "The Problem of Ritual Killing." In *Violent Origins. Ritual Killing and Cultural Formation*. Ed. R. Hamerton-Kelly. Stanford. 149–76.
Calame, C. 1976. "Mythe grec et structures narratives: Le mythe des Cyclopes dans l'*Odyssée*." *Ziva Antika* 26:311–28.
——. 1977. "L'univers cyclopéen de l'*Odyssée* entre le carré et l'hexagone logiques." *Ziva Antika* 27:315–22.
——. 1977b. *Les choeurs de jeunes filles en Grèce archaïque*. 2 vols. Rome.
——. 1986. *Le récit en Grèce ancienne: Enonciations et représentations de poètes*. Paris.
——. 1990. *Thésée et l'imaginaire athénien: Légende et culte en Grèce antique*. Lausanne.
Calder W., III. 1969. "The Date of Euripides' *Erectheus*." *GRBS* 10:147–56.
——. 1971. A reply to the article by Clairmont in the same issue. *GRBS* 12:493–95.
Camp, J. McK. II. 1979. "A Drought in the Late Eighth Century B.C." *Hesperia* 48:397–411.
Carpenter, R. 1960. *Greek Sculpture: A Critical Review*. Chicago.
Carrara, P. 1977. *Eretteo: Introduzione, testo e commento*. Papyrologica Florentina 3.
Casson, L. 1971. *Ships and Seamanship in the Ancient World*. Princeton.
Catling, H. "Archaeology in Greece, 1982–83." *Archaeological Reports for 1982–83* 29:3–62.

Chalkia, I. 1986. *Lieux et espace dans la tragédie d'Euripide*. Thessalonike.

Clairmont, C. 1971. "Euripides' *Erechtheus* and the Erechtheion." *GRBS* 12:485–93.

Clark, M. 1986. "Neoanalysis: A Bibliographical Review." *CW* 79:379–94.

Clay, J. 1980. "Goat Island: *Od.* 9.116–141." *CQ* 30:261–64.

——. 1983. *The Wrath of Athena: Gods and Men in the "Odyssey."* Princeton.

——. 1989. *The Politics of Olympus: Form and Meaning in the Major Homeric Hymns*. Princeton.

Coldstream, J. 1968. *Greek Geometric Pottery. A Survey of Ten Local Styles and Their Chronology*. London.

——. 1977. *Geometric Greece*. London.

——. 1983. "Gift Exchange in the Eighth Century B.C." In *The Greek Renaissance of the Eighth Century B.C.: Tradition and Innovation*. Proceedings of the Second International Symposium at the Swedish Institute in Athens, 1–5 June, 1981. Ed. R. Hägg. Stockholm. 201–7.

Connor, W. 1987. "Tribes, Festivals, and Processions: Civic Ceremonial and Political Manipulation in Archaic Greece." *JHS* 107:40–50.

Cook, A. 1914–40. *Zeus. A Study in Ancient Religion*. 3 vols. Cambridge, Eng.

Cook, E. 1990. Review of B. Fenik, *Homer and the "Nibelungenlied." JHS* 109:209–11.

——. 1992. "Ferrymen of Elysium and the Homeric Phaeacians." *JIES* 20:239–67.

Cook, J. 1962. Review of E. Brann, *The Athenian Agora*. *Gnomon* 34:820–23.

Crane, G. 1988. *Calypso: Backgrounds and Conventions of the "Odyssey."* Beiträge zur klassischen Philologie 191.

Crouwel, J. 1981. *Chariots and Other Means of Land Transport in Bronze Age Greece*. Amsterdam.

Damon, P. 1969. "Myth, Metaphor, and the Epic Tradition." *Orbis Litterarum* 24:85–100.

——. 1974. "The Cults of the Epic Heroes and the Evidence of Epic Poetry." *The Center for Hermeneutical Studies* 9:1–9.

Davies, J. 1971. *Athenian Propertied Families, 600–300 B.C.* Oxford.

Davies, M. 1987. "Description by Negation: History of a Thought-Pattern in Ancient Accounts of Blissful Life." *Prometheus* 13:265–84.

——. 1988. " 'Ere the World Began to Be': Description by Negation in Cosmogonic Literature." *Prometheus* 14:15–24.

Davison, J. 1958. "Notes on the Panathenaea." *JHS* 78:23–41.

——. 1962. "The Homeric Question." In *A Companion to Homer*. Ed. A. Wace and F. Stubbings. London. 234–65.

Dawe, R. 1993. *The "Odyssey": Translation and Analysis*. Lewes.

Dawkins, R. 1955. *More Greek Folktales*. Oxford.

Detienne, M. (see also Sissa, G.)

——. 1970. "L'olivier, un mythe politico-religieux." *Rev. Hist. Rel.* 178:5–23.

——. 1972. *Les jardins d'Adonis*. Paris.

——. 1977. *Dionysos mis à mort*. Paris.

Detienne, M., and J.-P. Vernant. 1974. *Les ruses de l'intelligence*. Paris.

——. 1979. *La cuisine du sacrifice en pays grec*. Paris. (= 1989. *The Cuisine of Sacrifice among the Greeks*. Trans. P. Wissing. Chicago.)

Deubner, L. 1932. *Attische Feste*. Berlin.

Dickinson, O. 1994. *The Aegean Bronze Age*. Cambridge, Eng.
Dietrich, B. 1973. "A Religious Function of the Megaron." *Rivista Storica Dell' Antichita* 3:1–12.
Dihle, A. 1970. *Homer-Probleme*. Opladen.
Dimock, G. 1989. *The Unity of the "Odyssey."* Amherst.
Dirlmeier, F. 1970. *Ausgewählte Schriften*. Heidelberg.
Dodds, E. 1951. *The Greeks and the Irrational*. Berkeley.
——1954. "Homer." In *Fifty Years of Classical Scholarship*. Ed. M. Platnauer. Oxford. 1–17. (= 1964. "Homer." In *The Language and Background of Homer*. Ed. G. Kirk. Cambridge, Eng. 1–21.)
Dunbabin, J. 1936–37. "Ἔχθρη παλαίη" *BSA* 37:83–91.
——. 1950. "An Attic Bowl." *BSA* 45:193–202.
——. 1953. "Bellerophon, Herakles, and Chimaera." *Studies Presented to David Moore Robinson on His Seventieth Birthday*. Ed. G. Mylonas and D. Raymond. St. Louis. 1164–84.
Durand, J.-L. 1986. *Sacrifice et labour en Grèce ancienne*. Paris.
Edwards, A. 1985. *Achilles in the "Odyssey."* Beiträge zur klassischen Philologie 171.
——. 1985b. "Achilles in the Underworld: *Iliad, Odyssey,* and *Aethiopis.*" *GRBS* 26:215–27.
Edwards, M. 1975. "Type-Scenes and Homeric Hospitality." *TAPA* 105:51–72.
——. 1990. "Neoanalysis and Beyond." *CA* 9:311–25.
Eisenberger, H. 1973. *Studien zur "Odyssee."* Palingenesia 7.
Erbse, H. 1972. *Beiträge zum Verständnis der "Odyssee."* Untersuchungen zur antiken Literatur und Geschichte 13.
——. 1986. *Untersuchungen zur Funktion der Götter im homerischen Epos*. Untersuchungen zur antiken Literatur und Geschichte 24.
Farnell, L. 1932. *The Works of Pindar*. 2 vols. London.
Felson-Rubin, N. 1994. *Regarding Penelope: From Character to Poetics*. Princeton.
Fenik, B. 1968. *Typical Battle Scenes in the "Iliad": Studies in the Narrative Techniques of Homeric Battle Description*. Hermes Einzelschriften 21.
——. 1974. *Studies in the "Odyssey."* Hermes Einzelschriften 30.
——. 1986. *Homer and the Nibelungenlied: Comparative Studies in Epic Style*. Cambridge, Mass.
Finley, M. 1979. *The World of Odysseus*. 2d ed. Dallas, Pa.
——. 1985. *The Ancient Economy*. 2d ed. Berkeley.
Fisher, N. 1976. "*Hybris* and Dishonour: I." *GR* 23:177–93.
Focke, F. 1943. *Die "Odyssee."* Tübinger Beiträge zur Altertumswissenschaft 37.
Foley, H. " 'Reverse Similes' and Sex Roles in the *Odyssey.*" *Arethusa* 11:7–26.
Fontenrose, J. 1959. *Python: A Study of Delphic Myth and Its Origins*. Berkeley.
Ford, A. 1992. *Homer: The Poetry of the Past*. Ithaca, N.Y.
Frame, D. 1978. *The Myth of Return in Early Greek Epic*. New Haven.
Fränkel, H. 1962. *Dichtung und Philosophie des frühen Griechentums: Eine Geschichte der griechischen Epik, Lyrik, und Prosa bis zur Mitte des fünften Jahrhunderts*. 2d ed. Munich.
Frazer, J. 1913. *Pausanias's Description of Greece*. 2d ed. 6 vols. London.
——. 1965. *Apollodorus. The Library*. 2 vols. The Loeb Classical Library.

Fredricksmeyer, E. 1996. "The Ambiguity of Helen from Homer to Isocrates." Diss., University of Texas-Austin.

French, A. 1964. *The Growth of the Athenian Economy*. London.

Freud, S. 1931. *Das Unbehagen in der Kultur.* 2d ed. Vienna. (= *Civilization and Its Discontents*. Trans. James Strachey. N.Y. 1961.)

Friedrich, R. 1989. "Zeus and the Phaeacians: *Odyssey* 13.158." *AJP* 110:395–99.

Gagarin, M. 1987. "Morality in Homer." *CP* 82:285–306.

Gantar, K. 1962. "Zu Aristoteles' *Poetik* 8, 1451a 23–25." *Ziva Antika* 11:294.

Garland, R. 1986. "Religious Authority in Archaic and Classical Athens." *ABSA* 79:75–123.

Garvie, A. F. 1969. *Aeschylus' "Supplices." Play and Trilogy*. Cambridge, Eng.

Gatz, B. 1967. *Weltalter, goldene Zeit und sinnverwandte Vorstellungen*. Spudasmata 16.

Gennep, van, A. 1960. *The Rites of Passage*. Chicago.

Germain, G. 1954. *Genèse de l' "Odyssée."* Paris.

Glenn, J. 1971. "The Polyphemos Folktale and Homer's Kyklōpeia." *TAPA* 102:133–81.

——. 1978. "The Polyphemus Myth: Its Origin and Interpretation." *GR* 25:141–55.

Goldhill, S. 1988. "Reading Differences: The *Odyssey* and Juxtaposition." *Ramus* 17:1–31.

——. 1991. *The Poet's Voice: Essays on Poetics and Greek Literature*. Cambridge, Eng.

Gray, D. 1974. *Seewesen:* Archaeologia Homerica I:G. Göttingen.

Grégoire, H., and L. Parmentier, eds. 1923. *Euripide,* vol. 3. Paris.

Griffith, M. 1990. "Contest and Contradiction in Early Greek Poetry." *Cabinet of the Muses: Essays on Classical and Comparative Literature in Honor of Thomas G. Rosenmeyer.* Ed. M. Griffith and D. Mastronarde. Atlanta. 185–207.

Grimm, W. 1857. *Die Sage von Polyphem*. Berlin.

Groeger, M. 1904. "Der Einfluss des Ω auf die Composition der *Odyssee*." *RhM* 59:1–33.

Groningen, B. A. van. 1946. "The Proems of the *Iliad* and the *Odyssey*." *Medelingen Ned. Ak., Afd. Letterk.* 9:279–94.

Güterbock, H. 1978. "Hethitische Literatur." In *Altorientalische Literaturen*. Ed. W. Röllig. Neues Handbuch der Literaturwissenschaft 1:211–53.

Habinek, T. 1990. "Sacrifice, Society, and Vergil's Ox-Born Bees." *Cabinet of the Muses: Essays on Classical and Comparative Literature in Honor of Thomas G. Rosenmeyer.* Ed. M. Griffith and D. Mastronarde. Atlanta. 209–23.

Hackman, O. 1904. *Die Polyphemsage in der Volksüberlieferung*. Helsingfors.

Hansen, W. 1972. *The Conference Sequence: Patterned Narration and Narrative Inconsistency in the "Odyssey."* University of California Press: Classical Studies 8.

Harder, R. 1988. "Nausikaa und die Palme von Delos." *Gymnasium* 95:505–14.

Harrison, E. 1967. "U and Her Neighbors in the West Pediment of the Parthenon." In *Essays in the History of Art Presented to Rudolf Wittkower.* Ed. D. Frazer et al. London.

Herman, G. 1987. *Ritualised Friendship and the Greek City State*. Cambridge, Eng.

Heubeck, A. 1954. *Der "Odyssee"-Dichter und die "Ilias."* Erlangen.

——. 1974. *Die homerische Frage: Ein Bericht über die Forschung der letzten Jahrzehnte*. Darmstadt.

———. 1978. "Homeric Studies Today: Results and Prospects." In *Homer, Tradition and Invention*. Ed. B. Fenik. Leiden. 1–17.
Hiller, S. 1973. "Bellerophon." *A&A* 19:83–100.
Hirzel, R. 1907. *Themis, Dike und Verwandtes*. Leipzig. (= 1966. Hildesheim.)
Hölscher, U. 1988. *Die "Odyssee": Epos zwischen Märchen und Roman*. Munich.
Holland, G. 1993. "The Name of Achilles: A Revised Etymology." *Glotta* 71:17–27.
Hommel, H. 1955. "Aigisthos und die Freier: Zum poetischen Plan und zum geschichtlichen Ort der *Odyssee*." *Studium Generale* 8. 237–45.
Hood, M. 1953. "A Mycenaean Cavalryman." *ABSA* 48:84–93.
Howland, R. 1958. *The Athenian Agora*. Vol. 4: *Greek Lamps and Their Survivals*. Princeton.
Hubbard, T. 1985. *The Pindaric Mind: A Study of Logical Structure in Early Greek Poetry*. Mnem. Suppl. 85.
———. 1986. "Pegasus' Bridle and the Poetics of Pindar's *Thirteenth Olympian*." *HSCP* 90:27–48.
———. 1992. "Nature and Art in the Shield of Achilles." *Arion* 2:16–41.
Imhoof-Blumer, F. 1964. *Ancient Coins Illustrating Lost Masterpieces of Greek Art. A Numismatic Commentary on Pausanias*. Chicago.
Immerwahr, W. 1891. *Die Kulte und Mythen Arkadiens*. Leipzig.
Jacoby, F. 1933. "Die geistige Physiognomie der *Odyssee*." *Die Antike* 9:159–94.
———. 1980. *Das Marmor Parium*. Chicago. (= 1904. Berlin.)
Jaeger, W. 1926. "Solons Eunomie." *Sitz.—Ber. d. Preuß Akad. d. Wiss., Phil.—hist. Kl.* 11:69–85 (= 1960. *Scripta Minora*. Rome. 315–17. = 1970. In *Antike Lyrik*. Ed. W. Eisenhut. Ars Interpretandi 2:9–31.)
Janko, R. 1982. *Homer, Hesiod, and the Hymns: Diachronic Development in Epic Diction*. Cambridge, Eng.
Jantzen, U., and R. Tölle. 1968. "Beleuchtungsgerät." In *Archaeologia Homerica*. Vol. 2:*P: Hausrat*. Ed. S. Laser. Göttingen. 83–98.
Jeanmaire, H. 1939. *Couroi et Courètes: Essai sur l'éducation spartiate et sur les rites d'adolescence dans l'antiquité hellénique*. Lille.
Jefferey, L. 1976. *Archaic Greece: The City-States c. 700–500 B.C.* New York.
Jensen, M. 1980. *The Homeric Question and the Oral-Formulaic Theory*. Opuscula Graecolatina 20. Copenhagen.
Jeppesen, K. 1987. *The Theory of the Alternative Erechtheion: Premises, Definition, and Implications*. Acta Jutlandica LXIII:1. Humanities Series 60.
Jörgensen, O. 1904. "Das Auftreten der Götter in den Büchern ι - μ der *Odyssee*." *Hermes* 39:357–82.
Jones, D. M. 1954. "Ethical Themes in the Plot of the *Odyssey*." Inaugural Lecture, Westfield College, London.
Katz, M. (see also M. Arthur)
———. 1991. *Penelope's Renown: Meaning and Indeterminacy in the "Odyssey."* Princeton.
Kirchhoff, A. 1879. *Die Homerische "Odyssee."* 2d ed. Berlin.
Kirk, G. 1962. *The Songs of Homer*. Cambridge, Eng.
———. 1970. *Myth: Its Meaning and Functions in Ancient and Other Cultures*. Berkeley.
Knox, M. 1979. "Polyphemos and His Near Eastern Relations." *JHS* 99:164–65.
Kraay, C. 1966. *Greek Coins*. New York.

Krischer, T. 1971. *Formale Konventionen der homerischen Epik*. Zetemata 56.

Kroll, J., and N. Waggoner. "Dating the Earliest Coins of Athens, Corinth, and Aegina." *AJA* 88:325–40.

Kron, U. 1976. *Die zehn attischen Phylenheroen: Geschichte, Mythos, Kult, und Darstellungen*. Berlin.

Kullmann, W. 1960. *Die Quellen der "Ilias."* Hermes Einzelschriften 14.

——. 1965. *Das Wirken der Götter in der "Ilias": Untersuchungen zur Frage der Entstehung des homerischen "Götterapparats."* Deutsche Akad. der Wiss. zu Berlin, Schr. der Sekt. für Altertumswissenschaft, Schr. 1.

——. 1977–78. "Die neue Anthropologie der *Odyssee* und ihre Vorausetzungen." *Didacta Classica Gardensia* 17/18:37–49.

——. 1981. "Zur Methode der Neoanalyse in der Homerforschung." *WSt* 15:5–42.

——. 1984. "Oral Poetry Theory and Neoanalysis in Homeric Research." *GRBS* 25:307–23.

——. 1985. "Gods and Men in the *Iliad* and the *Odyssey*." *HSCP* 89:1–23.

——. 1993. "The Concept of Man in the *Odyssey*." In *Spondes Ston Omero. Apo ta Praktika tou z' Sunedriou gia ten "Odusseia" (2–5 Septembriou 1990)*. Kentro Odusseiakon Spoudon. Ithake. 117–39.

Kurke, L. 1991. *The Traffic in Praise: Pindar and the Poetics of Social Economy*. Ithaca, N.Y.

Kyle, D. 1987. *Athletics in Ancient Athens*. Mnem. Suppl. 95.

Lang, M. 1969. "Homer and Oral Techniques." *Hesperia* 38:159–68.

Lenz, A. 1980. *Das Proöm des frühen griechischen Epos*. Bonn.

Lenz, J. 1993. "Kings and the Ideology of Kingship in Early Greece (c. 1200–700 B.C.): Epic, Archaeology and History." Diss., Columbia University. New York.

Lesky, A. 1961. *Göttliche und menschliche Motivation im homerischen Epos*. Sitz.-Ber. der Heid. Akademie der Wissenschaft, Phil.—hist. Kl.

——. 1967. *Homeros*. Stuttgart (= "Homeros." *RE Suppl. Bd.* 11.687–846).

Levin, K. 1964. "The Male Figure in Egyptian and Greek Sculpture of the Seventh and Sixth Centuries B.C." *AJA* 68:13–28.

Levy, H. 1963. "The Odyssean Suitors and the Host-Guest Relationship." *TAPA* 94:145–53.

Lincoln, B. 1975. "The Indo-European Myth of Creation." *History of Religions* 15:121–45.

——. 1976. "The Indo-European Cattle-Raiding Myth." *History of Religions* 16:42–65.

——. 1977. "Death and Resurrection in Indo-European Thought." *JIES* 5:247–64.

Lloyd-Jones, H. 1971. *The Justice of Zeus*. Berkeley.

——. 1987. "A Note on Homeric Morality." *CP* 82:307–10.

Long, A. 1970. "Morals and Values in Homer." *JHS* 90:121–39.

Looy, H. van. 1970. "L'*Erechthée* d'Euripide." *Hommages à Marie Delcourt*. Collection Latomus 114:115–22.

Loraux, N. 1981. *L' invention d'Athènes. Histoire de l'oraison funèbre dans la "cité classique."* Paris.

Lord, A. 1960. *The Singer of Tales*. Cambridge, Mass.

Lord, M. 1967. "Withdrawal and Return: An Epic Story Pattern in the *Homeric Hymn to Demeter* and in the Homeric Poems." *CJ* 62:241–48.

Lorimer, H. 1950. *Homer and the Monuments*. Oxford.

Luce, J. 1978. "The *Polis* in Homer and Hesiod." *Proceedings of the Royal Irish Academy* 78:1–15.

Lukermann, F., and J. Moody. 1978. "Nichoria and Vicinity: Settlements and Circulation." In *Excavations at Nichoria in Southwestern Greece, Vol. 1: Site, Environs, and Techniques*. Ed. G. Rapp and S. Aschenbrenner. Minneapolis. 78–112.

MacDowell, D. 1976. "*Hybris* in Athens." *GR* 23:14–31.

Macleod, C. 1982. *Homer, Iliad, Book XXIV*. Cambridge, Eng.

Mallory, J. 1989. *In Search of the Indo-Europeans. Language, Archaeology, and Myth*. London.

Malten, L. 1925. "Bellerophontes." *Jahrb. d. Deutsch. Arch. Inst.* 40:121–60.

Martin, R. 1989. *The Language of Heroes: Speech and Performance in the Iliad*. Ithaca, N.Y.

Mazarakis, A. 1987. "Geometric Eretria." *Antike Kunst* 30:3–24.

——. 1988. "Early Greek Temples: Their Origin and Function." In *Early Greek Cult Practice*. Proceedings of the Fifth International Symposium at the Swedish Institute in Athens, June 26–29, 1986. Ed. R. Hägg et al. 105–19.

McGlew, J. 1993. *Tyranny and Political Culture in Ancient Greece*. Ithaca, N.Y.

Meier, C. 1990. *The Greek Discovery of Politics*. Trans. D. McLintock. Cambridge, Mass.

Merry, W., and J. Riddell. 1886. *Homer's "Odyssey."* Vol 1: *Books 1–12*. Oxford.

Meuli, K. 1921. "'Odyssee' und 'Argonautica': Untersuchungen zur griechischen Sagengeschichte und zum Epos." Diss., Basel.

Michelini, A. 1978. "Ὕβρις and Plants." *HSCP* 82:35–44.

Micknat, G. 1986. "Die Frage der Kontinuität: Bemerkungen zum Thema 'Mykene und Homer.'" *Gymnasium* 93:337–47.

Mikalson, J. 1976. "Erechtheus and the Panathenaia." *AJP* 97:141–53.

Miller, D. 1982. *Improvisation, Typology, Culture, and the "New Orthodoxy": How Oral is Homer?* Washington, D.C.

Mondi, R. 1983. "The Homeric Cyclopes: Folktale, Tradition, and Theme." *TAPA* 113:17–38.

Morgan, C. 1990. *Athletes and Oracles: The Transformation of Olympia and Delphi in the Eighth Century B.C.* Cambridge, Eng.

Morris, I. 1986. "The Use and Abuse of Homer." *CA* 5:81–138.

——. 1986b. "Gift and Commodity in Archaic Greece." *Man*, n.s., 21:1–17.

——. 1988. "Tomb Cult and the 'Greek Renaissance': The Past in the Present in the 8th Century BC." *Antiquity* 62:750–61.

——. 1991. "The Early Polis as City and State." In *City and Country in the Ancient World*. Ed. J. Rich and A. Wallace-Hadrill. London. 25–57.

Morris, S. 1984. *The Black and White Style: Athens and Aigina in the Orientalizing Period*. Yale Classical Monographs 6.

Most, G. 1989. "The Structure and Function of Odysseus' *Apologoi*." *TAPA* 119:15–30.

Müller, M. 1966. *Athene als Göttliche Helferin in der "Odyssee": Untersuchungen zur Form der epischen Aristie*. Heidelberg.

Nagler, M. 1974. *Spontaneity and Tradition: A Study in the Oral Art of Homer*. Berkeley.

——. 1977. "Dread Goddess Endowed with Speech." *Arch. News* 6:77–85.

——. 1980. "Entretiens avec Tirésias." *CW* 74:89–106.

——. 1990. "Odysseus: The Proem and the Problem." *CA* 9:335–56.

——. 1990b. "Ethical Anxiety and Artistic Inconsistency: The Case of Oral Epic." In *Cabinet of the Muses. Essays on Classical and Comparative Literature in Honor of Thomas G. Rosenmeyer*. Ed. M. Griffith and D. Mastronarde. Atlanta. 225–39.

Nagy, G. 1979. *Best of the Achaeans. Concepts of the Hero in Archaic Greek Poetry*. Baltimore.

——. 1982. "Hesiod." In *Ancient Writers. Greece and Rome*. Vol 1: *Homer to Caesar*. Ed. T. J. Luce. New York. 43–73.

——. 1985. "A Poet's Vision of His City." In *Theognis of Megara. Poetry and the Polis*. Ed. T. Figueira and G. Nagy. Baltimore. 22–81.

——. 1989. "Early Greek Views of Poets and Poetry." In *The Cambridge History of Literary Criticism*. Vol. 1: *Classical Criticism*. Ed. G. Kennedy. Cambridge, Eng. 1–77.

——. 1990. *Greek Mythology and Poetics*. Ithaca, N.Y.

——. 1990b. *Pindar's Homer: The Lyric Possession of an Epic Past*. Baltimore.

——. 1992. "Homeric Questions." *TAPA* 122:17–60.

Nestle, W. 1942. "*Odyssee*-Interpretationen." *Hermes* 77.

Niles, J. 1978. "Patterning in the Wanderings of Odysseus." *Ramus* 7:46–60.

Nilsson, M. 1906. *Griechische Feste von religiöser Bedeutung mit Ausschluss der attischen*. Leipzig.

——. 1950. "Lampen und Kerzen in Kult der Antike." *Op. Arch.* 6:98–111.

Oberhuber, K. 1965. "Odysseus-Utis in altorienalistischer Sicht." In *Festschrift Leonhard C. Franz zum 70. Geburtstag*. Innsbrucker Beiträge zur Kulturwissenschaft 11:307–12.

——. 1974. "Der Kyklop Polyphem in altorientalistischer Sicht." In *Antiquitates Indogermanicae: Gedenkschrift für Hermann Güntert zur 25. Wiederkehr seines Todestages am 23. April 1973*. Innsbrucker Beiträge zur Sprachwissenschaft 12:147–53.

O'Conner-Visser, E. 1987. *Aspects of Human Sacrifice in the Tragedies of Euripides*. Amsterdam.

Olson, D. 1990. "The Stories of Agamemnon in Homer's *Odyssey*." *TAPA* 120:51–71.

Osborne, R. 1989. "A Crisis in Archaeological History? The Seventh Century B.C. in Attica." *ABSA* 84:297–322.

O'Sullivan, J. 1987. "Observations on the Kyklōpeia." *SO* 62:5–24.

——. 1990. "Nature and Culture in *Odyssey* 9?" *SO* 65:7–17.

Owen, A. 1939. *Euripides: "Ion."* Oxford.

Page, D. 1955. *The Homeric "Odyssey."* Oxford.

——. 1973. *Folktales in Homer's "Odyssey."* Cambridge, Mass.

Palagia, O. 1984. "A Niche for Kallimachos' Lamp?" *AJA* 88:515–21.

Parke, H. 1977. *Festivals of the Athenians*. Ithaca, N.Y.

Paton, J. 1927. *The Erechtheum*. Cambridge, Mass.

Pedrick, V. 1992. "The Muse Corrects: The Opening of the *Odyssey*." *YCS* 29:39–62.

Peppermüller, R. 1962. "Die Glaukos-Diomedes-Szene der *Ilias*." *WSt* 75:5–21.

Peradotto, J. 1990. *Man in the Middle Voice: Name and Narration in the "Odyssey."* Princeton.

Pfeiffer, R. 1928. Review of E. Schwartz, *Die "Odyssee,"* and of U. von Wilamowitz, *Die Heimkehr des Odysseus*. *DLZ* 49:2355–72.

——. 1935. Review of W. Jaeger, *Paideia*. *DLZ* 56:2126–34 and 2169–78.

——. 1960. "Die goldene Lampe der Athene (*Odyssee* 19, 34)." *Ausgewählte Schriften*. Munich. 1–7. (= 1956. *Studi Italiani di Filologia Classica* 27/8:426–33.)

Pitt-Rivers, J. 1977. *The Fate of Shechem: Or, the Politics of Sex: Essays in the Anthropology of the Mediterranean*. Cambridge, Eng.

Podlecki, A. 1961. "Guest-Gifts and Nobodies in *Odyssey* 9." *Phoenix* 15:125–33.

de Polignac, F. 1984. *La naissance de la cité grecque: Culte, espace, et société: VIIIe–VIIe siècles avant J.-C.* Paris.

Poljakov, T. 1983. "A Phoenician Ancestor of the Cyclops." *ZPE* 53:95–98.

Pötscher, W. 1960. "Moira, Themis, und τιμή im homerischen Denken." *WSt* 73:5–39.

Powell, B. 1977. *Composition by Theme in the "Odyssey."* Beiträge zur klassischen Philologie 81.

——. 1991. *Homer and the Origin of the Greek Alphabet*. Cambridge, Eng.

Pucci, P. 1982. "The Proem of the *Odyssey*." *Arethusa* 15:39–62.

——. 1987. *Odysseus Polutropos: Intertextual Readings in the "Odyssey" and the "Iliad"*. Ithaca, N.Y.

Puhvel, J. 1987. *Comparative Mythology*. Baltimore.

Quiller, B. 1981. "The Dynamics of Homeric Society." *SO* 56:109–55.

Raubitschek, A. 1949. *Dedications from the Athenian Akropolis: A Catalogue of the Inscriptions of the Sixth and Fifth Centuries B.C.* Cambridge, Mass.

Redfield, J. 1973. "The Making of the *Odyssey*." In *Parnassus Revisited*. Ed. A. Yu. Chicago. 141–54.

——. 1975. *Nature and Culture in the "Iliad": The Tragedy of Hector*. Chicago.

——. 1983. "The Economic Man." In *Approaches to Homer*. Ed. C. Rubino and C. Shelmerdine. Austin. 218–47.

Reiner, E. 1978. "Die akkadische Literatur." In *Altorientalische Literaturen*. Ed. W. Röllig. Neues Handbuch der Literaturwissenschaft 1:151–210.

Reinhardt, K. 1960. *Tradition und Geist: Gesammelte Essays zur Dichtung*. Göttingen. (Chapters 2–4 are reprinted from 1948. *Von Werken und Formen*. Godesburg.)

——. 1961. *Die "Ilias" und ihr Dichter*. Ed. U. Hölscher. Göttingen.

Robertson, N. 1985. "The Origin of the Panathenaea." *RhM* 128:231–95.

Röhrich, L. 1962. "Die mittel-alterlichen Redaktionen des Polyphem-Märchens (AT 1137) und ihr Verhältnis zur außerhomerischen Tradition." *Fabula* 5:48–71.

——. 1967. *Erzählungen des späten Mittelalters und ihr Weiterleben in Literatur und Volksdichtung bis zur Gegenwart*. 2 vols. Bern.

Rosaldo, R. 1987. "Anthropological Commentary." In *Violent Origins: Ritual Killing and Cultural Formation*. Ed. R. Hamerton-Kelly. Stanford. 239–44.

Roscher, W., ed. 1884–1937. *Ausführliches Lexicon der griechischen und römischen Mythologie*. Leipzig.

Rose, G. 1967. "The Quest of Telemachus." *TAPA* 98:391–98.

Rüter, K. 1969. *Odysseeinterpretationen: Untersuchungen zum ersten Buch und zur Phaiakis*. Hypomnemata 19.

Rutherford, R. 1986. "The Philosophy of the *Odyssey*." *JHS* 106:145–62.

Rutkowski, B. 1984. "Der Baumkult in der Ägäis." *Visible Religion* 3:159–65.

Saïd, S. 1979. "Les crimes des prétendants: La maison d'Ulysse et les festins de l'*Odyssey*." *Etudes de litterature ancienne*. Paris. 9–49.

Samuel, A. 1972. *Greek and Roman Chronology: Calendars and Years in Classical Antiquity*. Handbuch der Altertumswissenschaft 1:7. Ed. H. Bengtson. Munich.

Schachermeyr, F. 1950. *Poseidon und die Entstehung des griechischen Götterglaubens*. Vienna.

Schadewaldt, W. 1958. "Der Prolog der *Odyssee*." *HSCP* 63:15–32.

——. 1960. "Der Helioszorn in der *Odyssee*." In *Studi L. Castiglioni 2*. Florence. 861–76. (= 1970. *Hellas und Hesperien. Gessammelte Schriften zur Antike und zur neueren Literatur*. 2 vols. Stuttgart. 1.93–105.)

——. 1966. *Iliasstudien*. 3d ed. Darmstadt.

Schein, S. 1970. "Odysseus and Polyphemus in the *Odyssey*." *GRBS* 11:73–83.

Schröter, R. 1950. "Die Aristie als Grundform homerischer Dichtung." Diss., Marburg.

Scully, S. 1981. "The Polis in Homer: A Definition and Interpretation." *Ramus* 10:1–34.

——. 1987. "Doubling in the Tale of Odysseus." *CW* 80:401–17.

——. 1990. *Homer and the Sacred City*. Ithaca, N.Y.

Seaford, R. 1984. *Euripides. "Cyclops."* Oxford.

——. 1994. *Reciprocity and Ritual: Homer and Tragedy in the Developing City-State*. Oxford.

Segal, C. 1962. "The Phaeacians and the Symbolism of Odysseus' Return." *Arion* 1:17–64 (= chapters 2 and 3 of 1994.)

——. 1974. "The Raw and the Cooked in Greek Literature: Structure, Values, Metaphor." *CJ* 69:289–308.

——. 1994. *Singers, Heroes, and Gods in the "Odyssey."* Ithaca, N.Y.

Simon, E. 1965. "Das humanistische Programm der Tondi." *Jahrb. Berliner Mus.* 7:49–91.

——. 1981. *Die griechischen Vasen*. 2d ed. Munich.

——. 1983. *Festivals of Attica: An Archaeological Commentary*. Wisconsin Studies in Classics. Madison.

Simms, R. 1983. "Eumolpos and the Wars of Athens." *GRBS* 24:197–208.

Sissa, G., and M. Detienne. 1989. *La vie quotidienne des dieux grecs*. Paris.

Smith, J. 1987. "The Domestication of Sacrifice." In *Violent Origins: Ritual Killing and Cultural Formation*. Ed. R. Hamerton-Kelly. Stanford. 191–205.

Snell, B. 1964. "Göttliche und menschliche Motivation im homerischen Epos." In *Argumentation: Festschrift für Joseph König*. Göttingen. 249–55.

Snodgrass, A. 1980. *Archaic Greece: The Age of Experiment*. London.

——. 1983. "Two Demographic Notes." In *The Greek Renaissance of the Eighth Century*

B.C.: Tradition and Innovation. Proceedings of the Second International Symposium at the Swedish Institute in Athens, 1–5 June, 1981. Ed. R. Hägg. Stockholm. 161–71.
——. 1986. "The Greek City." *CR* 36:261–65.
——. 1991. "Archaeology and the Study of the Greek City." In *City and Country in the Ancient World*. Ed. J. Rich and A. Wallace-Hadrill. London. 1–23.
Sokolowski, F. 1962. *Lois sacrées des cités grecques*. Paris.
Sowa, C. 1984. *Traditional Themes and the Homeric Hymns*. Chicago.
Stanford, W. 1954. *The Ulysses Theme. A Study in the Adaptability of a Traditional Hero*. Oxford.
——. 1959. *The "Odyssey" of Homer*. 2 vols. London.
Stanley, K. 1993. *The Shield of Homer: Narrative Structure in the "Iliad."* Princeton.
Svenbro, J. 1976. *La parole et le marbre: Aux origines de la poétique grecque*. Lund.
Thompson, H. 1961. "The Panathenaic Festival." *AA* 76:224–31.
Thornton, A. 1970. *People and Themes in Homer's "Odyssey."* Dunedin.
Torr, C. 1964. *Ancient Ships*. Chicago.
Usener, H. 1898. "Göttliche Synonyme." *RhM* n.s. 53.
Usener, K. 1990. *Beobachtungen zum Verhältnis der "Odyssey" zur "Ilias"*. Tübingen.
Van der Valk, M. 1985. "On the God Cronus." *GRBS* 26:5–11.
Vermeule, E. 1974. *Götterkult*. Archaeologia Homerica 3:5. Göttingen.
——. 1979. *Aspects of Death in Early Greek Art and Poetry*. Berkeley.
Vernant, J.-P. (see also Detienne, M.)
——. 1972. "Le troupeaux du Soleil et la table du Soleil (*Odyssée* xii; Hérodote, iii, 17–26)." *REG* 85:xiv–xvii.
——. 1982. *The Origins of Greek Thought*. Ithaca, N.Y.
Vian, F. 1951. "Les ΓΗΓΕΝΕΙΣ de Cuzique." *Revue Archeologique* 37:14–25.
——. 1952. *La guerre des géants*. Paris.
Vidal-Naquet, P. 1986. *The Black Hunter. Forms of Thought and Forms of Society in the Greek World*. Trans. A. Szegedy-Maszak. Baltimore.
Watkins, C. 1987. "How to Kill a Dragon in Indo-European." In *Studies in Memory of Warren Cowgill*. Ed. C. Watkins. Berlin. 270–99.
Webster, T. 1967. *The Tragedies of Euripides*. London.
Weissenborn, W., and H. Müller. 1962. *Titi Livi ab Urbe Condita*. 10th ed. 10 vols. Berlin.
Welter, G. 1941. *Troizen und Kalaureia*. Berlin.
West, M. 1966. *Hesiod. "Theogony"*. Oxford.
——. 1978. *Hesiod. "Works and Days"*. Oxford.
——. 1983. *The Orphic Poems*. Oxford.
——. 1988. "The Rise of the Greek Epic." *JHS* 108:151–72.
——. 1992. "The Descent of the Greek Epic: A Reply." *JHS* 112:173–75.
Whitman, C. 1958. *Homer and the Heroic Tradition*. Cambridge, Mass.
Wide, S. 1893. *Lakonische Kulte*. Leipzig.
Wilamowitz-Moellendorff, U. von. 1884. "Homerische Untersuchungen." *Philologische Untersuchungen* 7.
——. 1926. *Euripides "Ion"*. Berlin.
——. 1927. *Die Heimkehr des Odysseus*. Neue Homerische Untersuchungen. Berlin.

——. 1931–32. *Der Glaube der Hellenen*. 2 vols. Berlin.
Will, E. 1955. *Korinthiaka*. Paris.
Williams, C. 1984. "Corinth, 1983: The Route to Sikyon." *Hesperia* 53:83–122.
Williams, F. 1978. *Callimachus "Hymn to Apollo". A Commentary*. Oxford.
Woodhouse, W. 1929. *The Composition of Homer's "Odyssey"*. Oxford.
Wright, H., Jr. 1972. "Vegetation History." In *The Minnesota Messenia Expedition*. Ed. W. McDonald and G. Rapp, Jr. Minneapolis. 188–95.
Yalouris, N. 1950. "Athena als Herrin der Pferde." *MH* 12–101.
Zimmern, A. 1915. *The Greek Commonwealth*. 2d ed. Oxford.

Index of Homeric Passages

Odyssey

General Index

MYTH AND POETICS

A series edited by

GREGORY NAGY

Helen of Troy and Her Shameless Phantom
by Norman Austin

The Craft of Poetic Speech in Ancient Greece
by Claude Calame
translated by Janice Orion

Masks of Dionysus
edited by Thomas W. Carpenter and Christopher A. Faraone

The Poetics of Supplication: Homer's Iliad *and* Odyssey
by Kevin Crotty

Poet and Hero in the Persian Book of Kings
by Olga M. Davidson

The Ravenous Hyenas and the Wounded Sun: Myth and Ritual in Ancient India
by Stephanie W. Jamison

Poetry and Prophecy: The Beginnings of a Literary Tradition
edited by James Kugel

The Traffic in Praise: Pindar and the Poetics of Social Economy
by Leslie Kurke

Topographies of Hellenism: Mapping the Homeland
by Artemis Leontis

Epic Singers and Oral Tradition
by Albert Bates Lord

The Singer Resumes the Tale
by Albert Bates Lord, edited by Mary Louise Lord

The Language of Heroes: Speech and Performance in the Iliad
by Richard P. Martin

Heroic Sagas and Ballads
by Stephen A. Mitchell

Greek Mythology and Poetics
by Gregory Nagy

Myth and the Polis
edited by Dora C. Pozzi and John M. Wickersham

Knowing Words: Wisdom and Cunning in the Classical Traditions of China and Greece
by Lisa Raphals

Heroic Poets, Poetic Heroes: The Ethnography of Performance in an Arabic Oral Epic Tradition
by Dwight Fletcher Reynolds
Homer and the Sacred City
by Stephen Scully
Singers, Heroes, and Gods in the Odyssey
by Charles Segal
The Mute Immortals Speak: Pre-Islamic Poetry and the Poetics of Ritual
by Suzanne Pinckney Stetkevych
Phrasikleia: An Anthropology of Reading in Ancient Greece
by Jesper Svenbro
translated by Janet E. Lloyd
The Jewish Novel in the Ancient World
by Lawrence M. Wills